Contents

The Library of Congress and the Center for the Book
Historical Essays in Honor of John Y. Cole
EDITED BY
MARY NILES MAACK

International Perspectives

Contributions and Legacy of John Y. Cole

VOYAGE

For John Cole

A boy climbs into a boat
and pushes off to the open sea

and when he loses sight of land,
the boat becomes a book

which the boy begins to read
as it carries him over the waves,

and when he has finished reading,
the boy becomes the book,

the wind from an illustration
in that book, blown

from the mouth of a cloud
with puffed-up cheeks,

and a rising moon drawn
at the top of the page

looks down with such
loving bemusement

on the night sea,
on the boat, the boy, and the book.

Billy Collins

Billy Collins

"Voyage," a poem dedicated to John Cole by Billy Collins, U.S. Poet Laureate 2001-2003. The poem was presented to Cole in 2003 as a surprise gift from the fifty state centers for the book to celebrate his twenty-five years as director of the Center for the Book. The original letterpress edition was printed in Alabama by Steve Miller on paper handmade by Frank Brannon. One hundred copies were struck in the Spring of 2003.

Introduction
John Y. Cole: Librarian, Bookman, and Scholar

Mary Niles Maack

Because the American Library Association held its annual conference in Washington, D.C., in 2007, the year that marked the thirtieth anniversary of the Library of Congress Center for the Book, it seemed most fitting to dedicate the Library History Round Table (LHRT) Research Forum to John Y. Cole. In his capacity as founding director of the Center for the Book, John has played a very significant role in sponsoring conferences, symposia, lectures, and publications related to book history and to library history. Known internationally as the foremost expert on the history of the Library of Congress, John has published widely in scholarly books and journals, in library periodicals, and in numerous reference books. The Research Forum was so well received by LHRT members and by John's colleagues at the Library of Congress that we decided to use the papers as the basis of a festschrift in his honor.

The Career and Research of John Cole

After heading the U.S. Army Intelligence School Library during his military service, John Cole came to the Library of Congress as an administrative intern in 1966. He later worked as an acquisitions librarian in the Library's Congressional Research Service and as a collections development librarian in the Reference Department. In 1969 he met Nancy E. Gwinn, a Library of Congress intern, and they were married in 1973. Since then Nancy and John have spent their professional lives in Washington, D.C., where both have had distinguished library careers. Nancy is the director of the Smithsonian Institution Libraries and for the past decade has been especially active as an officer in the International Federation of Library Associations and Institutions (IFLA).

In 1976, ten years after John Cole began his career at the Library, he was appointed by Librarian of Congress Daniel J. Boorstin (1975–87) to chair the Library of Congress Task Force on Goals, Organization, and Planning. Boorstin was aware of John's historical research and believed that his deep understanding of the institution's past especially fitted him to the work of planning for the future. In 1978, when John's duties with the task force ended, Boorstin named him executive director of the newly created Center for the Book in the Library of Congress. The Center's mandate, as envisioned by Boorstin, was to stimulate public interest in books and reading and to encourage the historical study of books and their influence. A passionate reader and bookman as well as a scholar, John Cole took up this challenge and has created an impressive array of programs that promote reading as well as scholarly reflection.

During more than four decades at the Library of Congress, John's duties have been varied as well as continually challenging. In addition to his many activities at the Center for the Book—from organizing scholarly programs to fundraising—he has played a key role in the National Book Festival since its establishment in 2001, serving as its author coordinator. In the course of his career John has traveled to every state and to almost every region of the world, touring libraries, representing the Library of Congress, giving scholarly papers, and participating in the work of the IFLA. John is known especially for his leadership on the Standing Committee of the IFLA Section on Reading (now the Section on Literacy and Reading); he served as chair from 1997 to 2001 and edited the section's newsletter from 1997 to 2008. He has been the major influence in the founding of centers for the book in all fifty states, the District of Columbia, and the Virgin Islands, and also has stimulated the creation of reading promotion activities abroad, especially national centers for the book in both South Africa and Russia.

Along with all these activities, John Cole has still made time to continue his historical research, which began with his dissertation on Ainsworth Rand Spofford, the sixth Librarian of Congress (1864–97), a bookman who greatly expanded the Library's collections and its national role. Since earning his Ph.D. in American civilization from George Washington University in 1971, John has pursued his study of the Library of Congress and lectured at several universities on the institution and its impact on librarianship and scholarly communication.

John has published more than one hundred articles on the Library of Congress and has written, edited, and contributed chapters to numerous books. Among his best-known books are two popular, beautifully illustrated histories of the Library of Congress: *Jefferson's Legacy: A Brief History of the Library of Congress* (1993) and *On These Walls: Inscriptions and Quotations in the Buildings of the Library of Congress* (1995), which in 2008 was issued in a revised, expanded edition. He has edited more than twenty books published by the Center for the Book, including *Television, the Book, and the Classroom* (1978), *Books in Our Future: Perspectives and Proposals* (1987), and *Books Change Lives* (1996). John has contributed articles to *Libraries & Culture* (now *Libraries & the Cultural Record*) and currently serves on the board of advisory editors of *Libraries & the Cultural*

Record. He also has published carefully researched studies on the Library of Congress in the *Quarterly Journal of the Library of Congress* and in other scholarly journals. Among his most cited publications is "Storehouses and Workshops: American Libraries and the Uses of Knowledge," which appeared in *The Organization of Knowledge in Modern America, 1860–1920,* edited by Alexandra Oleson and John Voss (1979).

John Cole has generously contributed to the reference literature of the field, writing articles for several encyclopedias and biographical dictionaries. His most ambitious publication to date is the well-reviewed *Encyclopedia of the Library of Congress* (2004), which he coedited with Jane Aikin. In addition to the editorial work on this impressive volume, John authored two major essays and wrote or coauthored more than three dozen shorter articles, including brief biographies of all thirteen Librarians of Congress.

Among his many honors over his forty-year career is the prestigious Joseph A. Lippincott Award given by American Library Association in 2000 for his distinguished service to the profession. The award statement highlights John Cole's indefatigable leadership on numerous library and reading promotion projects, especially the "Read More About It" series on CBS Television.

The Festschrift

The LHRT was very pleased to honor John Y. Cole in 2007 by holding an invitational research forum that brought together a distinguished panel to address topics representing different aspects of John's contributions and interests as a scholar and a librarian. Three of the papers from the forum were revised and expanded for publication in a special issue (volume 45, number 1, 2010) of *Libraries & The Cultural Record,* along with six additional essays from scholars and colleagues whose work has been influenced and inspired by John Cole. For this new cloth-bound edition, John has added an illustrated autobiographical essay and updated the bibliography of his writings, 1970–2010.

The essays are grouped according to four broad themes that characterize John's career and scholarly interests: "The History and Historiography of the Library of Congress," "The Center for the Book," "The History of Books, Reading, and Publishing," and "International Perspectives." The first section begins with an article by Jane Aikin, Director of the Division of Research Programs at the National Endowment for the Humanities and the author of a major biography of Librarian of Congress Herbert Putnam. Aikin's excellent article on the historiography of the Library of Congress is complemented by the first article ever to appear on the Library of Congress Archives—an essay that benefits from the deep personal knowledge of its author, Josephus Nelson, who worked in the Library's Manuscript Division for many years.

In the section focusing on the development of the Center for the Book, John Cole's work as director of the Center is discussed by his colleague Guy Lamolinara, the Center's communications officer. He offers a brief history of the Center for the Book, then discusses the formation of state centers as well as the Center's international influence. An article by Eleanor Shevlin and Eric Lindquist analyzes the role of the Center for the Book in promoting scholarship in the emerging interdisciplinary field that has become known as book history.

The history of reading and publishing is another abiding passion for John Cole, and we are pleased to have a particularly rich offering on these topics. Carl Ostrowski, a historian from Middle Tennessee State University, discusses Librarian Spofford's personal attitudes toward the dime novels and other popular fiction that he so conscientiously acquired for the Library's collections. An article by Michael Winship of the University of Texas at Austin shows the perspective of a publisher's clerk who visited the Library of Congress in 1892 and vividly described the state of the Library as well as his meetings with Spofford. In the next article Jean Preer of Indiana University covers a much more recent period, focusing on the first National Library Week in 1958 and other reading promotion activities of the National Book Committee, a group of publishers and librarians founded in 1954. Although this group disbanded in 1974, some of its most influential members later urged that the Library of Congress include reading promotion as one of the activities of the projected Center for the Book.

To honor John Cole's extensive work abroad we have entitled the final section of this festschrift "International Perspectives." Nancy Gwinn, whose research focuses on the history of the Smithsonian Institution, analyzes the roles that the Smithsonian and the Library of Congress played in the international exchange of publications during the late nineteenth century and thus offers yet another perspective on the work of Librarian Spofford. Donald G. Davis, Jr., professor emeritus at the University of Texas at Austin and former editor of *Libraries & Culture*, analyzes four important trends in the study of library history and pays tribute to John Cole's work in fostering international scholarship through both IFLA and the Center for the Book.

A Life at the Library of Congress[1]

John Y. Cole

Good Fortune from the Start

My enrollment in graduate library school at the University of Washington in 1962 turned out to be a critical, and indeed, as things happened, a life-changing decision. Subsequently, the same "good fortune" that Lawrence Clark Powell, one of my professional inspirations, proclaimed—and experienced—has accompanied my own career.[2]

As an undergraduate at the University of Washington in Seattle from 1958-1962, I pondered an uncertain professional future. I was a book-loving history major, but instinct steered me away from an academic career. When I was a senior, Dorothy Bevis, an indefatigable library school professor, persuaded me to take her course on the history of books and libraries as an enticement to enrolling the next year in the Graduate School of Librarianship. It worked. I postponed my ROTC-based active duty service in the U.S. Army for one year and obtained my graduate library degree in 1963.

In addition to Prof. Bevis, I was impressed by the ebullient personality of the School's dean, Irving Lieberman, an advocate of the new field of "media studies." He told students that even if we did not watch television, the new and controversial technology of the day, it was our responsibility as librarians and communicators to learn about it and to keep ourselves informed about it. This memory came back to me in 1979 when, as executive director of the new Center for the Book in the Library of Congress, I needed to find both support and a rationale for the Center's new "Read More About It" project, a pioneering reading promotion effort with CBS Television and the first such Library of Congress outreach venture.[3]

During my undergraduate and library school years at the University of Washington, I landed a part-time job, from 3:00 p.m. until closing at 9:00 p.m., as the evening manager of Hartman's, a university district bookstore that carried both new and used books. I spent most of the last hour of each day browsing the shelves while waiting on the occasional customer—a useful education that more than compensated for the necessarily administrative and technical nature of graduate library school.

Bookman and librarian Lawrence Clark Powell at a 1987 California Center for the Book event marking the publication of Powell's 1986 talk at the Library of Congress. John Cole is on the left, and Occidental College librarian Tyrus G. Harmsen on the right. Photo by Joe Friezer.

With my bookish interests and library school degree in hand, in November 1963, as a newly commissioned second lieutenant, I headed for training at the U.S. Army Intelligence School at Fort Holabird on the outskirts of Baltimore, Maryland. It was clear that most of the 125 members of my class were headed for Vietnam; soon after the start of our six-month class, however, I learned the true value of my library degree. I was a rarity: an army officer with a graduate library science degree. Without consulting with me, the astute army captain in charge of officer assignments appointed me the first qualified non-civilian to be Chief of the Library Branch of the Intelligence School. It was my first library job and an invaluable training ground for a "green" library professional and U.S. Army junior officer.

I soon realized that few of the officers at the Army Intelligence School knew much about the School's Library Branch or its resources, which, in addition to classified documents, specialized in foreign affairs and the history and practice of U.S. military intelligence and espionage, and even included some spy fiction. Thus I launched my first library public relations campaign, which incorporated posters, handouts, the creation of a library committee, and even an occasional theme-oriented library open house.

Most importantly, I quickly discovered what seemed to me to be an unbelievable privilege accorded the U.S Army Intelligence School Library. As a federal library, it was eligible to select volumes from the surplus book collections of the Library of Congress, which was only 35 miles away, straight down the Baltimore-Washington Parkway. I took advantage of both the opportunity and a U.S. Army car and driver every two months or so to make my first "acquisitions" trips. These visits introduced me to the Library of Congress, and it did not take long for me to decide where I wanted to spend the rest of my library career.

A "Bookie" Finds His Professional Home

In the summer of 1966, having completed my active duty obligation with the army, I knocked on the door of the personnel department of the Library of Congress and asked for a job. Anna Joseph, the Library's skilled chief personnel officer, immediately smiled, taking special note of my two years' experience as the head of a specialized U.S. Army library and a second master's degree I had obtained at Johns Hopkins University while stationed in Baltimore.

On the same day we met, she called Dean Irving Lieberman at the University of Washington Graduate School of Library Science and suggested that he recommend me as the school's candidate for the 1966-1967 "Special Recruit" class at the Library of Congress for recent and outstanding library school graduates. A potential problem was averted when Joseph, responding to Lieberman's observation that the school already had nominated a candidate, suggested that for this year the University of Washington might nominate two candidates; after all, she noted, it already was going to be the largest administrative recruit program in the Library's history.

Indeed, this is what happened, which is how the other University of Washington candidate, my colleague Mary Berghaus Levering, and I both joined the Library staff in 1966; moreover, today we are the only recruits from our 1966-1967 class still working at the Library of Congress.

Another recruit with whom I formed a close friendship was Arthur Plotnik, a journalist by training who remained at the Library of Congress for several years before becoming editor of the American Library

The new Library of Congress Building soon after it opened to the public on Nov. 1, 1897. Prominent architectural critic Montgomery Schuyler praised it as "a national possession, an example of a great public building monumentally conceived, faithfully built, and worthily adorned." Library of Congress Photograph.

Association's magazine, *American Libraries*. It was Plotnik who suggested that, as administrative recruits, the two of us should ask to spend the ten-day optional work experience at the end of our nine-month training program visiting the Library's newly opened shared cataloging office in London. L. Quincy Mumford, the Librarian of Congress, did not know quite how to react to our three-page written proposal, but William J. Welsh, the director of the Processing Department, did; he made a counter proposal. First of all, in order to obtain official support, we would need to pay all of the expenses personally. More important, we needed to develop a more creative and substantive proposal, one that included, for example, professional visits to institutions such as the British Museum Library, the British National Bibliography, and perhaps even the National Library of Ireland. We agreed, and took our trip in the spring of 1967. This firsthand experience was an unforgettable introduction for me to the rapidly growing international role of the Library of Congress and a memorable way to conclude the Special Recruit program. In fact, it set the pattern for solo trips I took to visit the overseas Library of Congress acquisitions and cataloging offices in Tokyo, Nairobi, and New Delhi between 1968 and 1970.

Ainsworth Rand Spofford (1825-1908), who as Librarian of Congress 1864-1897, transformed the Library of Congress from a library devoted primarily to serving the U.S. Congress into a national institution that also served the American public. Library of Congress Photograph.

Upon completing the recruit program, I became an acquisitions and reference librarian in the Congressional Research Service. Early in 1969, I moved to a broader-based policy position in the Library's Reference Department, a job concerned with collection development throughout the entire institution, and with foreign acquisitions as well. The expansion of my professional career in a Library-wide direction had been motivated by my increased interest in the institution's history, particularly the historical development of its national role. In 1968 I enrolled as a Ph.D. candidate in the George Washington University's program in American Civilization; my goal was a dissertation about how Ainsworth Rand Spofford, the Librarian of Congress from 1864-1897, turned what was essentially a legislative library in the U.S. Capitol into a national institution that eventually occupied its own monumental structure, a building that Spofford called "the book palace of the American people."[4]

In 1969 I met a new Library of Congress administrative recruit, Nancy E. Gwinn, who had come to the Library after graduating from the University of Wyoming and spending a year at Oxford University in England as a Fulbright scholar. Next she took advantage of a scholarship to complete a library degree at the University of Michigan Graduate School of Librarianship, and subsequently she was nominated for the Library of Congress' recruit program. She told me all about Oxford and I did my best to impress her with my (recently acquired) knowledge of England. Her first Library of Congress job was exciting and challenging: establishing the Congressional Research Services's new reference centers in the House of Representatives and Senate office buildings. I found myself balancing my new job with a new Ph.D. program, but we slowed down enough to get married in Washington, D.C. in 1973.

I first learned about Ainsworth Rand Spofford and his importance to the Library of Congress during my recruit year, when I read *The Story Up to Now: The Library of Congress, 1800-1946* (Washington, D.C.: Library of Congress, 1947) by David C. Mearns, a distinguished Library of Congress employee who had served the institution from 1918 until his retirement in 1967. If Spofford was as important to the Library as David Mearns said he was, why were there no major articles or books about him? Mearns, had spoken to our class, and I made an appointment to meet with him. After only a few minutes of conversation I knew Spofford indeed was my subject; moreover, by the end of our talk, Mearns had agreed to serve as an unofficial advisor for my Ph.D. work.

In June 1970, David Mearns surprised and encouraged me with a gift: one of Spofford's hand-written calling cards, slightly faded but clearly dated April 11, 1893. His accompanying note was brief and moving: "Dear Mr. Cole: This yellowed *carte de visite* belongs now more properly to you than it does to me. It was a gift about a quarter of a century ago. I have carried it in my pocket ever since." Both the framed note and the card have hung on my office wall since then. In 1971, the year I received my Ph.D., I recorded an extensive interview with Mearns for the Library of Congress Archives. He died in 1981; in 1993, I dedicated my book, *Jefferson's Legacy: A Brief History of the Library of Congress* (Washington, D.C.: Library of Congress, 1993) to his memory.

With Spofford, the Library's great "bookman" and collection-builder as both my research topic and inspiration, I looked at my job in the Library's Collection Development office with new eyes. I became especially interested in the arts collections of the 1930s generated by Project One of the Works Progress Administration (WPA) which, because of the lack of space on Capitol Hill, were stored at various sites in Maryland and Virginia. A few years later, these collections would become

David C. Mearns, a distinguished Library of Congress staff member and historian who encouraged John Cole's study of the career and influence of Ainsworth Rand Spofford. This photograph was taken in the 1950s, when Mearns held the position of chief of the Manuscript Division and assistant librarian for the American Collections. Library of Congress Photograph.

a resource and stimulus for several important Center for the Book collection-related projects that have continued until the present.[5]

L. Quincy Mumford retired as Librarian of Congress at the end of 1974, and on June 20, 1975, President Gerald R. Ford nominated historian and author Daniel J. Boorstin, senior historian at the Smithsonian Institution, to be the twelfth Librarian of Congress.

In the early 1970s, as my dissertation neared completion, I began writing articles about Spofford, focusing on how his achievements in centralizing copyright at the Library and then convincing Congress of the need for a separate Library building had secured the institution's national role. I did not know that in July 1975 a staff member in the office of the Librarian had included my most recent article, which traced the history of the Library's "dual" roles as both a legislative and a national institution, in a package of background materials sent to Dr. Boorstin to help him prepare for his forthcoming Senate confirmation hearings.[6]

Dr. Boorstin's nomination hearings before the U.S. Senate began on July 30, 1975, my 35th birthday. My wife Nancy and I were part of the audience. I was surprised (overwhelmed is closer to the truth) when he spotted and identified me, marched right up, and told me in a loud voice that he had read my article and found it to be "useful." Then he moved along to shake the next set of outstretched hands, and I quickly sat down.

Daniel Boorstin took the oath of office as the twelfth Librarian of Congress on Nov. 12. A week later he tracked me down, suddenly appearing in the lone chair next to my desk outside the office of my boss, John C. Finzi, director of Collection Development. He asked me to come to his ornate office down the hall, where he told me that he and William Welsh, now the director of the Processing Department, wanted me to head a year-long Library of Congress Task Force on Goals, Organization, and Planning. This was the Boorstin response, I later realized, to a study suggested by Senator Claiborne Pell at Dr. Boorstin's Senate confirmation hearings on July 30. From his office, Dr. Boorstin insisted I follow him up to the third floor "attic" of the Jefferson Building to see what would become my new office—if, of course, I took the job. It was a newly furnished conference room with a fancy table and twelve chairs, one for each of the Task Force members. My chair at the end of the table directly faced the U.S. Capitol across the street. I took a deep breath and managed to say that all of this seemed "OK." Nancy also encouraged me. The next day I told both Dr. Boorstin and Bill Welsh that we definitely were in business, and I began to learn what they had in mind.

The Task Force was launched in January 1976; its final report was due in January 1977. Its mission was ambitious: to "carry out a full-scale review of the Library of Congress" and to recommend changes that would "improve the effectiveness and the efficiency" of the institution. More than 160 Library staff members would eventually serve on the Task Force's fourteen subcommittees. With support from several private foundations, we established eight outside advisory groups: arts, humanities, law, libraries, media, publishers, science and technology, and social sciences. Seventy-five distinguished individuals from throughout the United States, plus four from abroad, served as advisors; nearly all of them participated during 1976 in the two meetings of their respective advisory groups held at the Library of Congress.[7]

The Task Force year was one of the busiest and most exhilarating years of my career. I was Dr. Boorstin's appointed "chair" of the entire endeavor, and he made a point of including me in many of the luncheons in his office with potential chairs and candidates for the Task Force's outside advisory groups. The distinguished guests I met under these circumstances included, for example, Gerard Piel, the publisher of

On Jan. 28, 1977, John Cole presented the final report of the Library of Congress Task Force on Goals, Organization, and Planning to Librarian of Congress Daniel J. Boorstin at a ceremony in the Library's Coolidge Auditorium. Library of Congress Photograph.

Scientific American, who had agreed to chair the Science and Technology Advisory Group, and who, at a second luncheon, brought with him his friend, the designer Charles Eames, a new member of the group. On three such luncheon occasions during the year I also met authors who would become friends and strong supporters of the Center for the Book: Barbara Tuchman, David McCullough, and Herman Wouk.

I presented the final Task Force report and all of its supplementary documents (a cart was needed!) to Dr. Boorstin in a staff ceremony in the Library's Coolidge Auditorium on Jan. 28, 1977.

The Center for the Book: 1977-1987

The Center for the Book in the Library of Congress was Daniel Boorstin's brainchild and creation. In 1974, the year before he was nominated to become Librarian of Congress, he had praised "the book" in its "wonderful, uncanny, and mystic simplicity" in an article in *Harper's* titled "A Design for an Anytime, Do-It-Yourself, Energy-Free Communication Device."[8] Once he became Librarian of Congress and established the Task Force process for improving the Library and its services, Dr. Boorstin himself proposed the Center for the Book idea for consideration by the Task Force and the outside advisory groups;

the recommendation went forward and was approved. After the Task Force's report had been accepted, Dr. Boorstin assigned me to a newly created Planning Office as the temporary assistant to the office's new director.

Once again, I had been fortunate. The new director of the Planning Office was Charles A. Goodrum, a friend, and indeed, a writer who shared my interest in the Library's history. He and I agreed that this was the opportunity for me to put together a book, eventually titled *The Library of Congress in Perspective*, about the work accomplished during the Task Force year. Published in 1978, it featured the Task Force's thirty-three major recommendations for the future of the Library as well as the recommendations of the outside Advisory Groups; as an introduction, I added a 75-page history of the Library. I also included three of the Planning Office's mid-1977 reports on the implementation of the Task Force recommendations, each published in the Library's *Information Bulletin*. In the June 3 issue, Goodrum reported: "The Librarian has asked the Planning Office to design a Center for the Book. With much help from units throughout the Library, this has been completed. Representative Nedzi has testified and the bill has been reported out of Committee for floor approval. If this is enacted, plans for staffing, programming, and funding are ready to go."[9]

Because of a rumor circulating that I might be selected to head the proposed new Center for the Book, I reviewed the proposed legislation. At first glance it struck me as both vague and a little disappointing. For example, the proposed center was described as a scholarly program for the "continued study and development of the written record as central to our understanding of ourselves and our world." It also appeared that the new director would need to raise private funds for the center's programming and staff, which certainly would be a new experience for me. However, I liked the notion of "stimulating public interest" in books, and only later noticed that the word "reading" was not mentioned anywhere in the legislation! A few weeks later, Dr. Boorstin offered me the Center for the Book job. With the positive Task Force experience under my belt, this time it was easy to agree.

With the enactment of Public Law 95-129, approved on Oct. 13, 1977, Congress endorsed a Center for the Book program that would "stimulate public interest and research in the role of the book in the diffusion of knowledge." President Jimmy Carter approved the legislation with a statement that happily included the word "reading," indicating his "commitment to scholarly research and to the development of public interest in books and reading." Only one salary, that of the director, was to be paid by the Library. However, the wording of P.L. 95-129 paved

Mickey Mouse and Fess Parker present a CBS Television/Library of Congress "Read More About It" message for the "Walt Disney: One Man's Dreams" broadcast in December 1981. Photo Courtesy CBS Television.

the way for the Center to become a true public-private partnership, authorizing the Librarian of Congress, in carrying out the Center's functions, to accept cash and other donations and the services of voluntary and noncompensated personnel, who could be reimbursed for travel and per diem expenses.[10]

Several members of the Task Force's outside advisory group were especially enthusiastic about the Center for the Book idea and were potential financial donors. Dr. Boorstin clearly was thinking along the same lines, since (I later learned) he already had obtained a pledge of initial financial support from the chairman of the Publishing Advisory Group, Dan Lacy, a senior vice-president at McGraw-Hill, Inc.

The Center owes a great deal to the members of the Task Force Advisory Groups for their ideas and support in shaping its early identity and program of activities. The Publishing Advisory Group was especially important. Members who became directly involved in the Center in our early years, in addition to Dan Lacy, were Simon Michael Bessie, senior vice president, Harper & Row Publishers; Carol A. Nemeyer, staff director for General Publishing, Association of American Publishers, and Theodore Waller, president, Grolier Educational Corporation.

On Nov. 13, 1981, actress Cicely Tyson taped a
"Read More About It" message for a forthcoming CBS
telecast of "The Marla Collins Story." Photo Courtesy
CBS Television.

Lacy, Bessie, and Waller had been active participants in the National
Book Committee (1954-1974), a reading promotion alliance of
publishers and librarians supported by the publishing community; each
was to become a member of the executive committee of the Center for
the Book's National Advisory Board (1977- 1985). Moreover, in 1978,
Virginia H. Mathews, the former staff director of the National Book
Committee, joined the Center for the Book as a part-time consultant,
specializing in projects relating to early childhood development, family
literacy, and library promotion. Mathews, whose work in developing the
"young reader" side of the Center's national reading promotion program
was a huge boost for our small endeavor, did not retire until 2008, and
the next year, she donated a small but important collection of National
Book Committee records and publications to the Library of Congress. [11]

Carol Nemeyer was a key participant for another reason. In late 1977,
Dr. Boorstin persuaded her to accept the job of Assistant Librarian for
Public Education—a new, high-level national outreach position. The
next year she became my boss, responsible for the general supervision

Cap'n O.G. Readmore, a reading promotion cat and the new host of ABC Television's Saturday afternoon children's programming, is introduced on April 27, 1983 by John Cole, Carol Nemeyer, Library of Congress associate librarian for national programs, and ABC Television vice-president Squire Rushnell. Library of Congress Photograph.

of the Center for the Book, along with her other duties.

More than a dozen other members of Task Force outside advisory committees were members of the Center for the Book's National Advisory Board during 1977-1982, our formative years. They were: Robert F. Aselson, president, R,R. Bowker, Co.; Edward E. Booher, director, National Enquiry into Scholarly Communication; Warren J. Haas, president, Council on Library Resources, Inc.; Neil Harris, director, National Humanities Institute, University of Chicago; Chester Kerr, director, Yale University Press; Jaroslav Pelikan, dean, Graduate School, Yale University, and chair of the Humanities Advisory Group; and the previously mentioned Gerald Piel, publisher, *Scientific American*, and chair of the Science and Technology Advisory Group.

The private funding aspect of the program, unusual at the time for a government agency, was of immediate help. A founding gift of $20,000 from McGraw-Hill, Inc., arranged through Dan Lacy, was used for four

Twenty-nine biographers were part of the audience in the Library's Mumford Room at the Center's 1983 symposium, "Biography & Books." Featured speakers were publisher Samuel S. Vaughan of Doubleday & Co. and biographers Edmund Morris, James Thomas Flexner, and David McCullough. Library of Congress Photograph.

planning meetings to discuss potential activities and initial organizational structure. The first session, held on Oct. 20, 1977, only one week after President Carter had approved the Center's creation, focused on "Potential Activities of the Center for the Book." Dr. Boorstin's carefully prepared statement explained why the Center for the Book was needed and why it should be at the Library of Congress.[12]

On Oct. 20, several individuals were invited to speak about what they would like to see the Center do—its potential in their respective areas of interest. Their talks provided the framework for the day's discussion. The topics and speakers were: "The Reading of Books," Robert Wedgeworth, Jr., executive director, American Library Association, Theodore Waller, president, Grolier Education Corporation, and Mrs. Robert McNamara, chair, Reading is Fundamental, Inc.; "The Creating of Books," Jaroslav Pelikan, dean, Graduate School, Yale University, author John Hersey, and William McPherson, editor, Book World, *The Washington Post*; "The Selling of Books," Dan Lacy of McGraw-Hill, Robert D. Hale, Hathaway House Bookshop, Wellesley, Mass., and president, American Booksellers Association, and Arthur Brody, chairman, Bro-Dart, Inc.; and "The Study of Books," G. Thomas Tanselle, professor of English, University of Wisconsin-Madison, and Terry Belanger, assistant professor, School

Three of the 21 members of the Center for the Book's 1984 "Advisory Committee on the Future of the Book," which met at the Library of Congress on March 7, 1984. They are, left to right, Warren J. Haas, president, Council on Library Resources, Inc.; author and historian Jacques Barzun; and Gerard Piel, publisher, Scientific American. *On Nov. 18, 1983, the U.S. Senate had authorized a study by the Library of Congress "of the changing role of the book in the future." The results were published in "Books in Our Future," a 49-page report from the Joint Committee on the Library of Congress (1984) and* Books in Our Future: Perspectives and Proposals *(Washington, D.C.: Library of Congress, 1987). Library of Congress Photograph.*

of Library Service, Columbia University. Specific luncheon discussion topics included television and the book, the state of book reviewing, how to improve book distribution, and encouraging reading through book festivals, prizes, and awards.[13]

Three additional meetings with advisors, most of whom became members of the Center's National Advisory Board, took place in the spring of 1978 and helped shape the Center's basic agenda. The topics were: "The International Flow of Books" (Feb. 23, 1978); "The Center's Organizational Structure" (March 23, 1978); and "The History of Books and Printing" (April 13-14, 1978).[14]

A National Advisory Board was formed during 1978. It was headed by George C. McGhee, former ambassador to Turkey and the Federal Republic of Germany, who chaired the board's first executive committee meeting on Sept. 7. The committee agreed that the Center should emphasize projects that would dramatize the importance of books and the printed word and serve as a catalyst to strengthen the programs of other organizations in the book and educational communities. Furthermore, initially it would focus on three of the many projects that had been recommended: development of an annual report on the state of the book, creation of a major television project emphasizing the importance of books and reading in society, and hosting a conference that would bring together practicing teachers and librarians to discuss the effective uses of books in elementary and secondary schools.[15]

These early planning meetings stimulated the Center's first two cooperative projects with other government agencies. The first was "Television, the Book, and the Classroom," a symposium at the Library of Congress with the U.S. Office of Education on April 26-27, 1978, which led directly to the "Read More About It" project with CBS Television and was the model for several symposia between 1978 and 1983.[16] The second, undertaken in partnership with the U.S. International Communication Agency (USICA), was "The International Flow of Information: A Trans-Pacific Perspective," an ambitious three-week program and "traveling seminar" that took place in Hawaii, New York City, Washington, D.C., and Dallas, Texas in June 1979. Additional sponsors were the Graduate School of Library Studies at the University of Hawaii, the Association of American Publishers, the R.R. Bowker Co., and the American Library Association.[17]

Other important private gifts, in addition to the initial $20,000 contribution from McGraw-Hill, benefited the Center in our early years. Joan Manley, president of Time-Life Books in Alexandria, Va., and a member of the Center's first National Advisory Board, wanted to make a $50,000 "thank you" gift to the Library of Congress for the valuable support that Time-Life Books had received through the years from the Library's special collections, particularly—but not exclusively—from the Prints and Photographs Division and the Geography and Map Division. She and Dr. Boorstin agreed that the gift should come to the new Center for the Book.

William Matheson, chief of the Library's Rare Book and Special Collections Division, proposed a project that resulted in another significant gift. I had worked closely with Matheson when I was in the Library's Collections Development Office, and when he learned that this new, uncertain creation called the Center for the Book was headed my way, he made a suggestion: the gift funds that his division received regularly from Mrs. Charles Engelhard should be used by the Center for the Book and the Rare Book and Special Collections Division for a jointly sponsored public lecture series about books, reading, printing, and bibliography. I gratefully agreed, realizing that I soon would need

Nancy E. Gwinn, assistant director for collections management at the Smithsonian Institution Libraries, at a Center for the Book reception in 1984. On the left is Ray Fry, U.S. Department of Education; on the right, Robert Gwinn (no relation), the chair of the Encyclopedia Brittanica, and a major supporter of the soon-to-be-established Illinois Center for the Book. Library of Congress Photograph.

Center for the Book "products" to demonstrate the Center's potential and practical worthiness to Dr. Boorstin, Center for the Book National Advisory Board members, and prospective donors. Why not handsomely produced lectures by prominent citizens of the book community, produced by well-known prominent designers, and published by the Center for the Book in a new publication series?

Thus began the Center for the Book's "Viewpoint Series" of talks and pamphlets.[18] The first, titled *The Book*, was presented on Oct. 17, 1977, by historian Barbara Tuchman, a member of the Center's National Advisory Board. This series of occasional invitational talks and attractive publications continued through 1996 with the publication of Viewpoint No. 31, *Readers & Libraries: Toward a History of Libraries and Culture in America*, by Kenneth E. Carpenter of the Harvard University Library.

In the same vein, Matheson opened my eyes to another possibility:

To John Cole
with best wishes,   Barbara Bush

At her request, First Lady Barbara Bush met with Dr. Billington and John Cole at the White House on January 30, 1989, to find out how she might help with the Center's forthcoming "Year of the Young Reader" campaign. White House Photograph.

using private sector funds donated to the Center for the Book for judicious and selective support of relevant symposia, publications, and projects organized by other organizations, both within and outside of the Library of Congress. In return, the Center for the Book would receive full recognition of its partnership role and good publicity as it attempted to establish a name for itself. I got the point and plunged ahead. The first such significant scholarly symposium, appropriately enough, was a May 30-31, 1980, meeting co-sponsored with the Rare Book and Special Collections Division that honored Lessing J. Rosenwald, one of the Library's most significant benefactors.[19] Only two months later, thanks to a cooperative arrangement with another government agency, the U.S. National Institute of Education, we hosted "Literacy in Historical Perspective," one of the first conferences to raise awareness about the growing problem of literacy in our society—albeit, in this instance, from a historical perspective.[20] The first project co-funded with a state center for the book was "Getting the Books Out," a conference co-hosted with the Illinois Center for the Book and the Graduate School of the University of Chicago, and held in Chicago in October 1985.[21]

These precedents, all successful, were significant. Co-sponsorship

First Lady Barbara Bush, honorary chairperson of the Center for the Book's "Year of the Young Reader," launches the campaign in the Great Hall of the Library's Jefferson Building in March 1989. Library of Congress Photograph.

arrangements, I realized, obviously were the key to the Center's potential success. And indeed, they became the basis for the creation of the Center's reading promotion networks of state affiliates (1984) and non-profit organizations (1987). Moreover, the need for partnerships beyond our formal networks became the rationale for supporting selected projects developed by other organizations.[22]

In 1975, my wife Nancy left the Library of Congress to become a program officer at the Council on Library Resources, located at Dupont Circle in downtown Washington, D.C. In 1980, she accepted a position as associate director, Program Coordination, at the Research Libraries Group, located on the Stanford University campus in Palo Alto, Calif. So I could join her for at least part of her California tenure, the Library of Congress generously gave me an unpaid one-year leave of absence from Sept. 1981-Sept. 1982. Each of us greatly enjoyed becoming temporary members of the northern California book and library community.

During my year in California, I worked half-time as acting director of the Special Collections Department of the Stanford University Libraries. I also collaborated with the Stanford University Libraries Associates, contributing articles to its quarterly publication *Imprint* about individual book collectors who had helped create Stanford

In this 1989 photograph, John Cole presents Librarian of Congress Emeritus Daniel J. Boorstin with a copy of the newly published volume, The Republic of Letters: Librarian of Congress Daniel J. Boorstin on Books, Reading, and Libraries, 1975-1987. *Observing are Librarian of Congress James H. Billington, and Ruth Boorstin. Edited by Cole, the book presents 17 speeches and public statements by Boorstin during the Center for the Book's first decade. Library of Congress Photograph.*

To mark the "Year of the Lifetime Reader" in 1992, the Center and the U.S. Postal Service, one of its reading promotion partners, issued a poster celebrating stamps that featured famous writers. Library of Congress Photograph.

In 1998, Friends of Libraries USA (FOLUSA) and the Center for Book awarded "Literary Landmarks Registry" status to the Thomas Jefferson Building of the Library of Congress. The plaque was unveiled on June 26 by FOLUSA president Sandy Dolnick on the plaza in front of the Jefferson Building. Library of Congress Photograph.

The five winners of the 1999 Illinois "Letters About Literature" contest proudly display their award certificates. Also in the photo in the back row are: Illinois Center for the Book president Alice Calabrese and Jesse White, Illinois Secretary of State and State Librarian. The Center's principal student reading and writing promotion program, "Letters About Literature" has been sponsored since 2004 by Target. In 2010-2011, more than 70,000 students throughout the nation wrote to authors describing how books have influenced their individual lives. Photo courtesy of the Illinois Center for the Book.

Through the years, the Center for the Book office in the Library's Madison Building has been a popular stop for international visitors. During her visit on March 26, 2001, Ellen Ndeshi Namhila, director of the Namibia National Library and Information Service, stocked up on publications and promotional materials. Photo by John Cole.

Since the first National Book Festival in 2001, the Center for the Book has coordinated the Festival's author program. It also has organized the Pavilion of the States since its debut in 2002. Representing Colorado in the Pavilion of the States at the 2009 National Book Festival were, from left to right, Shelley Walchak of the Colorado State Library, Colorado author Margaret Coel, and Maggie Coval, executive director of Colorado Humanities, the home of the Colorado Center for the Book. Photo by Pat Fisher.

On Oct. 23, 2009, the Library of Congress opened its Young Readers Center in the Thomas Jefferson Building. Administered by the Center for the Book, it is the first Library of Congress space ever devoted to promoting the reading interests of children and teens. After the ribbon-cutting, Librarian of Congress James H. Billington and his wife Marjorie read and explained a Finnish children's book to a young audience. Rep. Robert Aderholt (R-Ala.) and his son and Rep. Debbie Wasserman Schultz (D-Fla) and her children helped open the new center. Photo by Barry Wheeler.

On June 28, 2010, the Center hosted its annual "idea exchange" for affiliated state centers for the book. The first such meeing was held in 1987. Then, as now, major topics included fund-raising and promoting state and local writers. State representatives in the foreground, left to right, are Frannie Ashburn, North Carolina; Mary Menzel, California; Alice Beckwith, Rhode Island; and Norman Ferris, Tennessee. Photo by Abby Brack.

"River of Words" is an international youth poetry and art contest, cosponsored by the Center for the Book, that promotes literacy, the arts, and environmental awareness. At the 15ᵗʰ annual awards and recognition ceremony, held at the Library of Congress on June 30, 2010, poet Robert Hass presents a national grand prize to Zak Bye, age 7, for his poem, "The Bunny." Hass, named U.S. Poet Laureate for 1995-1997 by Librarian of Congress Daniel J. Boorstin, cofounded River of Words in 1995 with writer Pamela Michael. Photo by Abby Brack.

University. During the 1981-82 academic year, I also taught a course ("The Library of Congress and American Librarianship") at the School of Library and Information Studies at the University of California, Berkeley, and lectured on the same topic at the Graduate School of Library and Information Science, University of California, Los Angeles. In the summer of 1982, I taught a course, "Books and Libraries in the Electronic Age," at my alma mater, the School of Librarianship at the University of Washington in Seattle.[23]

During my one-year absence from the Library of Congress, Judith O'Sullivan, executive director of the Maryland Humanities Council, was hired as the acting director of the Center for the Book. Early in 1982, she managed the Center for the Book's successful move from the Jefferson Building into the newly opened Madison Building, making certain that the Center's director had a parking place in the building—for which (each day) I am still grateful! I returned to the Center for the Book in the fall of 1982. Nancy came back to Washington, D.C. in the fall of

1983, and in 1984 she accepted the position of assistant director for Collections Management of the Smithsonian Institution Libraries; she was named director of the libraries in 1997.

During my California "sabbatical," I decided that upon my return to the Library of Congress, I would try to move the Center for the Book ahead on several fronts: creating a system of affiliated state centers, reorganizing the large National Advisory Board into a smaller Advisory Council, and obtaining Library of Congress appropriated and permanent funding for as many Center for the Book staff positions as possible.[24]

Affiliated state centers were not part of the original Center for the Book plan. However, the idea came up forcefully in San Francisco at a November 26, 1979 luncheon meeting hosted by the California members of the Center's National Advisory Board. I was the principal speaker and it soon became clear that many of the more than eighty members of the northern California book community present expected the national center to have state affiliates and, of course, hoped California might be the first such affiliate.[25]

I had already received similar inquiries from other states, notably Missouri, Florida, and Illinois, and began to understand the need. A national "system" of self-funded, relatively independent state center affiliates would carry our national mission to the regional, state, and local levels. Their formal partnerships with the Library of Congress would serve as both incentive and leverage throughout the state. The plan was beginning to take shape when my California opportunity intervened. Furthermore, while in Palo Alto, I found myself discussing the "idea" of a California Center for the Book with many of my new colleagues and acquaintances.

Not long after my return to the Library of Congress, I heard from Jean Trebbi, a program coordinator for the Broward County Library in Fort Lauderdale, Florida, regarding the idea of a Florida Center for the Book, an affiliate that she hoped could be hosted by the Broward County Library. Initially I told her that I thought that state libraries, not public libraries, were the logical hosts for state centers; there could be only one such "home" in a state, and by their nature, state libraries were state-wide institutions. However, Trebbi talked to the Florida State Librarian and in the end he endorsed her Broward County Library proposal, even agreeing to serve on the new center's board of advisors to help ensure that the center's activities were as state-wide as possible.

Trebbi also noted that Carol Nemeyer was an old friend of her boss, Cecil Beach, the director of the Broward County Library, and that he loved everything about the idea, from the Library of Congress

On Jan. 5, 2010, John Cole gave an architectural tour of the Jefferson Building to newly appointed National Ambassador for Young People's Literature Katherine Paterson and her husband, John. Photo by Abby Brack.

partnership to specific proposals for honoring Florida writers and the state's literary heritage. Although I could see the direction in which this was going, I nevertheless asked the next "key" question on my list: how about funding? The Library of Congress could not provide any financial support to state centers, and we hoped that proposals from outside would provide for state center funding for at least three years. No problem, reported Trebbi: the Broward County Library was about to open a new building and the Broward County Library Foundation, as part of any Center for the Book proposal, planned (1) to provide funding for the center for the first three years and (2) to make the continuing support of the Florida Center for the Book one of its key objectives.

Our path had become clear. I consulted with Carol Nemeyer and she liked the idea. The two of us made minor changes to Trebbi's proposal, which was formally sent by Cecil Beach to the Library of Congress on January 20, 1984. Nemeyer soon obtained Dr. Boorstin's approval, and she announced the creation of the first state center for the book at Broward County Library on April 29, 1984, in conjunction with the

On April 14, 2010, John Cole pointed out the symbolic statues and quotations in the Library's Main Reading Room to Secretary of Agriculture Tom Vilsack and his wife Christie (second from left), who founded the Iowa Center for the Book in 1987. At the far left is Cindi Pederson, director of the Iowa Department of Cultural Affairs. Photo by Abby Brack.

dedication of the library's new $43 million building.

The gate for affiliated state centers for the book had been opened. Illinois was next, in 1985, followed in 1986 by Michigan, Oklahoma, Oregon, and Wisconsin. There also were early experiments that did not work, such as the short-lived Upper Midwest Center for the Book, an affiliation of the Minneapolis Public Library and the Minnesota Center for the Book Arts, which I proudly announced in Minneapolis on Nov. 5, 1986, as a regional partnership that would "promote books and reading in Minnesota, North Dakota, and South Dakota." However, it soon became clear that each state wanted its own affiliated center![26]

The funding side also showed both movement and concrete progress. Most significantly, in the mid-1980s, Dr. Boorstin persuaded his friend Walter Annenberg to begin what became a series of significant financial donations to the Center for the Book.[27] Then, in 1987, Dr. Boorstin decided to retire after twelve years as Librarian of Congress. He and his wife Ruth generously donated $100,000 to the Center for the Book to support our still nascent publishing program.

The same year, President Ronald Reagan nominated historian James H. Billington, the director of the Woodrow Wilson International Center for Scholars, to be the thirteenth Librarian of Congress. Nancy and I, of course, attended his confirmation hearings on July 14, 1987.

My first meeting with Dr. Billington took place soon thereafter; based on my earlier experience as chairman of Dr. Boorstin's Task Force on Goals, Organization, and Planning, he asked me to serve as one of two "special advisors" to his own Management and Planning Committee. At the end of our meeting, I brought up the subject of the Center for the Book and explained why I felt that unless the Library began supporting Center for the Book staff positions, the Center's future, and certainly its future success, was problematic. He immediately agreed to put two staff positions for the Center for the Book into his first (and forthcoming) budget, with encouragement for the future. He also said he wanted to offer me a new challenge: stimulating the creation of an official Center for the Book affiliate in each of the fifty states. Another lucky break. I nodded and smiled as I began my second decade as the director of the Center for the Book.

Notes

1. This essay ends in 1987 when a new Librarian of Congress, James H. Billington, provided new support and goals for the Center for the Book. For additional information about the Center's history and activities, see the articles in this volume by Guy Lamolinara (pp.69–87) and Eleanor F. Shevlin and Eric N. Lindquist (pp. 88–101), along with Selected Writings, (pp. 180–190).

I am immensely grateful to my friends and colleagues who contributed essays to the first version of this volume: the 2010 issue (volume 45, number 1) of *Libraries & the Cultural Record: Exploring the History of Collections of Recorded Knowledge.* I especially thank my long-time library history colleague Mary Niles Maack, who initiated and organized the 2007 Library History Round Table Research Forum that started the process, and then kept the project moving ahead for the next three years, in spite of her time-consuming responsibilities as the Associate Editor of the *Encyclopedia of Library and Information Sciences,* 3rd edition. Thanks also to *Libraries & the Cultural Record* editor David B. Gracy II and managing editor, the late Janelle Dupont (1948-2010), for their valuable suggestions in shaping the special issue, and to the Center for the Book's Staceya Sistare-Anderson for her help in preparing the manuscript for publication. Three veteran Center for the Book staff members have provided decades of dedicated service: Anne Boni (1987-present), Maurvene D. Williams (1988-2008), and Patricia White (1990-2006). Finally, I would like to acknowledge the friendship of Wayne Wiegand and Jane Aikin, two library history colleagues whose ideas and writings, through the years, have broadened my perspective about the role of the Library of Congress in American society and culture.

2. Lawrence Clark Powell, *Fortune & Friendship: An Autobiography* (New York: R.R. Bowker Co., 1968). I first came across Powell's name in 1961 while browsing in a military library during ROTC summer camp. I picked up an attractive-sounding volume, *Books in my Baggage: Adventures in Reading and*

Collecting (Cleveland: World Publishing Co., 1960) by Lawrence Clark Powell. The biographical information on the back said that he was the new dean of an institution that somehow was completely new to me: a graduate school of librarianship, this particular one at UCLA. It soon dawned on me that such a graduate school existed on my own campus at the University of Washington; in fact, I walked by it every day when I entered the university library. The ball started to roll.

3. "Library of Congress and CBS Launch Read More About It Project." *Library of Congress Information Bulletin (LCIB)* 38 (Oct. 5, 1979): 413-14. Other network television projects soon followed, including "Cap'n OG Readmore," a book-loving animated cat featured for several years on ABC Children's Television. Irving Lieberman himself came back into my life in 1983 as a participant in "Books in Action," the Center for the Book's symposium honoring the 40th anniversary of the Armed Services Editions, a project in which he had played an important role years earlier when he served in the U.S. Army. See John Y. Cole, "Tattered Copies in Action: The Armed Services Editions," *LCIB* 42 (Mar. 21, 1983): 105-108.

4. John Y. Cole, "Struggle for a Structure: Ainsworth Rand Spofford and a New Building for the Library of Congress," in *The Library of Congress: The Art and Architecture of the Thomas Jefferson Building*, ed. John Y. Cole and Henry Hope Reed, 30-63. (New York: W.W. Norton, 1997), 49.

5. In addition to the Federal Writers Project (FWP), Project #1 of the Works Project Administration included the Federal Art Project, Federal Music Project, Federal Theatre Project, and the Historical Records Survey. See John Y. Cole "Amassing American Stuff: The Library of Congress and the Federal Arts Projects of the 1930s," *Quarterly Journal of the Library of Congress* (*QJLC*) 40 (Fall 1983): 356-89; John Y. Cole, "The Best of Times for American Culture? LC's New Deal Arts Collections Displayed and Discussed," *LCIB* 54 (Feb. 6, 1995): 50-52. The FWP inspired other many other regionally based Americana book series of the 1930s-1950s. In the late 1980s I met Carol Fitzgerald, a collector and bibliographer of one of these series, "Rivers of America." The Center for the Book encouraged her work through a 1987 Library of Congress symposium and the 2001 co-publication of her definitive two-volume work, *The Rivers of America: A Descriptive Bibliography* (New Castle, Del.: Oak Knoll Press in association with the Center for the Book in the Library of Congress, 2001). In 2003, on the occasion of the center's 25th anniversary, Carol and her husband Jean donated their Rivers of America collection, correspondence, and archive to the Rare Book and Special Collections Division of the Library of Congress. In 2010, in the same spirit and following the publication of their next major work, *Series Americana: Post Depression-Era Regional Literature, 1938-1980* (New Castle, Del.: Oak Knoll Press in association with the Center for the Book in the Library of Congress, 2009), they donated their "Series Americana" collections, correspondence, and archive to the Library of Congress.

6. John Y. Cole, "Of Copyright, Men & a National Library," *QJLC* 28 (Apr. 1971): 114-36; "The Main Building of the Library of Congress: A Chronology, 1871-1980," *QJLC* 29: 267-70; "Smithmeyer & Pelz: Embattled Architects of the Library of Congress," *QJLC* 29 (Oct. 1972): 282-307; "For Congress and the Nation: The Dual Nature of the Library of Congress," *QJLC* 32 (Apr. 1975): 118-38.

7.Cole, John Y., ed. *The Library of Congress in Perspective: A Volume Based on the Reports of the 1976 Librarian's Task Force and Advisory Groups.* (New York: R.R. Bowker Co., 1978).

8. Daniel J. Boorstin, "A Design for an Anytime, Do-it-Yourself, Energy-Free Communication Device," *Harper's* 248 (Jan. 1974): 83-86.

9. Ibid., *Library of Congress in Perspective*, 5-83, 137.

10. John Y. Cole, "The Center for the Book in the Library of Congress," *QJLC* 36 (Spring 1979): 178-88

11. The National Book Committee was formally dissolved on Nov. 15, 1974. See John Y. Cole, "Is There a Community of the Book?" in John Y. Cole, ed., *The Community of the Book: A Directory of Selected Organizations and Programs* (Washington, D.C.: Library of Congress, 1986), 5-13; and John C. Frantz, "A Death in the Family," *American Libraries* 6 (April 1975): 206-7.

12. "The Center for the Book in the Library of Congress: A Prospectus," *LCIB* 37 (Jan. 20, 1978): 57-58.

13. "Advisors Plan Center for the Book," *LCIB* 36 (Nov. 11, 1977): 759-762. See also John Y. Cole, *The Center for the Book in the Library of Congress: The Planning Year* (Washington, D.C.: Library of Congress, 1978), 5-12.

14. Cole, *The Center for the Book in the Library of Congress: The Planning Year*, 13-27; also "Center for the Book International Committee Meets," *LCIB* 37 (Dec. 15, 1978): 756.

15. "Center for the Book Executive Committee Meets," *LCIB* 37 (Sept. 29, 1978): 593-94.

16. John Y. Cole, ed. *Television, the Book and the Classroom* (Washington, D.C.: Library of Congress, 1978), also was the first Center for the Book publication. Other early symposia, each leading eventually to a publication, included: "Reading in America," Oct. 25-26, 1978; "Responsibilities of the American Book Community," April 4-5, 1979; "The Textbook in American Society," May 2-3, 1979; "Books in Action: The Armed Services Editions," Feb. 17, 1983; and "Biography & Books," Nov. 9-10, 1983. A complete list of the more than 100 books and pamphlets published or co-published by the Center for the Book since 1978 can be found at www.loc.gov/cfbook.

17. John Y. Cole, ed. *The International Flow of Information: A Trans-Pacific Perspective* (Washington, D.C.: Library of Congress, 1981).

18. See the list in Section V of Selected Writings (pp. 189–190).

19. John Y. Cole, "The Rosenwald Symposium on the Illustrated Book: A Report on a Symposium Honoring Lessing J. Rosenwald, Library of Congress, May 30-31, 1980" (with William Matheson), *LCIB* 39 (Aug. 1, 1980): 271-76.

20. John Y. Cole, "Literacy in Historical Perspective: A Conference Sponsored by the Center for the Book and the U.S. National Institute of Education, Library of Congress, July 14-15, 1980," *LCIB* 39 (Oct. 10, 1980): 406-12.

21. Paul Koda, "Chicago Conference on the Book in the Nineteenth Century: A Report on Papers Presented on October 18 and 19, 1985," *LCIB* 45 (Feb. 3, 1986): 47-49.

22. The state affiliates network started in 1984, with the approval of a proposal for a Florida Center for the Book hosted by the Broward County Library. Early descriptions of the growth of the network can be found in Marlene Charnizon, "23 Progeny and Counting: Appreciation for Books, Reading and Libraries is the Mission; A Nonstop Flurry of Activities is the Method," *American Libraries* 21 (Oct. 1990): 906, 908, 910; also Barbara Bryant,

"State Centers for the Book Show How 'Books Change Lives'," *Wilson Library Bulletin* 68 (Dec. 1993): 33-35, 126-27.

The non-profit reading promotion partners network was started in 1987 to support The Year of the Reader, the Center's first national reading promotion campaign; the network grew rapidly during 1989, the Center's Year of the Young Reader, for which First Lady Barbara Bush served as honorary chair. For further information see John Y. Cole, "Reading Promotion Partners," *LCIB* 61 (June 2002): 122-23.

Center for the Book funding for projects not initiated or administered by the Library of Congress have included support to: the Rare Books and Manuscripts Section of the American Library Association for a planning meeting for the 1980 conference, "Books and Society in History"; the Penn State Center for the History of the Book at University Park (1992) for its early development; a 1996 conference in Vologda, Russia, on "Libraries and Reading in Times of Cultural Change"; the Center for the Study of Print Culture in Modern America (1993) at the University of Wisconsin at Madison for its early development; the American Antiquarian Society for planning conferences for the five-volume *A History of the Book in America* (published 2000-2010); Columbia University's Rare Book and Manuscript Library for a 1996 conference on publishing archives; the University of Luton in the United Kingdom for a 1999 conference on "Culture and Consumption"; and the Folger Institute at the Folger Shakespeare Library for conferences in 2001 and 2006 on "Transactions of the Book." In addition, as co-publisher, the Center for the Book has supported books published by the University of New Mexico Press (*Library: The Drama Within*, 1996); Oak Knoll Press (*The Rivers of America: A Descriptive Bibliography*, 2001; *Series Americana: A Descriptive Bibliography*, 2009); and the University of Massachusetts Press (*Perspectives on American Book History: Artifacts and Commentary*, 2002; *Agent of Change: Print Culture Studies After Elizabeth L. Eisenstein*, 2007).

23. The California experience also was a valuable year for reflection. I enjoyed representing and discussing the Library of Congress as both an instructor and lecturer at three graduate library schools, of course, never dreaming that UCLA would someday (2000-2009) be the "host" of a yet-to-be-established affiliate, the California Center for the Book. Largely through the Book Club of California, of which I am still a member, I gained a new appreciation of the potential role that private book clubs and topics such as the book arts and book collecting could play in the Center for the Book's future.

24. Most of my new thinking was reflected in "Center for the Book Restructured: Recent and Forthcoming Activities Described," *LCIB* 45 (Feb. 10, 1986): 56-59.

25. John Y. Cole. "A Report on a Meeting Sponsored by the Center for the Book, San Francisco, Calif., November 26, 1979," *LCIB* 39 (Jan. 18, 1980): 23-24.

26. The fiftieth state center, New Hampshire, was added to the network in 2002. See "CFB Reaches 50 State Affiliates: Six New State-Wide Centers Added in 2002," *LCIB* 62 (Jan. 2003): 6-8. Dr. Billington's encouragement of the state centers and of the Center's reading promotion partnership network opened up a whole new range of relationships among the Library of Congress, its Center for the Book, the nation, and the world. Projects such as "Letters About Literature" and "River of Words" were strengthened and expanded. Moreover, the groundwork was laid for the Center for the Book's involvement with several important new projects, including the South African Centre for

the Book in the National Library of South Africa, "reading centers" hosted by libraries throughout Russia, the National Book Festival (2001-), the National Ambassador for Young People's Literature (2008-), and the Young Readers Center (2009-).

27. In 1996, the Annenberg Foundation made a $1 million contribution to the Library of Congress Trust Fund to establish an endowment for the Center for the Book.

Histories of the Library of Congress

Jane Aikin

Much has been written about the Library of Congress (LC), but relatively little of it consists of the scholarly historical appraisals that are the primary focus here. The emphasis is on book-length treatments and significant articles; with limited space, it is impossible to even reference the numerous theses, memoirs, articles, guides, pictorial works, and exhibition catalogs as well as most of the descriptions of individual collections and individuals. A great deal of writing about the Library's history has come from the Library itself. One of the most important treasures is the *Library of Congress Information Bulletin* (1942–); its brief, fact-filled articles are gems recoverable chiefly through patience and indexes. Another publication, the *Quarterly Journal of the Library of Congress*, which began in 1943 as the *Quarterly Journal of Current Acquisitions* and ceased publication with the 1983 volume, is likewise valuable for its specialized articles, especially the detailed descriptions of the collections.

The first century of the Library's existence (1800–1900) produced nothing in the way of a full-length history. But in July 1900 Herbert Putnam, Librarian of Congress from 1899 to 1939, hired William Dawson Johnston, a former history instructor at Brown University, as the first assistant in the Division of Bibliography. His assignments included editing a series titled Contributions to American Library History. The first volume, *History of the Library of Congress, Volume I, 1800–1864,* Johnston's own history of the Library, appeared in 1904. He planned three volumes, with the second volume covering 1864 to 1900 and the third the history of other federal libraries.[1] The first volume, the only one published, reproduced "all documents of importance which relate to the history of the national library" (some complete, some excerpted), and the product seemed to some critics to be "a collection of documents strung together on a rather thin thread of narrative."[2] But Johnston's history also contained, as he noted, "many picturesque incidents, many antiquarian details, many expressions of contemporary opinion, which in the history of another library might be of merely local interest." That detail, together with its important documentary and tabular materials, assures the *History* continued prominence as a record of the Library's early years.[3]

In retrospect, Johnston's decision to end his first volume with 1864 was unfortunate, for it left untold the story of the remarkable ascendance of the Library in the late nineteenth century. Apart from the acquisition of Thomas Jefferson's books in 1815, the years prior to 1864 seemed undistinguished, and the reviewers of Johnston's book took notice. While one praised the book's attention to both political history and biography as well as its exposition of the history of the library and the grounds for its future development, others emphasized the failure to realize the promise of Jefferson's insistence that "there is no subject to which a Member of Congress may not have occasion to refer." They deplored early congressional unwillingness to support the purchase of notable collections, and one even commented that it was surprising that the Library had attained its current stature. Johnston's history also revealed that the Library had been hostage on occasion to partisan politics and sometimes suffered under humdrum administration. By ending the volume with 1864, Johnston could not provide the happy ending that the administrations of Librarians Ainsworth R. Spofford (1864–97), John Russell Young (1897–99), and Putnam gave the Library's first century, and the reviewers seemed to feel in some measure shortchanged.[4]

By the late 1920s a good number of written, on-the-spot observations of the LC began to appear. The line between memoir and history in this body of work is thin, with many of the texts marked by praise—sometimes hyperbolic—for Putnam's accomplishments. Most notably, on Putnam's thirtieth anniversary as Librarian former LC staff members William Warner Bishop and Andrew Keogh compiled a volume entitled *Essays Offered to Herbert Putnam by His Colleagues and Friends on His Thirtieth Anniversary as Librarian of Congress 5 April 1929*. In generally brief articles many of Putnam's associates aired their memories, from congressmen to library directors, LC associates, and scholars.[5]

Three Library staff members of the early and middle years of the twentieth century—Frederick William Ashley, Lucy Salamanca, and David Mearns—produced full histories of the Library. Ashley came to the Library in 1900 and filled a variety of posts, rising to become chief assistant librarian in 1927 and retiring in 1936. In a brief article for the 1929 Putnam volume he divided LC history into three eras: the pre-Spofford period; Spofford's administration; and the Young and Putnam administrations. Much admired at the time, this history exemplified the views of Putnam's contemporaries on the Library's development.[6] Ashley's lengthy manuscript history of the Library, unfinished and unpublished, today resides in the LC Manuscript Division. His work covers mainly the administrations of Young and Putnam. However, Ashley usually started his chapters with a brief survey of the earlier history of each administrative unit or subject and thus provided coverage of other administrations as well. The manuscript lacks documentation, but much of the material seems to come from division reports and the Librarian's annual reports, which for those administrations provide especially rich source material. Much of his text records day-to-day activities, including staff lists, descriptions of work routines, lists of acquisitions, and even details on items provided to readers. Nevertheless, if Ashley shows us mostly the soul of the scrupulous bureaucrat, eternally careful of detail, in the end his history provides a useful report.[7]

The next book-length history was Lucy Salamanca's *Fortress of Freedom*, published during World War II.[8] Salamanca, who served as head of the Inquiry Section of the Legislative Reference Service, set out to place the Library's history within the context of the identification of the Library by Librarian Archibald MacLeish (1939–44) with the Allied cause and with America as the arsenal of democracy. Indeed, in his foreword MacLeish described the LC as "a library of the people, by the people, and for the people, and as long as it exists as a free library and a people's library the intellectual and spiritual freedom which Jefferson and his colleagues proposed to establish will not perish from the earth."[9] The themes of democracy and freedom are prominent in Salamanca's undocumented narrative, but as a history it lacks extensive information on the mid-nineteenth-century period. *Fortress* is still worth reading for Salamanca's sometimes fulsome evocation of the Library's wartime aura.[10]

David Chambers Mearns entered the Library in 1918, just short of his nineteenth birthday. He rose to chief reference librarian, head of the Reference Department, and then assistant librarian, retiring in 1967 as chief of the Manuscript Division. His historical writings center on two passions: the Library of Congress and Abraham Lincoln; he was well respected in the circle of Lincoln scholars. After World War II, when Librarian Luther Harris Evans (1945–53) asked for almost double the Library's appropriation in his 1947 budget request in order to expand both the collections and national library activities, Congress abruptly refused, insisting on its own right to decide what the Library's role would be in the postwar world and thereby challenging its national library status. Evans turned to David Mearns to present the historical rationale for the Library's claim to a national role, and Mearns produced in just three months a preamble of more than two hundred pages to the Librarian's *Annual Report* for 1946 entitled *The Story Up to Now: The Library of Congress, 1800–1946*.[11]

From the first page it is evident that Mearns enthusiastically embraced his mission and that he would miss no chance to evoke the lessons of history for congressional contemporaries. When recording the debate that Librarian George Watterston (1815–29) raised regarding the Library of Congress's claim to be the national library, he referred to "ancient conflicts which have in the present day their surviving counterparts: the general library opposed to the special library; the great repository of national genius in all its forms ranged against the most authoritative records of other societies and other peoples; precedent versus possibility; wants known, and therefore wants precise, as distinguished from anticipated and consequently problematical, requirements; the claims of selection confronted by the claims of comprehensiveness."[12] Moreover, he commented:

> Then, as now, the annual book fund was sufficient only to the maintenance of subscriptions and to the procurement of the current products of the press. Then, as now, the lack of adequate provision forced neglect of materials of retrospective and antiquarian interest. Then, as now, there was that realization of "the absolute necessity of an extensive and judiciously selected library." Then, but fortunately now a little less, there were, in some quarters, misgivings concerning the actual utility of literature presented in languages other than our own. Then the problems were microscopic; now they are magnified; but they are the same problems and they are familiar.

He ended this passage by recalling approvingly the early (1824) congressional decision that "an extensive collection meant a comprehensive collection, with no exceptions save mediocrity," and he emphasized that in refusing several early opportunities to purchase fine private collections, "the cautious economies of 1836 merely transferred a burden to future generations. . . . Over and over again experience has made postponement profligate."[13]

When he came to the administration of Ainsworth Rand Spofford, Mearns developed in full his theme of the inevitability of national library status. The historical record, from Spofford's efforts to develop the national collections and then to house them, to the important initiatives of the Young and Putnam administrations to build on Spofford's foundations, confirmed that the Library of Congress was in fact the national library: the Librarians thought so, Congress thought so, and everyone else thought so too. And when citing congressional acceptance of the Gardiner Greene Hubbard bequest (1912) and the establishment of the Elizabeth Sprague Coolidge Foundation (1925), Mearns pressed his point ever more emphatically: "These activities constituted a departure from the philosophy of librarianship as ordinarily understood in terms of government subsidy and promotion. Under the earlier philosophy the Library's functions were, as is the case of most large public libraries, merely passive." While the word "passive" grates today because it surely misrepresents the pre-Hubbard and pre-Coolidge years, Mearns's chief concern here was to emphasize that "active participation in the cultural life of the community was both implied and intended through the purpose for which this [Coolidge] endowment was established." Moreover, he contended, the broadening of the Library's role was well understood by both the Library and the Congress in 1925, but no one could anticipate all the implications. Declaring that the Trust Fund Board (established in 1925) and the endowments "strengthened the Library of Congress as a cultural force in the lives of the American people," Mearns pointed out: "Similarly, it is difficult today to forecast the designs which these activities will fashion during the ensuing twenty-one years."[14]

This statement provided a lead-in to the World War II period, when the Library staff discovered that

> deficiencies were conspicuous in collections formerly believed to be adequate for any cause. The lack of specialists for the interpretation of materials in certain fields placed the national interest in jeopardy. Out of this, there grew upon the administrators of the Library a grim determination to lay at the first opportunity its case before Congress, set forth its needs as tragedy had marked them, and propose a plan which would, whether in war or peace, prevent recurrence.

Referring to Librarian Archibald MacLeish as "the 'front-line Librarian,'" Mearns evoked the wartime Library as "the Arsenal of Democracy, the City of the Mind, the Fortress of Freedom," and he averred that when MacLeish departed "the brush of the comet gave a new dimension to the Library. . . . It had become a cultural institution great among the great cultural institutions of the world. It could maintain that position." The sentence ends without a question mark, but the reader can almost see one in Mearns's thoughts. With only brief mention of MacLeish's successor, Luther Harris Evans, *The Story Up to Now* abruptly ends.[15]

Mearns's book did not immediately win the Library a large budget increase, but it drew significant praise: historian Lyman Butterfield declared that it set "a new standard for classic institutional history," and another historian, Julian Boyd, labeled it "a classic."[16] Its eloquent and persuasive construction of LC history seems to have forestalled any other comprehensive reassessment, even on an occasion as significant as the 1950 sesquicentennial, though an exhibition on the Library's history was mounted, and Mearns wrote a series of historical vignettes for the *Library of Congress Information Bulletin*. Dan M. Lacy, deputy chief assistant librarian, prepared a two-article series on the development and organization of the Library's collections that has proved to be a durable summary of the pre-1950 years.[17] The November 1950 issue of the *Quarterly Journal of the Library of Congress*, focusing on the founding of the Library, was the first of a few thematic issues on LC history.[18] But the most far-reaching of the sesquicentennial activities was the series of fifteen-minute intermission broadcasts at LC concerts surrounding the anniversary during which Mearns, Evans, and assistant librarian Verner W. Clapp discussed LC history, and other Library specialists presented remarks about the collections or the divisions.[19]

Through the years Mearns authored many articles about the Library and several Librarians, mostly as short pieces for the *Library of Congress Information Bulletin*. His articles about Librarian Emeritus Herbert Putnam—informed by conversations with Putnam—are particularly insightful, characterizing his contribution as "the gift of continuity and steady growth; the gift of the well set course and strength for its running." When Putnam died in 1955, Mearns produced a pamphlet entitled *Herbert Putnam, 1861–1955: A Memorial Tribute*. This slender volume included his essay "Herbert Putnam and His Responsible Eye," which, though subtitled "A Memorial Tribute," coupled reminiscence with Putnam's own words and an important summary of the Librarian's ideas and accomplishments.[20]

Putnam's death came a little less than a year after the appointment of Lawrence Quincy Mumford (1954–74), the first professional librarian to hold the office of Librarian of Congress. Following the administration of Luther Evans, who became unpopular with Congress, Mumford necessarily tended first to recovering and burnishing the Library's image on Capitol Hill, while the staff worked to modernize and even revolutionize some important elements of professional practice. Library colleagues, particularly research and academic librarians, criticized Mumford's disinclination to press for budget increases and ambitious projects that would benefit both the LC and the library community, but internal and external initiatives of the 1950s and 1960s propelled both the Library and the profession forward in the areas of computerized cataloging, massive foreign acquisitions, and preservation planning. Under Mumford the Library was extensively occupied with its own operations and their implications for the library community. But if that rather technically directed ménage mostly failed to inspire efforts to write the Library's larger history, it did result in some narratives and memoirs that focused on the history of important work to develop LC technical services and bibliographic systems. Much of this history came, appropriately, from yet another generation of in-house historians of the Library.[21]

In the latter years of the Mumford administration John Young Cole, then a staff member in the Reference Department, produced a 1971 dissertation on a distant, nearly untouched area of LC history: Ainsworth Rand Spofford's early career as Librarian. In comparison to his contemporaries (William Frederick Poole, Charles Ammi Cutter, and Melvil Dewey), Spofford had received little attention, and the dissertation represented, after Johnston's volume, the first fully documented appraisal of LC history by a trained historian. The study not only surveyed the nineteenth-century context of the Library's development but by extension provided a window on the early development of other Washington cultural institutions—chiefly the Smithsonian Institution and the National Archives—and thus contributed to understanding how the federal cultural institutional base emerged. It can also be read as a text on how one nineteenth-century federal agency head was able to originate and influence national policy.[22]

Frederick Ashley had characterized Spofford's administration as decisive, arguing in fact that the first sixty-four days of 1865 eclipsed the previous sixty-four years in terms of advancing the Library's role as a national library.[23] Proceeding from this observation, Cole's dissertation developed several themes: how the Library grew from a small legislative collection to an institution of national significance, how the idea of a national library developed in the United States, and how Spofford contributed to that development between 1861 and 1872.[24] He broadened Ashley's sixty-four days to the period 1865–70, pointing to six major acts that Spofford secured to establish precedents and the Library's national role: the 1865 appropriation to expand the Library's quarters in the Capitol; the 1865 return of copyright deposit to the Library; the Smithsonian Deposit of 1866, which brought the scientific library of the Smithsonian Institution to the LC; the 1867 purchase of the Peter Force library of Americana for $100,000; the international exchange resolution of 1867, which provided the means to develop a collection of foreign public documents; and the Copyright Act of 1870, which brought all U.S. copyright registrations and deposits to the Library. Among these, the most important was copyright deposit, which provided the means of rapidly expanding the collections. The logical conclusion to this succession of collection-building statutes was the construction of a separate building, which the Librarian first proposed in 1872.[25]

Spofford proceeded with a clear vision of the national library as a unique institution that would not be part of any system, "a single, comprehensive collection of national literature to be used both by Congressmen and by the American people." As Cole saw it, this "relatively narrow" view of the library's mission helped Spofford achieve his objectives, combined with the strictly pragmatic approach of proposing changes that (with the exception of the Force purchase) cost the government little. Spofford's successful strategy provided his successors with four essential preconditions for a national library: "(1) firm bipartisan support for the idea of the Library of Congress as both a legislative and a national library; (2) the beginning of a comprehensive collection of Americana; (3) a magnificent new building, itself a national monument; and (4) a strong and independent office of Librarian of Congress." Thus, Spofford "succeeded in establishing the national library as he envisioned it," and later Librarians' expansions of functions and services "have been based on his fundamental premise that a national library was a great national collection 'universal' in both its range and its usefulness."[26] As Cole claimed, "The extension of the services of the Library of Congress was a direct result of the expansion of the scope of the Library's collections; in other words, the functions of the Library have derived from its collections, not vice versa."[27] In this analysis it was Spofford who established the unique, dual role of the Library as a legislative and national institution. With its legislative responsibilities foremost but able also to pay attention to other constituencies, the Library could—and subsequently did, especially under Putnam's leadership—extend more elaborate services to the federal government, the public, authors and publishers, scholars and the research community, and the library community.[28]

If Spofford's role in building the national collections and reviving the national library idea had been overshadowed by more recent events, Cole's dissertation, his *Ainsworth Rand Spofford: Bookman and Librarian*, and his other writings on the nineteenth-century Library served to bring to light its post–Civil War history. The Library's national status resulted from the work of more than one Librarian but with Spofford as the key to its existence. And the emphasis on the historical grounding of national library status and the Library's dual focus was particularly timely given the twentieth-century context. Cole's new interpretation of LC history had followed four important initiatives, three nationally based and one congressionally inspired: the inception of the Machine-Readable Cataloging Program (1966), the National Advisory Commission on

Libraries' examination of the Library's national role (1966), the congressionally mandated expansion of the Congressional Research Service (1970), and the library community's pressure for a national preservation program (1960s).

Unlike the Library's 150th anniversary, the 175th, in 1975, included a major publication on LC history. The *Quarterly Journal of the Library of Congress* published a series of well-documented biographical articles on the eleven Librarians of Congress, from the first Librarian, John James Beckley (1802–7), through Mumford, mostly written by Library staff members.[29] Before this volume appeared biographical and other material about the Librarians was chiefly available through *Who's Who* entries, obituaries, and memorial volumes.[30] The essayists, whose articles were compiled into the volume *Librarians of Congress, 1802–1974*, were squarely in line with the standard approach to writing institutional history through analyzing the administrations of their chief executives. They provided a useful service by differentiating the Librarians, many of them scarcely remembered, and by providing generally balanced assessments of their accomplishments. The volume also helped to encourage professional historical study of the Library.[31] It appeared at a time when interest in library history was growing among both librarians and historians, and some scholars had already weighed in with well-documented appraisals.[32] Articles on some famous incidents in LC history also began to appear, signaling growing interest in examining particular aspects of the Library's development.[33]

When John Cole became chair of Librarian Daniel Boorstin's (1975–87) Task Force on Goals, Organization, and Planning in 1976, he drew on the past to inform the inquiry. The task force defined the role of the Library of Congress as a national cultural institution, extending Spofford's basic conception of the Library's responsibilities to both Congress and the American people. Its 1978 report, *The Library of Congress in Perspective*, included Cole's brief history of the Library to 1975 and a framework for thinking about its past and its future directions: the functions of the Library as having derived from the collections and the Jefferson Building (made necessary by those collections) as having been built specifically to serve as the American national library. The report also emphasized Herbert Putnam's initiative to establish an unusual working partnership between the national library and the library community in developing national library services. Here Cole also reiterated his understanding of the Library's dual role.[34]

In his analysis that role was perpetually in flux. "The normal pattern has been for the Library to grow in stages, usually with alternating emphases between legislative and national functions. . . . Congressional committees occasionally have expressed unhappiness with the Library, but such instances usually have been followed with a reemphasis on the institution's legislative role that eased the situation."[35] From the Putnam administration forward, the Library obtained outside funding for important projects that were later continued with appropriated funds, a technique that succeeded several times in the 1950s and 1960s just as it had in the 1920s and 1930s. But the paradox of national library status remained: Congress always refused to relinquish its ownership of the Library or to allow changing its name while simultaneously providing increasing support, which enabled the LC to strengthen its national and international influence and to provide services to its other constituencies. Three Librarians whose administrations Cole characterized as expansionist—Spofford, Putnam, and Mumford—all notably refused to advocate changing either the Library's name or its status within the federal government but at the same time exerted leadership to enlarge its national responsibilities.[36]

Cole's gift for extending his knowledge of LC history to a wide audience emerged in the many articles he wrote for the *Library of Congress Information Bulletin*, and when we became acquainted in the early 1980s, he invited me to meetings he was hosting for LC staff who had read those articles and had become interested in LC history. In 1979 he published *For Congress and the Nation: A Chronological History of the Library of Congress*, a documented chronology (1774–1975) of the notable dates in LC history, which has provided a baseline for coverage of the Library's past.[37] As a reference work this book has been enormously valuable internally, but it also encouraged the study of LC history, as did *The Library of Congress: A Documentary History*, a microfiche series that provides scholars and students with a massive base of primary source material. Cole's introductory essay contributed both a brief history and some much-needed guidance for future users of the huge, complex, and sprawling Library of Congress Archives and related collections in the Manuscript Division.[38]

Librarian Boorstin brought not only a historian's perspective to the Library but also an interest in bringing books and reading to public attention. One result was the establishment of the Center for the Book in the Library of Congress in 1977, with Cole as founding director. In 1981 the Library appointed the first full-time specialist in Library of Congress history and archives in the Manuscript Division and took steps toward establishing its own records as the Library of Congress Archives. This in turn led to the transfer of the massive Putnam and MacLeish-Evans records to the division as well as the processing and preservation of the large group of records pertaining to the construction of the Jefferson Building. These initiatives both centralized the Library's records and began the preparation of the mass of documentation for scholars' use. The LC Archives specialists have since undertaken initiatives to gather in more material and to complete some oral histories, as Cole continually urges them on. Recent efforts have been directed toward persuading the developers of the digital library collections to add material dealing with LC history, while the Library's own Web site has become an increasingly useful record of the factual history of its development.

The history of the Library is both intertwined with and sheds light on larger aspects of American culture, especially the work of Congress and the federal government; authorship, printing, and publishing; scholarship and literature; the arts; and libraries and librarianship. Cole has written on all these subjects, demonstrating in the process the Library's pervasive influence in American cultural life. For example, he characterized the age of Spofford and Putnam as the age not only of the emergence of the great American library but also of the library's transition from storehouse to workshop, and he showed how the work of both men shaped and supported American scholarship. A short piece on LC's relations with the American Library Association provided important perspectives on their sometimes vexed relationship as well as LC's relations with the library community as a whole.[39] Cole's article in the final issue of the *Quarterly Journal* focused on the Library's initiatives to gather in and preserve the rich cultural legacy of the Great Depression.[40] His scholarship also has extended to the comparative history of national libraries and the Library's international role.[41]

In *Jefferson's Legacy: A Brief History of the Library of Congress* Cole emphasized that not only do the functions of the Library derive from the expansion of the collections from Jefferson's time forward, but the development of the library also has reflected the continuing influence of Jeffersonian ideals. Both Jefferson and James Madison traced a direct link between knowledge and democracy; Cole pointed out that Librarians of Congress have all, in different ways, emphasized the belief that the democratic form of government depends on fostering knowledge and sharing information. Wide recognition of the Library as a symbol of democracy emerged in the wake of nineteenth-century cultural nationalism and pervaded the twentieth-century institution, from the exhibition of the Declaration of Independence and the Constitution (1921–52) in the Jefferson Building's Great Hall, through World War II and the subsequent emphasis on internationalism. But these themes in LC history were not much elaborated until *Jefferson's Legacy* demonstrated that the collection-building initiatives of several Librarians followed the theme of Jeffersonian comprehensiveness.[42] Two years later, in *On These Walls: Inscriptions and Quotations in the Buildings of the Library of Congress*, Cole revealed how democratic references and principles and also the ambitions to amass and share the wisdom of all civilizations were incorporated into the decoration of not just the Jefferson Building but also the Adams and the Madison buildings.[43] In a more recent article Cole asserted that the LC has become "the largest and most international of the world's major libraries" primarily because Librarians Spofford, Putnam, Evans, and James H. Billington (1987–), in particular, adhered to and expanded Jeffersonian ideas. As Cole noted, for example, Spofford adopted Jefferson's early vision of a broad scope for the Library, even paraphrasing him: "There is almost no work, with the vast range of literature and science, which may not at some time prove useful to the legislature of a great nation." In more recent years the Library's Web site has been the chief vehicle for expanding knowledge of its resources, helping to achieve Librarian Billington's ambition to make the Library "an important catalyst for the educational, competitive, and creative needs of our nation" and to increase the knowledge readily available to Americans in their local communities.[44]

For the Library's most recent anniversary in 2000 Cole cochaired the Bicentennial Committee. The Bicentennial slogan, "Libraries—Creativity—Liberty," continued the themes of *Jefferson's Legacy*: that the Library's development rests on Jefferson's and Madison's conviction that democracy depends "on the mutual support of liberty & learning"; Spofford's insistence that because the United States was "a Republic which rests upon the popular intelligence" the Library should serve the American people; Putnam's initiatives to share LC collections and products widely through national services; and Billington's particular talents for building private support for the Library and developing the resources required to harness electronic technologies.[45] For the Library's bicentennial, as David Mearns had done for the sesquicentennial, Cole wrote a series of articles entitled Bicentennial Background for the *Library of Congress Information Bulletin,* and the Library sponsored the publication of a one-volume popular illustrated history.[46]

Work on the *Encyclopedia of the Library of Congress: For Congress, the Nation and the World* has straddled the twentieth and twenty-first centuries. Designed as a one-volume reference on the Library that reflects on its history and evolution, the coedited volume consists of thematic articles and encyclopedia-type entries on the Library's history. The themes of John Cole's earlier work—the Jeffersonian legacy, the Library's dual role, its identification with American democracy, and its international scope—recur in the article on the Library's overall history, particularly in the sketches of the individual Librarians. The work of the individual divisions is covered extensively by different authors, mostly Library of Congress staff members whose descriptions of both historical and recent operations provide (often for the first time) each of these smaller histories with its own continuous narrative. An article on the organization of the Library provides an unusual overview of its evolution.[47] Perspectives on the Library's relations with other federal cultural institutions appear in articles on the National Archives and the Smithsonian Institution; other essays address the Library's international role and its relationship to scholarship and to other libraries and librarians. The volume also features extensive tabular and bibliographical material.[48]

Recent years have seen new appraisals of LC history. Library staff members, as in the past, have contributed to the new work, for example, Josephus Nelson and Judith Farley's illustrated volume on the Main Reading Room and Charles Goodrum and Helen Dalrymple's article on the first years of LC automation. Their account was followed by several more that discuss the LC experience with formulating and disseminating the MARC format, the development of networking activities, and increased interlibrary cooperation, together, as always, with reminiscences and staff observations.[49]

A few scholars have examined periods of the Library's history in book-length treatments. Carl Ostrowski, a scholar of American literature, proceeded from a book culture perspective in *Books, Maps and Politics: A Cultural History of the Library of Congress, 1783–1861*, exploring the relationship between the establishment of the Library and the expansion of print culture and public discourse in the colonies and the early republic. He found that resistance to establishing a library for Congress rose less because the members objected to the associated costs than from their conviction that building a comprehensive library was a luxury unnecessary to the diffusion of knowledge among the citizenry—such diffusion could be readily accomplished through the growing traffic in newspapers and pamphlets. Thus, the Library of Congress during its first sixty-plus years was limited for the most part to the essential titles required to serve legislative needs.[50] Several article-length studies on other aspects of the Library's eighteenth- and nineteenth-century past have also appeared.[51]

The Nation's Great Library: Herbert Putnam and the Library of Congress, 1899–1939 is my own attempt to place in perspective Herbert Putnam's vision of growth and development for the national library. Putnam extended the concept of a national library far beyond that of its European counterparts by organizing cataloging, bibliographic, and interlibrary loan services that served Congress, other libraries, and the public at large. The book also appraises congressional relations under Putnam; LC relations with libraries, librarians, and the American Library Association; and the difficult years of the post–World War I period, when reduced funding limited the ability to provide for the Library's own needs and those of its various constituencies. This changed when Elizabeth Sprague Coolidge's gift and the establishment of the Library of Congress Trust Fund Board encouraged private contributions to increase collections and services and to further the Library's role as a cultural institution.[52] Several analyses of initiatives of that period provide insights into the ways in which the Putnam administration fostered that development.[53]

Twentieth-century LC history continues to draw historians' attention, in particular, investigations of topics related to technical services and World War II and the postwar periods.[54] Fred Stielow, for example, discussed the American Library Association's eventual rapprochement with Archibald MacLeish after its protest against his nomination and the Librarian's subsequent leadership in the library community and among federal libraries during World War II. "Preparing for a National Emergency: The Committee on Conservation of Cultural Resources, 1939–1944" also analyzes MacLeish's wartime activities, focusing on the interagency effort to protect federal cultural collections against invasion or air attack. Louise Robbins probed the Library's experience with the 1947 Federal Loyalty Program, concluding that the Library influenced the ALA to "moderate, then to more closely define, its objections to loyalty programs in libraries."[55]

In *Poetry's Catbird Seat* William McGuire focused on the Library's involvement with poetry, "up to 1937 . . . primarily custodial," until Librarian Putnam appointed Joseph Auslander as the first consultant in poetry, thus making the LC "a principal vehicle of the poetic tradition."[56] McGuire's lightly documented history is a chronological exposition focusing on the poets themselves and their activities at the Library. He designated Archibald MacLeish's appointment of Allen Tate as consultant in 1943 as an important turning point. The well-respected Tate became a magnet, attracting his poet colleagues to the Library and making it for a few years a center of Washington literary culture. McGuire also discussed the 1948 controversy over the LC poetry fellows' decision to award the Bollingen Prize for poetry to Ezra Pound, a choice that became so controversial because of Pound's fascist and anti-Semitic views that Congress discontinued the Library's involvement with the prize.[57]

Writing the history of the Library of Congress presents the challenge of analyzing a gigantic institution with records of mammoth breadth and depth. From past to present its collections and interests have been deeply engaged with not only American culture broadly but any and every other culture worldwide. Considering the mass of documentation available to them, historians writing during the past two decades have, perhaps wisely, confined their investigations chiefly to topical analyses or limited periods. John Cole, whose writings range across the entirety of LC history, is, of course, the exception. The professional historical analysis of this institution is becoming broader and deeper; it includes a number of fine-grained, well-documented treatments of significant aspects of the Library's past. We look forward to more of these as scholars continue to balance LC achievements against the constraints on the Library's activities as an institution, as a federal agency, as a cultural actor, and as part of the global library establishment.

Notes

1. William Dawson Johnston, *History of the Library of Congress, Volume I, 1800–1864* (Washington, D.C.: Government Printing Office, 1904). Notes for volume 2 are in Box 14, William Dawson Johnston Papers, Manuscript Division, Library of Congress (hereafter LC).

2. Johnston, *History*, 5; the quote is from Aksel Josephson's review in *The Dial*, February 1, 1905, 81–82.

3. Johnston, *History*, 5.

4. Reviews are in Box 14, Johnston Papers.

5. William Warner Bishop and Andrew Keogh, eds., *Essays Offered to Herbert Putnam by His Colleagues and Friends on His Thirtieth Anniversary as Librarian of Congress 5 April 1929* (Freeport, N.Y.: Books for Libraries Press, 1967).

6. Frederick W. Ashley, "Three Eras in the Library of Congress," in ibid., 57–67.

7. Frederick William Ashley Papers, Manuscript Division, LC.

8. Lucy Salamanca, *Fortress of Freedom: The Story of the Library of Congress with a Foreword by Archibald MacLeish* (Philadelphia: J. B. Lippincott Company, 1942). The typescript version is in the Manuscript Division, LC.

9. Salamanca, *Fortress*, 9.

10. The LC's online collection "Freedom's Fortress," *American Memory*, draws on Salamanca's work. See http://memory.loc.gov/ammem/collections/freedoms_fortress.

11. David Chambers Mearns, *The Story Up to Now: The Library of Congress, 1800–1946* (Washington, D.C.: Library of Congress, 1947).

12. Ibid., 30.

13. Ibid., 33–34, 49.

14. Ibid., 195.

15. Ibid., 214–15; see also David Chambers Mearns, "The Brush of the Comet: Archibald MacLeish at the Library of Congress," *Atlantic Monthly* 215 (May 1965): 90–92.

16. John Broderick, "David Chambers Mearns," in *Supplement to the Dictionary of American Library Biography*, ed. Wayne A. Wiegand, 72 (Englewood, Colo.: Libraries Unlimited, 1990).

17. Dan Lacy, "The Library of Congress: A Sesquicentenary Review. The Development of the Collections," *Library Quarterly* (hereafter *LQ*) 20 (July 1950): 157–79; *LQ* 20 (October 1950): 235–58.

18. Others were the Jefferson Building (October 1972) and the 1975–76 articles about the Librarians of Congress.

19. Recordings are available in the Library. Other articles revealing sesquicentenary interest are Richard G. Wood, "Librarian-in-Arms: The Career of John G. Stephenson," *LQ* 19 (October 1949): 263–69; Fred Shelley, "Manuscripts in the Library of Congress, 1800–1900," *American Archivist* 11 (1948): 3–19.

20. David C. Mearns, "Herbert Putnam and His Responsible Eye," in *Herbert Putnam, 1861–1955: A Memorial Tribute*, 1–52 (Washington, D.C.: Library of Congress, 1956); see also Mearns, "Ainsworth the Unforgettable," *Quarterly Journal of the Library of Congress* (hereafter *QJLC*) 25 (January 1968): 1–4; Mearns, "Herbert Putnam: Librarian of the United States," *DC Libraries* 26 (January 1955): 1–24; and Mearns, "The Brush of the Comet." The quote is from Mearns, "Herbert Putnam: Librarian of the United States: The Minneapolis Years," *Wilson Library Bulletin* 29 (September 1954): 63.

21. Paul Edlund, "A Monster and a Miracle: The Cataloging Distribution Service of the Library of Congress, 1901–1976," *QJLC* 33 (October 1976): 383–421; Mary Kay Daniels Gunning, "Library of Congress Cataloging Distribution Services, 1901–1976," *Library Resources and Technical Services* 21 (Fall 1977): 317–25; John P. Comaroni, "'Knowledge Organized Is Knowledge Kept': The Dewey Decimal Classification, 1876–1976," *QJLC* 33 (1976): 311–31; Verner W. Clapp, et al., "The Age of Cronin," Aspects of the Accomplishments of John W. Cronin, Library of Congress, 1925–1968," *Library Resources and Technical Services* 21, no. 4 (Fall 1968): 385–405; John Cronin, "History of the National Union Catalog, Pre-56 Imprints," in *Book Catalogs*, ed. Maurice B. Tauber and Hilda Feinberg, 118–32 (Metuchen, N.J.: Scarecrow Press, 1971); Henriette D. Avram, *MARC: Its History and Implications* (Washington, D.C.: Library of Congress, 1975); John M. Dawson, "The Library of Congress: Its Role in Cooperative and Centralized Cataloging," *Library Trends* 16 (July 1967): 85–96.

22. John Young Cole, "Ainsworth Spofford and the 'National Library,'" Ph.D. diss., George Washington University, 1971; Cole, ed., *Ainsworth Rand Spofford: Bookman and Librarian* (Littleton, Colo.: Libraries Unlimited, 1975); see also Cole, "Ainsworth Rand Spofford: The Valiant and Persistent Librarian of Congress," in *Librarians of Congress, 1802–1974*, 119–41 (Washington, D.C.: Library of Congress, 1977); Cole, "The Library of Congress in the 19th Century: An Informal Account," *Journal of Library History* (hereafter *JLH*) 9 (July 1974): 222–40; Cole, "A Congenial Intellectual Occupation," *Manuscripts* 26 (Fall 1974): 247–53; Cole, "A National Monument for a National Library: Ainsworth Rand Spofford and the New Library of Congress, 1871–1897," *Records of the Columbia Historical Society of Washington, D.C.* 48 (1971–72): 468–507.

23. Ashley, "Three Eras," 57–62.

24. Conversation with John Y. Cole, February 27, 2009.

25. John Y. Cole, "Ainsworth Spofford and the Copyright Law of 1870," *JLH* 6 (1971): 34–40; Cole, "Of Copyright, Men, & a National Library," *QJLC* 28 (April 1971): 114–36; Cole, "Smithmeyer & Pelz: Embattled Architects of the Library of Congress," *QJLC* 29 (October 1972): 282–307.

26. Cole, "Ainsworth Rand Spofford: The Valiant and Persistent Librarian of Congress," 129; Cole, *Ainsworth Rand Spofford: Bookman and Librarian*, 32, 44; and Cole, "The Library of Congress and the Democratic Spirit," in *Libraries and Democracy: The Cornerstones of Liberty*, ed. Nancy Kranich, 169–82 (Chicago: American Library Association, 2001), 172.

27. John Y. Cole, "The Library of Congress in American Life," *Advances in Librarianship* 8 (1978): 57. Verner Clapp made the same observation in "The Library of Congress and the Other Scholarly Libraries of the Nation," *College & Research Libraries* 9 (April 1948): 117.

28. See Cole, "Library of Congress in American Life"; Cole, "For Congress and the Nation: The Dual Nature of the Library of Congress," *QJLC* 32 (April 1975): 118–38; Cole, "LC and ALA, 1876–1901," *Library Journal* 98 (October 15, 1973): 2965–70; Cole, "The Library of Congress and American Research Libraries," in *University Library History*, ed. James Thompson, 187–207 (New York: K. G. Saur, 1980).

29. *Librarians of Congress, 1802–1974*. The volume lacks an editorial statement, but John Cole did much to organize it. See also Keyes D. Metcalf, "*Librarians of Congress, 1802–1974*: A Review Essay," *JLH* 14 (Winter 1979): 43–55.

30. Newer works are Scott Donaldson, *Archibald MacLeish: An American Life* (Boston: Houghton Mifflin, 1992); and William H. MacLeish, *Uphill with Archie: A Son's Journey* (New York: Simon and Schuster, 2001). Also see Edmund Berkeley and Dorothy Smith Berkeley, *John Beckley: Zealous Partisan in a Nation Divided* (Philadelphia: American Philosophical Society, 1973).

31. It also encouraged some reflections on the role of the Librarian: see Metcalf, "*Librarians of Congress*." An earlier appraisal is Jerrold Orne, "The Annual Reports of the Librarian of Congress," *LQ* 14 (1944): 239–45.

32. John Cole, "Herbert Putnam and the National Library," in *Milestones to the Present: Papers from Library History Seminar V*, ed. Harold Goldstein, 109–24 (Syracuse, N.Y.: Gaylord Professional Publications, 1978); Eva Goldschmidt, "Archibald MacLeish, Librarian of Congress," *College & Research Libraries* 30 (January 1969): 12–24; Betty Milum, "Choosing MacLeish's Successor: The Recurring Debate," *JLH* 12 (Spring 1977): 86–109; Betty Schwartz, "The Role of the American Library Association in the Selection of Archibald MacLeish as Librarian of Congress," *JLH* 9 (July 1974): 241–64; Dennis Thomison, "F.D.R., the ALA and Mr. MacLeish: The Selection of the Librarian of Congress, 1939," *LQ* 42 (1972): 390–98; Dennis Thomison, "Trouble in Camelot: An Early Skirmish of Kennedy's New Frontier," *JLH* 13 (Spring 1978): 148–56; Wayne A. Wiegand, "Herbert Putnam's Appointment as Librarian of Congress," *LQ* 49 (July 1979): 255–82.

33. Elizabeth Snapp, "Acquisition of the Vollbehr Collection of Incunabula," *JLH* 10 (April 1975): 152–61; Frederick R. Goff, "Uncle Sam Has a Book," *QJLC* 38 (Summer 1981): 123–33; Milton O. Gustafson, "The Empty Shrine: The Transfer of the Declaration of Independence and the Constitution to the National Archives," *American Archivist* 39 (July 1976): 271–85.

34. John Y. Cole, ed., *The Library of Congress in Perspective: A Volume Based on the Reports of the 1976 Librarian's Task Force and Advisory Groups* (New York: R. R. Bowker Company, 1978).

35. Ibid., 2.

36. Ibid., 2, 5–83.

37. John Y. Cole, *For Congress and the Nation: A Chronological History of the Library of Congress* (Washington, D.C.: Library of Congress, 1979).

38. John Y. Cole, ed., *The Library of Congress: A Documentary History* (Bethesda, Md.: CIS Academic Editions, 1987); Cole, ed., *The Library of Congress: A Documentary History. Guide to the Microfiche Collection* (Bethesda, Md.: Congressional Information Service, Inc., 1987); Cole, "Studying the Library of Congress: Resources and Research Opportunities," *Libraries & Culture* (hereafter *L&C*) 24 (Summer 1989): 357–66.

39. John Y. Cole, "The Library of Congress and American Scholarship, 1865–1939," in *Libraries and Scholarly Communication in the United States*, Beta Phi Mu Monograph 2, ed. Phyllis Dain and John Y. Cole, 45–61 (New York: Greenwood Press, 1990); Cole, "LC and ALA."

40. John Y. Cole, "Amassing American 'Stuff': The Library of Congress and the Federal Arts Projects of the 1930s," *QJLC* 40 (Fall 1983): 356–89.

41. John Y. Cole, "The International Role of the Library of Congress: A Brief History," *Alexandria: The Journal of National and International Library and Information Issues* 1 (December 1989): 43–51; Cole, "Cross-Currents: BL and LC in Historical Perspective," *Library Review* 32 (Winter 1983): 247–58; Cole, "The National Libraries of the United States and Canada," in *Century of Service: Librarianship in the United States and Canada*, ed. Sidney L. Jackson, Elinor B. Herling, and E. J. Josey, 243–59 (Chicago: American Library Association, 1976); Cole, "Library of Congress in American Life."

42. John Y. Cole, *Jefferson's Legacy: A Brief History of the Library of Congress* (Washington, D.C.: Library of Congress, 1993); see also John Y. Cole, "Thomas Jefferson and the Library of Congress," in *Jefferson the Man: In His Own Words*, ed. Robert C. Baron, xii–xv (Golden, Colo.: Fulcrum/Starwood Publishing with the Library of Congress, 2009).

43. John Y. Cole, *On These Walls: Inscriptions and Quotations in the Buildings of the Library of Congress* (Washington, D.C.: Library of Congress, 1995); see also Cole, "A National Monument." The large literature on the art and architecture of the buildings is outside the scope of this article.

44. John Y. Cole, "The Library of Congress Becomes a World Library, 1815–2005," *L&C* 40 (Summer 2005): 385; the Spofford quote is in Cole, *Jefferson's Legacy*, 18; the Billington quote is in Cole, "Library of Congress and the Democratic Spirit," 179.

45. Cole, "Library of Congress and the Democratic Spirit," 169–82.

46. James Conaway, *America's Library: The Story of the Library of Congress, 1800–2000* (New Haven, Conn.: Yale University Press, 2000). Bicentennial Background articles appeared in the *Library of Congress Information Bulletin*, April 1999 through January 2001.

47. Charles A. Goodrum and Helen W. Dalrymple, *The Library of Congress*, 2nd ed. (Boulder, Colo.: Westview Press, 1982) contains only a brief history. Goodrum authored short articles on the LC and several works of mystery fiction set there; an investigation of one of his tales is Charles A. Seavey, "Did the

Library of Congress Survive the 1814 Fire?" *Government Publications Review* 19 (January–February 1992): 75–85.

48. John Y. Cole and Jane Aikin, eds., *Encyclopedia of the Library of Congress: For Congress, the Nation and the World* (Lanham, Md.: Library of Congress in association with Bernan Press, 2004).

49. Josephus Nelson and Judith Farley, *Full Circle: Ninety Years of Service in the Main Reading Room* (Washington, D.C.: Library of Congress, 1991); Charles A. Goodrum and Helen W. Dalrymple, "Computerization at the Library of Congress: The First Twenty Years," *Wilson Library Bulletin* 57 (October 1982): 115–21; Peter T. Rohrbach, *FIND: Automation at the Library of Congress, the First Twenty-five Years and Beyond* (Washington, D.C.: Library of Congress, 1985); Suzanne E. Thorin, ed., *Automation at the Library of Congress: Inside Views* (Washington, D.C.: Library of Congress Professional Association, 1986); Alva T. Stone, ed., *The LCSH Century: One Hundred Years with the Library of Congress Subject Headings System* (Binghamton, N.Y.: Haworth Information Systems, 2000); Karen M. Spicher, "The Development of the MARC Format," *Cataloging and Classification Quarterly* 21, nos. 3–4 (1996): 75–90; William Welsh, "ARL/LC, 1932–1982," *Advances in Library Administration* 3 (1984): 287–94.

50. Carl Ostrowski, *Books, Maps and Politics: A Cultural History of the Library of Congress, 1783–1861* (Amherst: University of Massachusetts Press, 2004); see also Ostrowski, "James Alfred Pearce and the Question of a National Library in Antebellum America," *L&C* 35 (Spring 2000): 255–77.

51. Tom Glynn and Craig C. Hagensick, "Books for the Use of the United States in Congress Assembled, 1783 and 1800," *L&C* 37 (Spring 2002): 109–22; Harry Clark, "The Library of Congress in 1880: A User's Report," *JLH* 16 (Summer 1981): 523–30; Anne-Imelda Radice et al., *The Original Library of Congress: The History (1800–1814) of the Library of Congress in the United States Capitol*, U.S. Senate Committee Print, 97th Cong., 1st sess., August 1981 (Washington, D.C.: Government Printing Office, 1981); Aaron D. Purcell, "Abstractions of Justice: The Library of Congress's Great Manuscripts Robbery, 1896–1897," *American Archivist* 62 (Fall 1999): 325–45.

52. Jane Aikin Rosenberg, *The Nation's Great Library: Herbert Putnam and the Library of Congress, 1899–1939* (Urbana: University of Illinois Press, 1993); also Rosenberg, "Foundation for Service: The 1896 Hearings on the Library of Congress," *JLH* 21 (Winter 1986): 107–30; Rosenberg, "Patronage and Professionals: The Transformation of the Library of Congress Staff, 1890–1907," *L&C* 26 (Spring 1991): 251–68; and Jane Aikin, "Women and Intellectual Resources: Interpreting Print Culture at the Library of Congress," in *Women in Print: Essays in the Print Culture of American Women from the Nineteenth and Twentieth Centuries*, ed. James P. Danky and Wayne A. Wiegand, 179–207 (Madison: University of Wisconsin Press, 2006).

53. Debora Kodish, "'A National Project with Many Workers': Robert Winslow Gordon and the Archive of American Folk Song," *QJLC* 35 (October 1978): 218–33; Jane Aikin, "High Culture, Low Culture: The Singular Duality of the Library of Congress," *American Studies* 42 (Fall 2001): 43–61. See also Kodish, *Good Friends and Bad Enemies: Robert Winslow Gordon and the Study of American Folksong* (Urbana: University of Illinois Press, 1986); Cole, "Amassing American 'Stuff.'"

54. D. A. Smith, "Processing Services 1905: Putting the Library's [LC's] House in Order and the Country's Cataloging in Gear," *Library Resources & Technical*

Services 29 (July/September 1985): 248–63; Martha M. Yee, "Attempts to Deal with the 'Crisis in Cataloging' at the Library of Congress in the 1940s," *LQ* 57 (January 1987): 1–31.

55. Frederick J. Stielow, "Librarian Warriors and Rapprochement: Carl Milam, Archibald MacLeish, and World War II," *L&C* 25 (Fall 1990): 513–33; Jane Aikin, "Preparing for a National Emergency: The Committee on Conservation of Cultural Resources, 1939–1944," *LQ* 77 (July 2007): 257–85; Louise Robbins, "The Library of Congress and Federal Loyalty Programs, 1947–1956: No Communists or Cocksuckers," *LQ* 64 (October 1994): 381.

56. William McGuire, *Poetry's Catbird Seat: The Consultantship in Poetry in the English Language at the Library of Congress, 1937–1987* (Washington, D.C.: Library of Congress, 1988), 432.

57. William McGuire, "The Bollingen Foundation: Mary Mellon's 'Shining Beacon,'" *QJLC* 39 (Fall 1982): 200–211; William McGuire, "The Bollingen Foundation: Ezra Pound and the Prize in Poetry," *QJLC* 40 (Winter 1983): 16–25.

Properly Arranged and Properly Recorded: The Library of Congress Archives

Josephus Nelson

In the 1940s Library of Congress managers began an effort to bring order to the Library's historic records, and in 1946 the chief of the Manuscripts Division wrote: "Many years ago there was sent to the Division, material of an archival nature, representing old records of the Librarian's office . . . and I have consistently upheld as wise the establishment of an archival unit in the Library and have noted the advantages that would be derived from the accumulation of such records in one place. . . . I recommend that the care and management of archival holdings be made the duty of one high grade position in the Division of Manuscripts."[1]

St. George Sioussat's report to the Librarian of Congress was an early appeal for a more systematic approach to record keeping at the Library of Congress—a move away from the informal and haphazard approach of the past. This effort by Library administrators to methodically collect and preserve the Library's organizational records is a rich tale, reflecting the growth and development of the institution.

Library records were not carefully preserved until the end of the nineteenth century, and by then a large body of material had accumulated, such as nineteen volumes of Librarians' letterbooks (official correspondence), thirteen volumes of incoming correspondence, "a volume of extracts from the minutes of the Joint Committee on the Library, 1861–98, . . . and a group of ledgers, receipts, and correspondence relating to the construction of the Main Building of the Library, 1889–97."[2] During the administration of Librarian Herbert Putnam (1899–1939) these and other records were for the most part the responsibility of the Library's Office of the Secretary. During this period that office "not only prepared the Librarian's correspondence and maintained his files but also carried on much of the Library's correspondence from memoranda written in the divisions. . . . As time went on the Librarian began more and more to communicate directly with the divisions and these offices began to receive the right to establish their own divisional files."[3] However, it was not until 1944 that Librarian Archibald MacLeish (1939–44) officially placed the record-keeping responsibility in the Office of the

Secretary: "The Secretary will maintain the General Files of the Library, and will arrange with directors of departments, subject to the approval of the Chief Assistant Librarian, for the establishment, organization, and maintenance of files in various departmental, divisional, and other offices of the Library."[4]

On March 1, 1945, Luther H. Evans, acting Librarian of Congress, announced that Richard G. Wood, National Archives archivist, would work with the Office of the Secretary to survey records in all units of the Library. Wood's "Inventory of the Records of the Library of Congress," completed in June 1945, offered a detailed picture of the Library's records. For each of the forty-nine administrative units surveyed, Wood prepared summaries containing a brief history of the unit and a listing of the variety of records it held. The Manuscripts Division (since 1957 called the Manuscript Division), for example, kept not only the records of the division's foreign copying program and the World War II evacuation records but also a daily list of absentees. John C. L. Andreassen, director of the Library's Administrative Department, had reservations about the value of the Wood survey: "The records which have been deposited in the Manuscripts Division are of considerably more historical interest and relatively, of greater significance than the great bulk of the records which are described in the ten hundred and eighty-five series entries in the 162 page Inventory."[5]

Throughout the early 1950s Library administrators continued to debate the location and the role of the archives of the Library of Congress. In January 1950 Manuscripts Division curator Henry B. Dillard acknowledged that parts of the archives came to his division at intervals from 1944 to 1948 and that these allocations were probably based on the recommendations of Sioussat in the hope that "the Library would provide a security area in the north stack." Unfortunately, this never proved feasible, and Dillard reported, "The materials were therefore fitted into available empty areas. . . . Most of it is rarely used. Some of it has never been used."[6] In July 1950 Dillard noted that he received forty-one volumes of Library of Congress records for the years 1913 through 1948. The record does not show that Library officials made any definitive decision at this point about the Library's historic material.

Throughout the 1950s the Office of the Secretary continued to grapple with the management of the Library's official records. Mildred C. Portner, head of the office from 1946 to 1969, reported in 1956 that her staff "studied the use of the Manuscripts Division as the depository for Library of Congress files of exclusively archival character, specifying what kinds of documents should appropriately be transferred there."[7]

The following year Portner noted that progress had been made in administering the records program but that "there are in the central files and in the Library of Congress archives in the Manuscripts Division sizeable quantities of older records which must be sifted for background documentation on the Library's development."[8]

A September 10, 1964, memorandum, "Notes on L.C. Archives," by Frank G. Burke of the Manuscript Division indicates that the collection was still in limbo: "A survey of the L.C. Archives reveals that it is not a true archive, but an archival collection which because of the nature of the materials involved, is housed among the manuscript collections. . . . There is little continuity of materials received from the same office at different times. The physical condition of recently received material is good, becoming worse as one goes back to earlier deposits."[9]

Portner and the staff of the Office of the Secretary—following the lead of other federal agencies in standardizing record keeping—continued in the 1960s to pull together the Library's records. In 1968 the staff organized records from the administration of Luther H. Evans, Librarian of Congress from 1945 to 1953, and microfilmed records documenting the establishment and growth of the Library's gift and trust fund program.

Division of Responsibility: The Central Services Division and the Manuscript Division

In 1969 Librarian L. Quincy Mumford (1954–74) abolished the Office of the Secretary, replacing it with the Central Services Division, which became responsible for records management at the Library of Congress. The staff of the new unit actively carried out its records management work. In 1971 they completed "29 records reviews in various departmental and divisional offices," transferred more than 650 cubic feet of records "from active files to storage or to the Library of Congress archives, and almost 1,300 cubic feet of obsolete records were destroyed."[10] The Central Services Division continued to share responsibility for the Library's historic records with the Manuscript Division.

A request from a Columbia University student in 1970 prompted a renewed discussion of the nature and the role of the Library's archives. Hermine Watterson, studying the reorganization of the Library of Congress in the 1940s, "arrived at LC bearing two letters from Luther Evans, authorizing her use of his personal papers," then housed in the Manuscript Division. Not only was the Library's collection of Evans's papers restricted, but the papers had remained in the Manuscript

Division vault, never having been open to researchers. In pondering Watterson's request, Roy P. Basler, chief of the Manuscript Division, noted that "in addition to personal papers of Evans and MacLeish in this Division, there are undoubtedly many documents in LC's files in the Central Services Division relevant to the study of this topic." He then wrote Paul Berry, his supervisor and the director of the Reference Department, recommending that "inactive, historical LC files in the custody of the Central Services Division be transferred to this Division for service to researchers who otherwise qualify for use of our collections." Basler reminded Berry that the historic records in the Central Services Division complemented those papers of the earlier Librarians of Congress housed in the Manuscript Division and that researchers needed them in order to gain a complete picture of Library of Congress history: "The presence in this Division of personal papers of A. R. Spofford, John Russell Young, Herbert Putnam, Archibald MacLeish, and Luther Evans provides opportunities for some study of the history of LC but without the supplementary contribution of official files of historic interest—including the Putnam archives—only a partial understanding can emerge." The Manuscript Division chief pointed out too that the recently established George Washington University and Library of Congress joint doctoral program in American thought and culture would cause more researchers to delve into library history: "Already one of their number, John Cole, is well advanced toward a study of Ainsworth Spofford and the idea of a national library. . . . [M]oreover, as recent requests concerning the roles of James Agee and Robert Penn Warren in the Library indicate, such interest will not be limited to those specifically interested in library history, but intellectual and cultural historians will find much of profit in the activities of the national library."[11]

Basler's memorandum to Berry prompted discussion among Library administrators. Ida F. Wilson, former assistant secretary in the Office of the Secretary and recently appointed chief of the Central Services Division, said her division expected to have enough space in the Library's new James Madison Memorial Building to house the Library's archival records. She noted that the Manuscript Division "became the repository because of lack of space" and that "as the Library's policy is presently defined Manuscript Division has no assigned responsibility for LC official records, archival or other."[12] Basler, of course, questioned the need for the shared responsibility of the historic records by the Central Services Division and the Manuscript Division.

Interestingly enough, Berry, who had responsibility for the Manuscript Division, indicated that he did not support the idea of the records being housed in that division and that the real issue was whether the Library had an institutional policy about the archives of the Library of Congress.

It is my personal view—not that of the Ref. Depart—that LC archives are institutional and should be handled at the highest administrative level possible. I do *not* see the LC archives as belonging in the collections of the Library (i.e. in Mss. Div.). If the decision were made that they cannot be treated administratively, and are best handled as collections, the Mss Div. staff is certainly competent to perform the service. The question here is one of institutional philosophy for its administrative records.[13]

In late 1971 responsibility for the archives was transferred to the Central Services Division. Division chief Wilson advised the appropriate supervisors that "effective as of December 1, 1971, the Central Services Division will discontinue organizing and transferring from Central Files archival material for deposit in the Manuscript Division. It has been determined that the Central Services Division will be the custodian of the institution's administrative archives—such documents will not be added to the Library's 'collections' which are administered by the Manuscript Division."[14] Despite this decision, material from across the Library continued to be added to the archives in the Manuscript Division. For example, the records of the Library's Poetry Office and the records created from various literary events held at the Library were sent to the archives during the 1970s.

Official Transfer of the Archives to the Manuscript Division

This long and simmering debate about the future of the Library of Congress Archives continued through the 1970s, coming to a head in 1981. Elliott Finley, chief of the Central Services Division, vigorously sought to have his division declared the chief custodian of the Library's historic records once and for all. In April 1981 he told Glen A. Zimmerman, associate librarian for Management, that his division had *always* had control of those records and that the Library's regulations clearly showed that for more than thirty-five years the chief of the Central Services Division and his predecessors—the supervisors of the Office of the Secretary—were the Library's records managers. To support his argument, Finley gave credit for the founding of the Library of Congress Archives to one of his forerunners, Mildred Portner. Portner, he said, saw the "need to preserve many of the records of former Librarians as well as other supporting documentation generated at departmental and divisional levels. Great concern was voiced by the Secretary from the outset about the security and preservation of the records of the current and former

Librarians. It was from this concern and the persistence of the Secretary that the Library of Congress Archives was born."[15]

John C. Broderick, assistant librarian for Research Services with authority over the Manuscript Division, entered the discussion. Writing to William J. Welsh, deputy Librarian of Congress, he declared that "the transfer of responsibility of the archives from Central Services Division to the Manuscript Division is a logical move of the Library's permanently valuable records—its archives—from one legitimate custodian to another." He also pointedly noted that neither the Office of the Secretary, the Central Services Division, nor the Manuscript Division had taken good care of the records: "No effort by the Manuscript Division or other responsible office of the Library (to my knowledge) has been made to see that the permanently valuable records are in good order. . . . As a consequence, a measure of disarray in the so-called LC Archives is now apparent. . . . The first order of business is to see that the Library's records in the custody of the Manuscript Division be brought into good order and control."[16]

Control of the historic records of the Library passed to the staff of the Manuscript Division in 1981. According to the Library's 1981 annual report, "Since the early 1940s the Manuscript Division has had physical custody of many of the Library's permanent valuable records—its archives—with primary responsibility for their control and management being assigned the Central Services Division. This responsibility has now been transferred to the Manuscript Division."[17]

Another important change occurred in 1981: the assigning of a curator for the Library of Congress Archives. Marlene D. Morrisey was transferred to the Manuscript Division as the specialist in Library history and archives and given the task of analyzing and interpreting the historic records in the Library of Congress Archives. Her appointment finally fulfilled Sioussat's 1946 recommendation that "the care and management of archival holdings be made the duty of one high grade position in the Division of Manuscripts."[18] Morrisey, a Library staff member since 1941, had served as executive assistant to two Librarians of Congress—Luther Evans and L. Quincy Mumford—and as special assistant to Barbara Ringer, register of copyrights. She brought to her new position wide-ranging knowledge of the Library, a wealth of experience, and high-level organizational skills.

After surveying the holdings of the Library's archives, Morrisey reported that the collection was in "varying stages of disrepair. Although the letterbooks are boxed for the most part, some of the bindings are broken, some backs off, and some pages too faded to be fully legible. Some of the record books . . . are loose on the shelves. There are out-size books that will require cleaning and wrapping." Even more important, Morrisey reminded Paul T. Heffron, Manuscript Division acting chief, that the Library lacked a definite policy about adding material to its archives. "Such policies and procedures would seem to be one of the first needs if the archive is to have any real meaning. There appears to be only a small amount of material from the 1940s and almost nothing from the 50s and 60s." She suggested that the Library issue "a policy statement and a directive to departments to comply with the Library's policy of turning over non-current departmental records to the Central Services Division and the eventual transfer of those records identified for the permanent historical archive to the Manuscript Division."[19]

By June 1981 Morrisey had completed her study of the Library of Congress Archives. Breaking the study into seventeen subject areas with the amount of material listed in each area, she was able to determine the gaps in the coverage of the Library's past. She discovered, for example, that the archives held only a few administrative records, very few acquisition records, and almost nothing about the Copyright Office, the Congressional Research Service, or the other major Library departments. Morrisey concluded that Library departments must begin the regular transfer of historic records to the Library of Congress Archives, or the "Archive will remain only an assembly of miscellaneous records of varying degree of historical value."[20]

Morrisey began at once to urge Library officials to regularize the acquisition of historic material for the Library of Congress Archives. In October 1981 she suggested that departmental officials talk with the staff of the Central Services Division to find out what procedures were in place for transferring historic records from the departments to the archives. Officials and staff should discuss preservation of historic materials, she believed, as well as whether there needed to be changes in procedures or "a revision of policy directives to assure retention and transfer of important Library archival materials."[21]

Morrisey's efforts to encourage Library officials to act were aided by the fact that staff members had raised questions about the retention and disposition of records such as Copyright Office telegrams (1911–30) and 1904 Louisiana Purchase Exposition material. Responding to the request by Central Services Division staff to destroy certain records, Peter VanWingen, rare book curator, suggested that the forty-six boxes and thirty-four bound volumes recording the names of readers and the books they used from 1926 to 1975 should be retained "for their intrinsic historical value."[22] Alan Fern, director of Special Collections, queried Morrisey for advice on what to do with certain preservation materials.

In preparation for a March 8, 1982, meeting she and Heffron would have with Fern, Morrisey drafted a memorandum in which she stressed six points needed to build the Library of Congress Archives:

1. Need for criteria to determine what records should be transferred to the LC Archives.
2. Need for procedures for transferring records to the LC Archives.
3. Need for a policy for microfilming certain LC records.
4. Need for an LC regulation governing the transfer of materials to the LC Archives.
5. Need for guidelines governing the transfer of LC non-current records.
6. Need for a meeting of administrators to discuss these issues and formulate basic policies and procedures.[23]

With Morrisey's memorandum in hand and considering issues raised by staff, Broderick wrote Finley about "the need to meet with you to work out procedures that would enable us to enhance the Archives and facilitate the disposition of records that divisions are ready to relinquish."[24] After the March 8 meeting Morrisey reviewed the Library of Congress regulations as well as the federal acts affecting the retention and disposition of records, concluding that "there is no LC Regulation detailing the procedures followed by Central Services Division in maintaining and disposing of LC records nor any LC Regulation on the selection of records for and transfer to the LC Archives."[25]

While Morrisey worked to gather support for her position, Finley petitioned Zimmerman to uphold his right to be the sole arbiter of records management in the Library of Congress: "I am greatly concerned that, by sinister design, there are plans to evade the issue and Library of Congress Regulations that place with the Chief, Central Services Division, the 'responsibility for developing complete historical records of the Library's policies and programs.' . . . I am therefore seeking your official position on this issue, and whether or not you intend to support my right and responsibility."[26]

Neither Zimmerman nor Broderick immediately addressed the Central Services Division/Library of Congress Archives issues before them. In June 1982 James H. Hutson, chief of the Manuscript Division, reminded Broderick that the length of time that the Central Services Division held records before sending them to the Library of Congress Archives had to be decided: "Until such a policy is adopted, announced, and implemented the LC Archives will not reach its potential, and researchers cannot expect to find here the full history of any part of the Library's activities."[27]

Finally meeting in October 1982, the assistant librarian for Research Services, the associate librarian for Management, and the chief of the Central Services Division agreed to cooperate "in implementing the provisions of directives pertaining to LC archives, including the development of appropriate criteria to govern the retirement of current records to the archives."[28]

Before Morrisey retired in April 1983, she completed a number of important tasks. In a manuscript entitled "Descriptive Guide to Library of Congress Archives" she detailed the general scope of the collections in the archives, the development of the archives, and general information about its record groups.[29] With the Central Services Division she helped plan the transfer of Librarian Herbert Putnam's material to the archives as well as the microfilming of that collection. She also made suggestions for the future care and service of the Library of Congress Archives.

The Library of Congress Archives: 1983–2008

John D. Knowlton, formerly the head of the Manuscript Division's Preparation Section, succeeded Morrisey as the specialist in Library history and archives. Knowlton recognized that the Library of Congress Archives had reached a turning point as a result of Morrisey's efforts: "Prior to Mrs. Morrisey's extraordinary analysis of them . . . description of these records had only shown them in silhouette. Her analysis and recent major additions to the Archives are forcing an alteration of such views."[30] Knowlton perceived that the cataloging of these historic records and the preparation of detailed guides to this material could greatly alter the perception of the Library of Congress Archives by historians.

Making use of the new and developing technology, Knowlton created a series of computer-generated finding aids to the collections in the archives. These aids cover the Poetry Office, the Manuscript Division, the Exchange and Gift Division, the Consultants and Fellows program, gifts and deposits, and photographs—but probably most important, the Central File: Young, Putnam, MacLeish, Evans, since it could be considered "the nucleus of the Library's archives."[31] Knowlton's guides helped make the Library's history far more accessible to researchers than it had ever been.

Working with John Y. Cole, the unofficial historian of the Library of Congress, Knowlton as early as 1986 attempted to improve the position and condition of the Library of Congress Archives by linking it with the Library's bicentennial celebration in the year 2000: "I believe that if the Library's archives are to be positioned to play a role in supporting this event, their present unstable foundation should receive expert and broad based attention."[32] He also suggested to Broderick that the Library's regulations on records management be reviewed and revised and that the archival specialist position and that of the Library's records officer be defined.

Knowlton retired in 1992, leaving the Library of Congress Archives at a critical juncture. Not permitted to fill his position, Manuscript Division administrators began looking for ways to keep the archives afloat. It was recommended that the archives be transferred to the custody and administration of the Office Systems Services Division, the unit in the Library now responsible for records management. "The care of an institution's archives is, after all, a records management function," Manuscript Division chief Hutson wrote. "Transferring the Archives to OSS will serve the additional purpose of liberating a substantial section of stack spaces for the processing of large arrearage collections." Hutson commented on another suggestion that the National Archives take charge of the Library archives: "The National Archives already receives considerable amounts of material from the legislative Branch and may welcome the opportunity to become the custodian of our Archives."[33] Nevertheless, the approach of the Library of Congress's bicentennial in 2000 dictated that these two suggestions would not be adopted.

Toward the end of the 1990s two new curators were assigned responsibility for the archives: William Mobley (1998–2000) and Josephus Nelson (2000–2005). Mobley had worked in the Manuscript Reading Room and had served as an editor for the Manuscript Division's Presidential Papers Project. Nelson, a reference librarian (and author of this article), had come to know the archives well while preparing a history of reference service in the Library's Main Reading Room. Not only did the new curators work to have new collections added to the archives and cataloged, but they also lobbied to have their records management colleagues provide additional storage space. However, lack of space, lack of staff, and the huge workload of the Manuscript Division precluded much being done in the archives.

New possibilities exist for the Library of Congress Archives in the twenty-first century. In 2008 the archives contained more than 3.5 million items; its curator, Cheryl Fox, has added collections and created new finding aids and is using current technology to support the archives. There are, for example, discussions about creating a digital history collection about the Library of Congress that would include material from the archives covering the development of the Library's collections, services, and administration from the early years to the present. In the coming years the curators of the Library of Congress Archives are likely to continue to search—just as their predecessors did—for new and varied ways to ensure that the archives are properly arranged and properly recorded.[34]

Notes

1. St. George L. Sioussat, "Annual Report, Division of Manuscripts, 1945–1946," 5, in "Annual Reports 1946, Reference," part 1, Library of Congress Archives, Manuscript Division, Library of Congress, Washington, D.C. (hereafter LC Archives).

2. John Y. Cole, *For Congress and the Nation: A Chronological History of the Library of Congress* (Washington, D.C.: Library of Congress, 1979), 177.

3. Richard G. Wood (for the Office of the Secretary), "Inventory of the Records of the Library of Congress" (1945), 63, Central File: Young, Putnam, MacLeish, Evans, Container 999, Wood, Richard G., report on LC records, 1945, LC Archives.

4. General Order No. 1225, Office of the Secretary of the Library, July 10, 1944, LC Archives.

5. John C. L. Andreassen, "Archives in the Library of Congress," *American Archivist* 12, no. 1 (1949): 21.

6. H. B. Dillard to Arthur E. Young, January 13, 1950, memorandum about additional stack space on Deck 8, South, Case File: LC Archives.

7. *Annual Report of the Librarian of Congress for the Fiscal Year Ending June 30, 1956* (Washington, D.C.: Library of Congress, 1957), 50 (hereafter *Annual Report*).

8. *Annual Report*, 1957, 57.

9. Frank G. Burke, "Notes on L.C. Archives," September 10, 1964, Case File: LC Archives.

10. *Annual Report*, 1971, 73.

11. Roy P. Basler to Paul L. Berry, February 13, 1970, memorandum about the opening of the LC Archives for historical research, Case File: LC Archives.

12. Ida F. Wilson to Fred E. Croxton, November 19, 1971, memorandum about the criteria for determining archival material to be transferred from the Central Services Division, Case File: LC Archives.

13. Ibid.

14. Ida F. Wilson to the head of the Paperwork Management Section of the Central Services Division, December 13, 1971, memorandum about transferring archival material to the Manuscript Division, Case File: LC Archives.

15. Elliott C. Finley to Glen A. Zimmerman, April 27, 1981, memorandum about the responsibility for the records management program, Case File: LC Archives.

16. John C. Broderick to William J. Welsh, May 19, 1981, memorandum about Library of Congress records and archives, Case File: LC Archives.

17. *Annual Report*, 1981, 11.

18. "Annual Report, Division of Manuscripts, 1945–1946," 6, in "Annual Reports 1946, Reference," part 1, LC Archives.

19. Marlene Morrisey to Paul T. Heffron, May 18, 1981, memorandum about the content of the LC Archives in the Manuscript Division, Case File: LC Archives.

20. Marlene Morrisey to Paul T. Heffron, June 18, 1981, memorandum about the present content of the Library of Congress Archives in the Manuscript Division, Case File: LC Archives.

21. Marlene Morrisey to Paul T. Heffron, October 21, 1981, memorandum about the acquisition of department historical materials, Case File: LC Archives.

22. Elliott C. Finley to William Matheson, February 23, 1982, memorandum about the reader registers of the Rare Book and Special Collections Division, Case File: LC Archives.

23. Marlene Morrisey to Paul T. Heffron, March 5, 1982, memorandum about issues that could be discussed at March 8 meeting in Dr. Fern's Office, Case File: LC Archives.

24. John C. Broderick to Elliott C. Finley, March 16, 1982, memorandum about the disposition of the register of readers' materials and related LC Archives issues, Case File: LC Archives.

25. Marlene Morrisey to John C. Broderick, March 29, 1982, memorandum about the authority and regulations concerning the disposition of the Library's records, Case File: LC Archives.

26. Elliott C. Finley to Glen A. Zimmerman, March 25, 1982, memorandum about historical records, Case File: LC Archives.

27. James H. Hutson to John C. Broderick, June 28, 1982, memorandum about the systematic transfer of LC archival materials from the Central Services Division to the LC Archives, Manuscript Division, Case File: LC Archives.

28. James H. Hutson to John C. Broderick, October 19, 1982, memorandum about the Library of Congress Archives, Case File: LC Archives.

29. Marlene D. Morrisey, "Descriptive Guide to Library of Congress Archives," January 1983, Case File, LC Archives.

30. John D. Knowlton, July 11, 1986, memorandum about the Library of Congress Archives, Case File: LC Archives.

31. *Library of Congress Acquisitions: Manuscript Division, 1987* (Washington, D.C.: Library of Congress, 1989), 32.

32. John D. Knowlton to John C. Broderick, November 21, 1986, memorandum about the Library of Congress Archives, Case File: LC Archives.

33. James H. Hutson to Glen A. Zimmerman, October 28, 1992, memorandum about the future of the Library of Congress Archives, Case File: LC Archives.

34. The title of this essay was inspired by John Knowlton's July 1964 *American Archivist* article, "Properly Arranged and So Correctly Recorded," about Richard Varick, the compiler of George Washington's wartime papers.

The National and International Roles of the Center for the Book

Guy Lamolinara

Librarian of Congress James H. Billington has called the Center for the Book "a remarkably effective national, and indeed international, catalyst for promoting books, reading, literacy and libraries and for encouraging scholarly research about the role of books and print culture in our society."[1] Over the course of more than thirty years the Center has played a pivotal national role in these distinct but complementary areas of activity and study. Today through its state center network the Center's influence reaches into every state, the District of Columbia, and the U.S. Virgin Islands; moreover, the Center for the Book concept has spread to South Africa, Russia, and other nations around the world. Within the Library of Congress the Center is well known for its sponsorship of book talks, its key role in the National Book Festival, and its cooperative programs with other library offices as well as with other institutions in the United States and abroad.

Founding Principles

At the urging of Daniel J. Boorstin, the distinguished historian who served as the twelfth Librarian of Congress from 1975 to 1987, Congress established the Center for the Book in 1977 through Public Law 95-129. Boorstin's initiative was supported by the 1976 Task Force on Goals, Organization, and Planning, which the librarian set up soon after his appointment. Believing that such a body should be informed by an understanding of the history of the Library, Boorstin named as task force chair John Y. Cole, a seasoned staff member and scholar who had recently completed his doctoral dissertation about how Ainsworth Rand Spofford, the sixth Librarian of Congress (1864–97), had shaped the Library into an institution of national significance. Soon after the Center for the Book was established, Boorstin named Cole as its founding director.

Among its many recommendations, the task force urged the Library to play a more prominent educational role, particularly in enhancing appreciation of the book and the printed word. Therefore, it heartily endorsed Boorstin's proposed legislation to establish a program "for the investigation of the transmission of human knowledge and to heighten public interest in the role of books and printing in the diffusion of knowledge."[2] In October 1977, when Boorstin addressed the members of the newly created Center for the Book's National Advisory Board, he spelled out both the rationale for and the purpose of the Center: "You may wonder why the Library of Congress, which of all places, is a center for the book should now become a place for the establishing of the Center for the Book. It is to organize, focus and dramatize our nation's interest and attention on the book, to marshal the nation's support—spiritual, physical and fiscal—for the book."[3]

Although it was Boorstin's vision that led to the creation of the Center for the Book, it is through the leadership of its founding director, John Y. Cole, that the Center has grown from a modest organization into a nationwide network of literacy and reading advocates who share the Center's zeal for the importance of books, reading, and book culture. In addition to recruiting support from institutions and organizations within the broader community of the book, John Cole has obtained funding from a wide variety of corporate sponsors and individual donors. This is possible because the Center was established as a public-private partnership; the Library of Congress funds its four staff positions (whose number has remained constant for more than twenty years), but all of its activities, publications, and programs are supported by gifts, endowments, or other outside funds. Approximately $20 million has been donated to the Center since its founding. While much of that funding has been devoted to reading promotion activities, support from the private sector also has gone to underwrite scholarly symposia and publications.

Promoting Scholarship on Books, Reading, and Literacy

The statute that established the Center for the Book in 1977 specifically prescribes that the Center "shall stimulate . . . research in the role of the book in the diffusion of knowledge." Over the past thirty years the Center has fulfilled that mission through its numerous symposia on book culture in the United States and abroad. These activities began in 1978, when two days of meetings were held in cooperation with the Book Industry Study Group; participants discussed a wide range of topics related to American book-reading and book-buying habits. During its first year of operation the Center sponsored a series of lectures on the role of the book in society, featuring topics such as early illustrated books and their great artists, early American print shops, and masters of modern typography. (Many other symposia sponsored by the Center are highlighted in this festschrift in an article by Eleanor F. Shevlin and Eric N. Lindquist, "The Center for the Book and the History of the Book.")

A number of programs the Center sponsored in the 1980s were scholarly in nature but featured contemporary rather than historical topics. "The Public Lending Right"—the notion of an author's right to compensation for multiple use of his or her books by libraries—was discussed at a forum in 1983. Later that year authors, publishers, critics, and filmmakers gathered for a two-day symposium on the nature and influence of biographical works. A concurrent resolution in the House and Senate was the impetus for "The Book in the Future" study undertaken by the Center in 1983. Senator Charles Mathias, Jr., of Maryland told members of the Library's advisory committee charged with studying the issue: "Set no limits to your visions . . . for perhaps the future of the book is not as solid as it might appear," an eerily prescient statement in view of the current state of book publishing and sales today.[4] At a 1987 symposium, "The Subtle Danger: Reflections on the Literacy Abilities of America's Young Adults," Secretary of Labor William E. Brock III delivered the keynote address.

Several programs the Center sponsored in the 1990s focused on history as the Library celebrated the renovation and centennial of the Jefferson Building and prepared for its bicentennial. In 1993, to honor the 250th anniversary of Thomas Jefferson's birth, the Center held a three-day event that attracted more than twenty-five scholars, historians, and writers to discuss Jefferson's views on the links between education, citizenship, and democratic government. "Thomas Jefferson and the Education of a Citizen in the American Republic" was complemented by a special exhibition of sixteen volumes from Jefferson's personal library, which he sold to Congress in 1815 after the British burned the U.S. Capitol (which then housed the Library of Congress). Today a permanent exhibition of the Jefferson library is on view in the building of the same name as well as online at www.loc.gov/exhibits.

Several symposia were held during the Library's celebration of its bicentennial in 2000, including "National Libraries of the World: Interpreting the Past, Shaping the Future." More recently, the Center has sponsored such diverse projects as a 2006 art exhibition (with Meridian International) called "This Is Our Land: Discovering America and the World through Original Illustrations from Children's Books." In 2007 the Center hosted a program on library accessibility in celebration of Disability Awareness

Month. A program on deaf perspectives on library research, in partnership with the National Literary Society of the Deaf, was held in 2008.

Center for the Book Publications

Since its founding the Center for the Book has published or collaborated on the publishing of more than one hundred books and pamphlets that address topics related to reading and libraries. Several Center for the Book publications have focused on the Depression era New Deal and the related collections at the LC. John Cole wrote "Amassing American 'Stuff': The Library of Congress and the Federal Arts Projects of the 1930s" in 1983, and in 1994 a program of the same name brought together twenty-one veterans or observers of New Deal arts projects. In 2008 the American Folklife Center cosponsored with the Center the symposium "Art, Culture and Government: The New Deal at 75." The Center also has published collections of papers from symposia hosted at the Library, and it often has copublished conference proceedings or special collections of papers such as the 2006 festschrift in honor of library historian Donald G. Davis, Jr. (A number of the Center publications that deal with book or library history are discussed in greater detail in the article by Shevlin and Lindquist.)

The Center for the Book has worked with the Library's Publishing Office on publications related to the Library's history, architecture, and collections. Some works are published or copublished by private firms such as Bernan. A recent highlight is the *Encyclopedia of the Library of Congress: For Congress, the Nation and the World*, edited by Cole and Jane Aikin. Published in 2004, this authoritative one-volume reference work contains original, carefully documented essays, articles, and statistical appendixes. Other Center for the Book publications include *On These Walls: Inscriptions and Quotations in the Buildings of the Library of Congress* by Cole, which was republished (with Scala Publishers) in 2008 in a revised edition with more than one hundred full-color illustrations by noted photographer Carol M. Highsmith. Cole also contributed a new introduction to *Library: The Drama Within* with photographs by Diane Asséo Griliches; it was reprinted in 2008 in an edition from Bunker Hill Publishing.

Book and Reading Promotion Themes

While the goal of promoting scholarship was clearly stated in the legislation that created the Center for the Book, the efforts to promote reading came a bit later. Cole wrote: "The concept of 'reading promotion,' while not well known when the Center . . . was established, nevertheless was an 'implied' natural mission for the new organization. In 1981 the Center launched 'Books Make a Difference,' the first of a series of reading promotion projects."[5] The idea was to heighten awareness of the important role that books play in shaping people's lives. As activities developed around the theme, an oral history project was launched in which more than three hundred people were interviewed about books that changed their lives. The Center also reached out to television producers, and this theme became the basis for a Library of Congress–NBC series of public service announcements extolling the pleasures of reading. The announcements featured stars of all ages from the network's most popular programs at the time such as *Cheers*, *The Cosby Show*, and *St. Elsewhere.*

In 1985 the Center teamed with the Association of American Publishers (AAP) for the "I'd Rather Be Reading" campaign. Parker Ladd of AAP said, "At exactly the right moment in the development of this important program, the Center for the Book has come aboard with its strength, convictions and prestige."[6]

To mark its tenth anniversary in 1987 the Center chose the "Year of the Reader" as its promotional theme. The United Nations-affiliated International Book Committee, which endorsed the slogan in a resolution, recalled the success of UNESCO's "Year of the Book" international campaign and hoped the new campaign would produce similar results. For the first time, the White House became an active supporter of the Center for the Book when President and Nancy Reagan signed pledges to read at least one additional book in 1987, inaugurating the "Year of the Reader" project. President Reagan invited all Americans to "restore reading to a place of preeminence in our personal lives and in the life of our nation."[7]

Two years later the Center celebrated the "Year of the Young Reader." First Lady Barbara Bush continued the tradition of White House participation and support of the Center's activities when she agreed to chair the "Year of the Lifetime Reader" campaign in 1991.[8] "Explore New Worlds—Read!" carried the campaign through 1992, and "Books Change Lives" was chosen as the theme for 1993–94. "Reading teaches us about the world," said Cole when he announced the 1995–96 theme, "Shape Your Future—Read!" "It helps us make wise choices and prepare ourselves for the path we have chosen, and it tells us of the achievements of the courageous men and women who have contributed to our society."[9]

The Library has always made the point that reading and literacy are fundamental elements of a strong democracy, so it was only natural that "Building a Nation of Readers" would be the campaign for 1997–2000, a theme appropriate for celebrating the Library's bicentennial in 2000. When he announced that "Telling America's Stories" would be the 2001–3 reading promotion theme, Cole noted that the slogan took advantage of the newly launched "America's Story from America's Library" Web site (www.americaslibrary.gov), designed to stimulate interest in history among families and young people through the lively stories it presents using unique materials from the Library's collections. Following her mother-in-law's example, First Lady Laura Bush agreed to serve as honorary chair of the campaign.

Special Programs for Young Readers

The Center places special emphasis on young readers and on instilling a love of reading from an early age. These youth-oriented programs encourage reading activities that engage children as well as their families.

Letters About Literature

The concept behind this reading and writing program for students is simple: every reader can point to at least one book that profoundly affected him or her. The Letters About Literature program (www .lettersaboutliterature.org) began in the early 1980s as "Books Change Lives," an essay-writing contest sponsored by the Center for the Book in association with *Read* magazine, published by *Weekly Reader* for students in grades six through nine. The top winner received a trip to Washington to visit the Library of Congress, courtesy of the publisher, and all winners were showcased in *Read* magazine in an April edition called "The Student Issue."

In 1993 the "Books Change Lives" contest was retooled to emulate more closely the reader-response approach of teaching reading in middle schools. Letters About Literature challenged young readers to write a personal letter to an author—past or present—describing a book's effect on the reader. In 1997 the program moved from *Weekly Reader* to the Center for the Book, which hired a consultant to be the national director of the program. Although *Weekly Reader* continued as a program sponsor, management and promotion of the program shifted to the national director working with affiliate state centers for the book. In 2003 Target Stores Inc. became a partner, giving the program a new national identity; a year later, Target became the exclusive sponsor. Prizes currently are $10,000 for the six national winners (two in each of three competition levels), who can name a community or school library as the receiver of this reading promotion grant.

River of Words

Each year, in affiliation with the Center for the Book, the organization River of Words (www.riverofwords.org) conducts an international poetry and art contest for students ages five through nineteen. Former Poet Laureate Robert Hass (1995–97) and Pamela Michael, former director of the United Nations Task Force on Media and Education, cofounded River of Words in 1995 as a California-based 501(c)(3) nonprofit organization. A year later the River of Words poetry and art competition was launched, inviting K–12 students to submit a poem or picture on the theme of watersheds.

Lifelong Literacy

The Center for the Book is an important contributor to the Library's public awareness campaign, "Explore New Worlds. Read," which offers resources online at www.read.gov. The Ad Council and the Library have teamed together to promote literacy through a series of public service announcements.

National Ambassador for Young People's Literature

In January 2008 the Library named its first National Ambassador for Young People's Literature, Jon Scieszka. The position was created to raise national awareness of the importance of young people's literature as it relates to lifelong literacy, education, and the betterment of the lives of young people. During the two-year term the national ambassador travels the country to promote the importance of reading by young people. The program (www.childrensbookambassador.com) is administered in collaboration with the Children's Book Council. Scieszka introduced himself in a January 27, 2008, op-ed piece in the *New York Daily News*: "Kids are reading less and getting worse at it. So the Library of Congress and the Children's Book Council have created a new position and named our first National Ambassador for Young People's Literature. That's me—the guy with the impossible-to-pronounce last name. . . . And my new job is to get our kids jazzed about reading."

Young Readers Center

The Young Readers Center is a new place in the Library's Jefferson Building that welcomes children and adults to the wonderful world of books. Here they find a comfortable space to read aloud to young people, to access kid-friendly sites on the Internet, and to attend programs featuring the nation's best children's authors. The center also features a theater for special readings and information on how young readers can participate in Center for the Book activities in Washington and across the country.

Using Technology to Promote Reading

From its very beginning the Center has employed a variety of media to educate people about books, and it was a pioneer in using television to promote books and reading. Although television has been used to promote reading since the late 1950s, under Boorstin's leadership the Center's goal was to find ways to more effectively "integrate television and the printed word within the educational process."[10] In April 1978 the Center held its first symposium, "Television, the Book and the Classroom." A publication related to television, "Books and Cable Television Enrich Your Life," a sixteen-page reading and viewing guide, was issued by the Arts and Entertainment Network in 1987. Actor E. G. Marshall prepared a thirty-second video to announce the project on the cable channel.

Systematic use of television to foster reading began in 1979 when the first "Read More About It" segments appeared on CBS. The first thirty-second spot was aired at the conclusion of *All Quiet on the Western Front*, and its star, Richard Thomas, gave readers a list of related books to read, including Erich Maria Remarque's book, on which the film was based. The Center realized early on the power of celebrities to persuade Americans. Cable television joined the "read more" family in 1982, when Showtime's *Faerie Tale Theatre* provided names of stories in print similar to those presented in the TV program.

By the time the "Read More About It" project ended in 1999 nearly four hundred CBS television programs had exhorted viewers to "read more" about what they had just seen. The basic message remained the same: to read more about the topic, viewers could obtain LC's suggested titles from their local libraries and bookstores. During its twenty-year history "Read More About It" reached millions of Americans. In a record for the series, more than 70 million viewers saw the "Read More About It" segment that followed the 1992 Super Bowl.

The project attracted other networks, and in the mid-1980s the Center worked with NBC Television and ABC Children's Television, which debuted the character Cap'n O. G. Readmore in an April 1983 ceremony at the Library. "Our joint commitment is to bring books and television together to stimulate the widest possible interest in reading," Cole said at the time.[11] The Center worked with the news division of CBS beginning in 1985 for its "American Treasure" series of one-minute spots about unusual people, places, and events in life and fiction. Each of the one hundred segments was based on the collections of the Library of Congress.

A glittering affair that could rival any held in Hollywood took place in 1985, when the Library hosted some thirty-five stars to celebrate their contributions to the "Read More About It" series. Douglas Fairbanks, Jr., Helen Hayes, Marsha Mason, Jean Stapleton, and Ben Vereen were among the actors who attended, as did then Chief Justice of the United States Warren Burger. The "Read More About It" series won an award in 1986 from the National Education Association, and its success was the impetus for public television's requirement that producers provide reading lists for their programs—which they still do today.

"Read More About It" continues online by offering reading lists to accompany the thematically organized collections of the Library's "American Memory" Web site (www.read.gov/booklists). A selection of these historic TV spots is available at www.youtube.com (search "read more about it"). Today the Center embraces technology through its Web site (www.read .gov/cfb) and through the Ad Council–supported www.read.gov.

The Third Decade: New Initiatives

Celebrating Books and Authors

At the Library of Congress the Center is a focal point for public programs that celebrate authors, books, and reading and that encourage the study of books and print culture. The Books & Beyond author series, which began in 1996, has brought writers from all genres and from across the country and around the globe to the Library to talk about their work. These writers have used the incomparable collections of the Library in their research, and they are more than eager to exalt the treasures they can access here as well as the staff members who bring them to life. Since 2000 these discussions have been recorded for later Webcast, and more than one hundred are available from the Center's Web site at www.read.gov/webcasts. These Webcasts include programs as diverse as "An Evening with Chinua Achebe" (2008), whom many consider to be the father of the African novel in America; a visit from Stephen King, his wife, and his son, during which they discuss their writing styles (2008); mystery writer Sara Paretsky on her thriller *Fire Sale* (2007); Harold Bloom on his book *How to Read and Why* (2000); and Robert Caro on his multivolume biography of Lyndon Johnson (2002). Appropriately, best-selling author David Baldacci launched his 2006 novel, *The Collectors*, at the Library of Congress—the scene of the book's crime.

The Center has also organized special author tributes, most recently for Herman Wouk. The first Library of Congress Award for the Writing of Fiction was given to the novelist in 2008, and John Cole emceed the event that brought such luminaries to the Coolidge Auditorium as Supreme Court Justice Ruth Bader Ginsburg, journalist William Safire, ABC News correspondent Martha Raddatz, and musician Jimmy Buffett, whose musical *Don't Stop the Carnival* is based on Wouk's novel of the same name. Also in 2008 the Center organized a tribute to Louis L'Amour (1908–88), one of the most prolific and best-selling authors of all time. He was honored by the Center for the Book as its inaugural "Champion of the Book"—a designation reserved for those who have made an important contribution to the world of books.

National Book Festival

First Lady Laura Bush, who initiated the Texas Book Festival, brought the festival idea to Washington in 2001 and invited the Library of Congress to sponsor and organize a National Book Festival, which she would host. Supported by private funds, the National Book Festival (www.loc.gov/bookfest) is held on the National Mall and now draws more than 120,000 book lovers annually to hear their favorite authors talk about their books and sign their works. The Center for the Book develops and coordinates the roster of authors, illustrators, and poets, who are nominated by their publishers for participation. The writers are from all fields of literary endeavor, and their works are aimed at audiences of all ages.

The Center also sponsors the popular Pavilion of the States, in which representatives from the fifty states, the District of Columbia, and U.S. territories speak to festival goers about their state's unique literary heritage. The Book Festival Web site features a "Young Readers' Toolkit," with instructions on hosting local book festivals, age-specific reading lists, and suggested topics by festival authors for writing, illustrating, and storytelling.

Going Nationwide with State Centers

When the Center for the Book was founded in 1977 there was no plan for establishing affiliated centers, but in 1984 a proposal from Broward County Library in Fort Lauderdale, Florida, sparked what was to become a remarkable burst of activity nationwide to develop state centers for the book. Just as the Center for the Book uses the prestige and resources of the Library of Congress in fulfilling its mission, Florida wanted to use the prestige of the national Center (and the Library) in promoting books and reading in that state, especially its local literary heritage. That same year Pennsylvania joined the state center family. State centers are approved for a three-year period and must reapply for approval for subsequent three-year periods; they are financially self-supporting. The state centers are expected to actively promote books and reading in their states through activities such as book festivals, author presentations, and reading promotion campaigns.

Illinois, Michigan, Oklahoma, Oregon, and Wisconsin brought the number of state centers to seven in 1985. The push to spread the state center initiative continued in 1987, when eight states—the most in a single year—joined the fold: California, Connecticut, Indiana, Iowa, Kansas, Ohio, Texas, and Virginia. By 1992 twenty-six states had Center for the Book affiliates, with the addition of Arizona and Colorado (1988); Washington (1989); Alaska, Minnesota, Montana, Nebraska, New Jersey, and Rhode Island (1990); and Kentucky and North Carolina (1992). Cole, who personally worked to establish state centers nationwide, continued to push on. Missouri and North Dakota signed up in 1993, followed by Idaho, Louisiana, and Vermont a year later. Wyoming joined in 1995 and in 1996 Maryland, New Mexico, South Carolina, and Tennessee. Georgia, Maine, and Nevada set up their centers in 1998. Utah came on board in 1999 and was followed by Arkansas, the District of Columbia, Massachusetts, and Mississippi the next year. West Virginia and Alabama joined the fold in 2001, then Hawaii, New York, and South Dakota (2002). Finally, in 2003 Delaware and New Hampshire joined, bringing the total to fifty-one. In 2009 the U.S. Virgin Islands Center for the Book was established.

With a grant from the Lila Wallace–Reader's Digest Fund, the Washington Center for the Book at the Seattle Public Library in 1998 developed the project "If All Seattle Read the Same Book." Since then nearly five hundred communities have been logged in on the national center's Web site with "One Book" projects, in which a community or state chooses to read a single book. The Center for the Book began promoting this idea that same year, and through the network of state centers this program is promoted nationwide and in the overseas affiliates. Sixteen are statewide efforts implemented by a state center for the book affiliate.

Since 1987 representatives of state centers have gathered annually at the Library of Congress to exchange ideas and share information. The presentation of the Boorstin State Center Awards has been an annual meeting highlight since 1997. Supported by funds donated by Daniel J. Boorstin and his wife, Ruth, the awards recognize and support the achievements of individual state centers. The national center occasionally is able to support projects that benefit state centers directly. In 1992 the Center for the Book received a grant from the Lila Wallace–Reader's Digest Fund for The Literary Heritage of the States, a three-year education and traveling exhibition program. The first phase was Language of the Land: Journeys into Literary America, a traveling exhibition (www.loc.gov/exhibits) of literary maps that was hosted by sixteen state centers and nine other libraries across the country between 1993 and 1997. Twelve state centers took advantage of grants to produce new literary maps for their states. Eight state centers have since produced online, interactive literary maps.

Eleven states now administer, plan, and stage state book awards programs. Oklahoma, the first state to establish such a program, had its 20th Oklahoma Book Awards ceremony in April 2009. Florida, the latest with a statewide awards program, had its first ceremony in April 2007. Other states with book awards programs are Connecticut, Indiana, Massachusetts, Nebraska, New Hampshire, Pennsylvania, Utah, Vermont, and Washington. Twelve states sponsor statewide book festivals, including Nebraska since 1991 and Wyoming with its first in September 2007.

Capitalizing on its dynamic network of fifty-two affiliated centers, the Center for the Book was the lead organizer behind "National Treasures, Local Treasures: The Library of Congress at Your Fingertips," a pilot educational program, designed to bring the riches of the Library to selected cities across the country. The program traveled to Broward County, Florida, Denver, Dallas, San Francisco, and Los Angeles in 2008. Events were held in cooperation with the state centers for the book.

Reading Promotion Partner Network

In addition to the network of state centers, the Center for the Book has organized a nationwide network of reading promotion partners— other organizations dedicated to advocating books, reading, and literacy.

These partners (www.read.gov/cfb/affiliates.html) also meet annually at the Library of Congress to hear what other organizations are doing and to discover new ways to collaborate. There are currently more than eighty organizations in this network.

International Activities and Influence of the Center for the Book

Almost from the beginning of its establishment in 1977 the Center for the Book has played an international role. In a recent interview John Cole recalled its origins:

> During the initial planning meetings for the Center in 1978, it was clear that American publishers were eager for the Center to promote books and reading internationally and that they would fund our initial projects. As a historian of the Library of Congress, I was well aware of the institution's growing international role in the twentieth century and sensed that this was a key area for the Library in the future. Moreover, since my arrival at the Library of Congress in 1966, I had developed a personal interest in collection development, particularly the Library's blossoming foreign acquisitions program, and I was eager to make use of my new knowledge and contacts.[12]

In February 1978 the Center, in cooperation with the Association of American Publishers, sponsored a meeting to explore international issues relating to book and reading promotion, including how information flows among nations. This meeting and another on the history of books and printing were held to help determine the Center's potential international activities. Nine years later, in 1987, the Center's role in international literacy and reading efforts was so well known that it received the International Book Award from the International Book Committee, a UNESCO-affiliated body. The award recognized the Center's "imaginative and practical campaigns on behalf of books and reading in all their diverse aspects, which have inspired similar efforts in the United States and internationally."[13]

International activities of the Center for the Book fall into three general categories: 1) sponsoring awards, conferences, symposia, and other meetings; 2) issuing publications on international topics; and 3) fostering the development of Center affiliates overseas. Because a number of the symposia and publications are discussed elsewhere in this festschrift, the following presentation is selective and organized by region.

International and Regional Conferences, Symposia, and Awards

Asia

In 1979 the Center for the Book hosted its first international conference, held at the East-West Center in Hawaii. With the advice of publishers, the theme selected was "The International Flow of Information: A Trans-Pacific Perspective." The conference culminated in a two-week tour of the United States for the seventeen participants from twelve East Asian and Pacific Rim nations. Also in 1979 the Center and the Library's Asian Division sponsored a two-day meeting on Japanese literature in translation. It was followed by the 1984 symposium "Calligraphy and the Japanese Word," which featured calligraphy demonstrations by two eminent Japanese artists.

Russia and Eastern Europe

"Book Studies in the Soviet Union and Eastern Europe" was the topic of a 1985 symposium that examined the "history and present state of book studies" in these areas. The symposium papers noted that while there was a great growth in literacy in the USSR during its early decades, there was also "accelerated politicization of book studies beginning in the late 1920s."[14] After the fall of the Soviet Union the opportunities for research and travel increased dramatically, and the Center was able to sponsor a number of programs and exchanges, drawing on Librarian of Congress Billington's extensive knowledge of Russian history and culture and his many contacts in the region. In 1993 a Center-sponsored conference was entitled "Publishing and Book Culture in Russia and the New States: Challenges of the West." Participants spoke of the "crisis in Russian book culture" and noted that because Russian society had virtually no history of private entrepreneurship, post-Soviet publishing in Russia was in peril. The lack of government subsidies for the industry, as one participant put it, had "turned publishing on its head."

Billington continued to welcome Eastern European visitors, and in 1994 and 1995 the Center for the Book hosted one-day programs for publishers from that part of the world who wished to learn about U.S. publishing practices. Cole spoke about the Center's international activities at the 1995 Warsaw International Book Festival and at the National Library of Poland. The following year Billington and Cole traveled to Vologda, Russia, to speak at the international conference "Libraries and Reading in Times of Cultural Change." The conference, which received a small subsidy from the Center for the Book, gave librarians, scholars, and administrators from Russia and the United States an opportunity to exchange information about recent changes in libraries, reading habits, and book culture in those countries.

South Africa

In 2003 the Center for the Book organized "South Africa: A Journey to Promote Reading & Literacy," a program that featured events of special interest to librarians, educators, and reading and literacy promoters. It included working visits to the South African Centre for the Book in Cape Town, the National Library of South Africa, the South African Children's Book Forum, and *Sesame Street South Africa*, where an initiative was developed to help children appreciate all of South Africa's eleven official languages. Discussions with South African government officials, educators, authors, librarians, publishers, and reading professionals were part of the program, and three symposia were held: "Reading Promotion Strategies," "'Book Famine' in South Africa," and "The Digital Divide."

Latin America

The Center for the Book, along with the Library's Hispanic Division and the Consortium of the Latin American Studies Program at the University of Wisconsin–Milwaukee, hosts the Américas Awards for Children's and Young Adult Literature. Held annually at the Library of Congress, the awards honor outstanding U.S. works of fiction, poetry, folklore, or selected nonfiction that "authentically and engagingly portray Latin America, the Caribbean or Latinos in the United States." In 2007 Margarita Engle and illustrator Sean Qualls were honored for their book *The Poet Slave of Cuba*, and Jennifer Riesmeyer Elvgren and illustrator Nicole Tadgell received an award for *Josias, Hold the Book*. In 2008 author Pat Mora and illustrator Rafael Lopez were honored for *Yum! Mmmm! Que Rico! America's Sproutings*, and Laura Resau was recognized for her book *Red Glass*.

International Programs

In 1985 the Center began a long partnership with the International Reading Association for the celebration of International Literacy Day. The program focused on a new report by the Commission on Reading, "On Becoming a Nation of Readers." Other international programs hosted by the Center included a 1993 conference to celebrate the fiftieth anniversary of American libraries overseas. Cosponsored by the Center and the U.S. Information Agency, this program, featuring Librarian of Congress Emeritus Boorstin, studied how technology could help strengthen U.S. libraries abroad and the formation of new partnerships, among other topics.

When the Library celebrated its bicentennial in 2000, the Center for the Book sponsored a four-day international conference, "National Libraries: Interpreting the Past, Shaping the Future," which drew 150 participants from around the globe. According to Billington, the goal was to "reach out both internationally and back into the past to broaden and enrich all of us." Participants included both library historians and thirty-two current library directors. Reminding them that the digital future would greatly affect libraries, especially national libraries, Billington asked participants to explore the potential of new technology to create a global library while preserving, restoring, and honoring historical collections and unique traditions.

International Publications

Many of the conferences and other meetings that the Center has sponsored have resulted in publications. Such was the case in 1984, when a series of discussions organized by Curtis G. Benjamin, former president of McGraw-Hill Book Company, led to Benjamin's volume *U.S. Books Abroad: Neglected Ambassadors*. The Center sponsored both the discussions and the volume's publication. John Cole wrote in the preface that "the role of the book in the future, both nationally and internationally, is a prime concern of the Center for the Book."[15] The study was done to "stimulate renewed and wider awareness, first, of the dire need for U.S. books in less developed countries and second, of possible ways and means by which this need may be met."

The Indivisible World: Libraries and the Myth of Cultural Exchange by Boorstin was the result of a paper presented at the International Federation of Library Associations and Institutions (IFLA) General Conference in Chicago in 1985. The Center published the paper, which contended that [although] the world's cultures—and the culture of books—may be defined by languages, by traditions and by historical movements, they are not confined by national boundaries: All boundaries in the world of culture and ideas are artificial and all are doomed to be dissolved. We, the librarians of the world, are servants of an indivisible world. Though some of us are national librarians, culture is not national. All culture belongs to all people. Books and ideas make a boundless world. To try to confine the reading or the thinking of any people violates the very nature of culture.[16]

A booklet entitled *International Library Horizons: Some Personal Observations* by Robert Vosper was published in 1989. One of the outstanding library leaders in the United States from the 1950s to the 1980s, Vosper was a key participant in international library activities, including those of IFLA. The booklet, sponsored by the Center for the Book, contains his recollections and observations on topics such as post–World War II library acquisitions from Europe, the international activities of the American Library Association and the Association of Research Libraries, U.S. involvement in IFLA, and many of the IFLA general conferences in the 1960s and 1970s.

A 1990 symposium sponsored by the Center for the Book and the Library of Congress African/Middle Eastern Division led to the 2005 publishing of *The Book in the Islamic World: The Written Word and Communication in the Middle East.* Its thirteen papers examine the book not as an artifact but in terms of its intellectual and social influence in the Islamic world.

The Center for the Book, the British Council, and the Pushkin Library Foundation in Russia in 2007 published *Building Nations of Readers: Experience, Ideas, Examples,* a handbook on reading promotion. Produced in cooperation with the Section on Reading of IFLA, the illustrated volume, written in both English and Russian, describes reading promotion and reader development in the United Kingdom, Russia, and the United States.

Center for the Book Affiliates in Other Nations

The Center for the Book has been an inspiration and a model not only for the state centers in the United States but also for similar initiatives in Britain, Canada, Russia, and South Africa. In some cases these efforts were short-lived or were limited in scope, yet in other cases their success has been considerable.

The earliest attempt occurred in 1989, when the Board of the British Library "gave its blessing to the idea of a Centre for the Book to be established within the library." According to Tim Rix, who was chairman of the consultative committee, the Centre eventually was to be housed in the new British Library building at St. Pancras, which opened in 1993. Through its various programs the Centre's goal was to "protect and promote the rightful place of books in our society."[17] The British Centre for the Book had a very successful program of book promotion, but it never made it to St. Pancras; a lack of sufficient funding forced its closing in 1993.

In 1995 Canada considered developing its own Center for the Book but opted instead to begin a program akin to the "Read More About It" series of thirty-second television spots that the U.S. Center for the Book created in cooperation with CBS. In Canada the project, cosponsored by the Canadian Broadcasting Corporation, was called "Read Up on It," and television viewers were encouraged to read more books by Canadian authors.

A more successful effort occurred in Russia that came about as a result of contacts that date from 1991, when Librarian Billington asked John Cole to help organize a ten-person American delegation that would attend a three-day conference in Moscow in late October. During that meeting, "The National Library in the Life of the Nation: The Lenin State Library and the Library of Congress," Cole met his Lenin State Library reading promotion counterpart, Valeria Stelmakh, with whom he remained in contact. After the collapse of the Soviet Union in December 1991, the national library scene in Russia changed drastically. Over the next decade more Russian librarians were able to participate in international meetings and travel to the United States. Then in June 2002 the Center for the Book led a seven-member delegation of U.S. librarians and reading promotion experts to an international conference, "Reading World and World of Reading," in St. Petersburg. The visit, which included tours of libraries in St. Petersburg, Moscow, and Vladimir, completed the first phase of an international project developed by the Open Society Institute (OSI, Soros Foundation–Moscow), the institute's Pushkin Library Megaproject, and the Center for the Book. This collaboration resulted in an OSI project that created twenty-two Centers for the Book (called "reading centers") throughout Russia. Stelmakh played a major role in the establishment of the system of Russian Centers for the Book that exists today. With John Cole she also coedited the 2007 handbook *Building Nations of Readers: Experience, Ideas, Examples.*

The creation of the South African Centre for the Book as a unit of the National Library of South Africa was a long and sometimes difficult process. Discussions began with a visit to the Center for the Book by staff of the National Library in 1989; in 1995 the South African national librarian announced that a Centre for the Book would open there. It was established in 1997 under the new democratic regime and vigorously undertook, among other projects, a major literacy promotion project, "First Words in Print," that won an award in 2004 from the International Board on Books for Young People.

The Center for the Book in the Library of Congress had helped to firmly establish what is often taken for granted: that books, reading, and literacy are inextricably bound to a strong democracy, no matter where in the world that democracy might be.

Notes

The author gratefully acknowledges early assistance in developing this essay from Maurvene D. Williams, former Center for the Book program officer.

1. Helen Dalrymple, "The Center for the Book's 25th Birthday: Dr. Boorstin and 50 State Affiliates Honored," *Library of Congress Information Bulletin* (hereafter *LCIB*) 62 (January 2003): 3.

2. John Y. Cole, "The Center for the Book in the Library of Congress," *Quarterly Journal of the Library of Congress* 36 (Spring 1979): 178.

3. Daniel J. Boorstin, "A Center for the Book in the Library of Congress," in *The Republic of Letters: Librarian of Congress Daniel J. Boorstin on Books, Reading, and Libraries 1975–1987*, ed. John Y. Cole, 40 (Washington, D.C.: Library of Congress, 1989).

4. "The Book in the Future Discussed," Library of Congress press release, March 15, 1984.

5. John Y. Cole, "Promoting Books and Reading: Nationally, Internationally, and in the States," *LCIB* 62 (January 2003): 11.

6. "Center for the Book to Co-Sponsor 'I'd Rather Be Reading' Promotion Theme," Library of Congress press release, April 26, 1985.

7. "President and Mrs. Reagan Sign 'Year of the Reader' Pledges," Library of Congress press release, May 5, 1987.

8. "Barbara Bush Receives Women's National Book Association Award," Library of Congress press release, July 19, 1990.

9. "'Shape Your Future—READ!' To Be Library of Congress National Reading Promotion Theme for 1995–1996," Library of Congress press release, November 7, 1994.

10. John Y. Cole, "CFB on TV: Center for the Book Begins Third Decade of Promoting Reading on Television," *LCIB* 57 (December 1998): 290–92.

11. "Joys of Reading to Be Given Lively Boost by Cap'n O. G. Readmore in New Library of Congress/ABC Television Venture," Library of Congress press release, April 21, 1983.

12. John Y. Cole to author, interview, April 6, 2009.

13. Citation, International Book Award, London, August 20, 1987.

14. Edward Kasinec and Robert A. Karlowich, "Book Studies in the Soviet Union and Eastern Europe: A Symposium at the Library of Congress, October 30, 1985," *LCIB* 45 (February 3, 1986): 51.

15. Curtis G. Benjamin, *U.S. Books Abroad: Neglected Ambassadors* (Washington, D.C.: Library of Congress, 1984), v, 1.

16. Daniel J. Boorstin, *The Indivisible World: Libraries and the Myth of Cultural Exchange* (Washington, D.C.: Library of Congress, 1985), 12.

17. Tim Rix, "In the Cause of Books: The British Library Centre for the Book," *British Book News*, 1991.

The Center for the Book and the History of the Book

Eleanor F. Shevlin and Eric N. Lindquist

In the three decades and more since its creation, the Center for the Book has benefited immensely from John Cole's leadership in executing its broad public mandate. During these same decades the history of the book has become firmly established as a significant field of study, yielding an abundance of innovative scholarship.[1] The development of the Center not only coincided but also intertwined with the emergence of book history as a field, especially from 1977 to 1980, years that were foundational for both. What has not been sufficiently recognized is the important role Cole and the Center have played in nurturing book history in the United States and indeed internationally.

In Anglo-American scholarship the history of printing and the history of books in the form of analytic and descriptive bibliography are venerable subjects.[2] Not until the late 1970s, however, did a subject identified as "the history of the book" (or "book history") emerge in the English-speaking world. French scholars pioneered what they called *l'histoire du livre*, and the 1976 appearance of *The Coming of the Book*, the English translation of Lucien Febvre and Henri-Jean Martin's groundbreaking *L'apparition du livre* (1958), is usually considered the first major event in the development of the new field. In 1979 two American scholars who had trained as historians of France published major works now also seen as seminal—Elizabeth Eisenstein's monumental *The Printing Press as an Agent of Change* and Robert Darnton's *The Business of Enlightenment: A Publishing History of the Encyclopédie, 1775–1800*. These works, as bibliographic scholar and textual critic G. Thomas Tanselle has remarked, "reflect . . . widened interest [in book history] and at the same time have served to stimulate it."[3] (Eisenstein's work has been particularly instrumental in the formation of "print culture studies," a rubric that some see as defining a field related to but nevertheless distinct from "book history.") Within a few years the terms "history of the book" and "book history" had become widely current among English-speaking scholars. Integrating French sociological approaches with Anglo-American bibliographic traditions, book history as a field attempts to combine many long-existing strands of scholarship (such as the history of printing and publishing, analytical bibliography, and library history) with newer concerns (such as the history of reading and sociological approaches to literacy).[4]

In 1977, a year after the publication of *The Coming of the Book*, the Center for the Book was established by act of Congress (Public Law 95-129). The text of the act encapsulated tenets that print culture studies and book history, inchoate fields at the time, would soon come to embrace: "the importance of printing and its impact"; "the importance of . . . the continued study and development of the written word as central to our understanding of ourselves and our world"; and "a program for the investigation of the transmission of human knowledge and to heighten public interest in the role of books and printing in the diffusion of this knowledge."[5] To head the Center for the Book and direct the formulation and implementation of its goals, Daniel J. Boorstin, Librarian of Congress and a noted historian himself, appointed John Y. Cole as its first executive director. The wisdom of that decision is evident in the Center's record of accomplishments over the past three decades and its vibrant health today. But the suitability of Boorstin's choice was no doubt evident even at the time.

At the time of his appointment in 1977 Cole had already spent a decade at the Library of Congress working in several units, including the Collection Development Office. He also had chaired the Library of Congress Task Force on Goals, Organization, and Planning, and it was from this task force's recommendations that Boorstin conceived the idea of establishing a Center for the Book. Cole's extensive working knowledge of the Library and firsthand familiarity with its collections were complemented by his scholarly insights drawn from his own historical research. His dissertation on Ainsworth Rand Spofford, the sixth Librarian of Congress (1864–99), reflected Cole's deep interest not only in the man who transformed "the small Library of Congress into an institution of national significance" but also in the broader context of that transformation—the historical connections between the Library and American culture.[6] This latter perspective embodies a foundational tenet of early articulations of book history as a field: "The history of the book is fundamental to the historical study of society."[7] In appointing Cole to lead the Center, then, Boorstin had selected a director equipped with a historian's eye, a collection librarian's expertise, and an administrator's skill in collaborating with disparate groups and successfully navigating projects from implementation through completion. Most important to our focus here, he had chosen a practitioner of book history.

Cole's commitment to encouraging book history research was apparent early on both in his own scholarship and in his inaugural writings about the Center for the Book. In a March 13, 1978, article in *AB Bookman's Weekly*, the trade journal of U.S. antiquarian book dealers, Cole provided one of the earliest public announcements about the Center. Book history, according to the article, was a paramount concern. His purpose in writing, Cole noted, was to "ask for ideas about what long-range, substantive contributions the center might make to the history of books and printing." The Center's interests, he continued, "cover a broad range of subjects related to the book, including the book in society, authorship and writing, the book as a physical object, publishing and bookselling, libraries and book use, reading, and international book programs." At a time when book history was still in the process of being defined, this statement was remarkably comprehensive and forward looking.[8]

Assembling an impressive range of consultants, Cole held planning meetings in 1978 to identify the activities the Center would undertake. The plans articulated at these gatherings are recorded in a 1978 booklet, *The Center for the Book in the Library of Congress: The Planning Year*. From these meetings two topics emerged as the focus for initial program plans: the history of books and printing and the international flow of books. A year later these subjects had been translated into concrete conferences, lecture series, and programs. The energy exhibited by this initial activity was sustained over the ensuing thirty years and shows no signs of abating.

The roster of names associated with the Center at its start included many who have contributed and continue to contribute significantly to the field of book history, bibliography, and print culture studies. In 1979 Elizabeth Eisenstein was in residence at the Library of Congress as a part-time consultant to the Center for the Book. Robert Darnton served on its national advisory board, as did Richard D. Altick, Terry Belanger, John Bidwell, Priscilla C. Clark, G. Thomas Tanselle, John W. Tebbel, and William B. Todd. The full list of advisory members—notable librarians, scholars, booksellers, and publishing and media executives—illustrates the range of expertise and interests sought from the outset and speaks to an approach that contributed appreciably to the Center's success in its promotion and advancement of book history pursuits: the forging of collaborative partnerships between the public and private spheres.

In 1979, the same year Eisenstein's seminal work was published, *The Center for the Book in the Library of Congress* by John Cole appeared as a handsome pamphlet.[9] Although the two works differ starkly in genre, purpose, and scope, Cole's twenty-page pamphlet and Eisenstein's two-volume masterwork are nevertheless linked by a deep conviction that print matters and that the study of print is crucial to our understanding of Western civilization. In its own way Cole's early treatise on the Center for the Book also performed a foundational role.

The Center's interests and mission as articulated in the 1979 booklet offered a blueprint for studying the history of the book and print culture. A key aim was to serve as a "national forum for exploring issues related to the essential role of the book and the printed word in our culture." The Center, moreover, was not conceived as simply a central clearinghouse for the study of books and print but instead was envisioned as a means of fortifying the efforts of those scholarly and book-related organizations engaged in similar pursuits and "to stimulate research about books and about reading."[10] Cole has frequently described one of the Center's roles as that of a "catalyst." Situated in the Library of Congress, the Center is well placed to play that role. An extensive institutional infrastructure for the study of book history in the United States already existed, notably, several divisions within the Library of Congress itself as well as other important research libraries such as the American Antiquarian Society, one of whose main missions since its founding in the early nineteenth century has been fostering the study of American print culture, and organizations devoted to specific aspects of book history and culture, including the American Library Association's Library History Round Table and Rare Books and Manuscripts Section and the American Printing History Association (founded in 1974). The Center for the Book would associate with these organizations and others such as state centers for the book to further the study of book history.[11]

From its first days, then, the Center saw its role as encompassing a significant outreach mission. That the Center could "receive money and other property donated, bequeathed, or devised" for its mission and accept volunteer services afforded it a unique position as a public-private hybrid.[12] Although housed within the Library, the Center could seek private funds to finance its activities, collaborations, and other innovative projects—and it could work with scholars, librarians, publishers, book collectors, educators, and others in ways that would not have been possible otherwise. McGraw-Hill's contribution of $20,000, for instance, funded the early planning meetings for the Center.[13] The effective execution of its outreach and the concrete results these efforts have yielded owe much to the energy and vision of John Cole.

On December 15, 1978, when the Center for the Book was barely a year old, it engaged in an especially important collaboration with

the Rare Books and Manuscripts Section of the American Library Association when it lent its support and hosted a planning meeting for
the conference "Books and Society in History," which would figure
significantly in the emergence of book history as a field of study.[14] The
conference, whose participants included Henri-Jean Martin, Elizabeth
Eisenstein, and Robert Darnton, took place in Boston in 1980; it has
been identified by Robert A. Gross, a prominent American historian of
the book, as "arguably the birthplace of an international field." Furthermore, it was at this seminal meeting that "A Statement on the History
of the Book," what Gross has called "the manifesto for a new field," was
promulgated.[15] Published with eight papers from the conference, this
statement offers a definition of the history of the book as "meaning all
aspects of the history of production, publication and distribution, from
the stage of authorship on through to the impact of books on readers
and, ultimately, on society."[16]

Also central to the Center's early efforts in advancing book history was
the spate of conferences and lectures that took place in 1978 and the
following year on topics now associated with book historians. Consider
the titles for events the Center for the Book arranged in 1979: "The
Textbook in American Society," "The Audience for Children's Books: A
Trans-Atlantic Perspective," "Japanese Literature in Translation," "The
Book in Mexico," "The International Flow of Information: A Trans-
Pacific Perspective," and "Function and Form in Bookbinding." As this
list indicates, the topics covered in these inaugural years reflected both
the widely diverse subjects that the history of the book as a discipline
has come to encompass and a long-standing belief in the international
dimensions of the field. The events also attest to the collaborations that
were present from the start. The lectures on bookbinding, for instance,
were organized by the Center for the Book and the Library's Rare Book
and Special Collections Division and featured bookbinding historian
Mirjam Foot of the British Library and the British typographer and book
designer John Dreyfus.

In the years that followed, forming partnerships with other Library
of Congress divisions as well as with book historians and institutions
at home and abroad continued to be an important component of
the Center's efforts. In 1980 the Center hosted "The Early Illustrated
Book," "its first major scholarly conference."[17] Paying tribute to Lessing
J. Rosenwald and the remarkable collection of manuscripts and books
he had donated to the Library, the conference attracted distinguished
scholars such as the medievalist Sandra Hindman, a historian of early
printed books who would later edit the volume of essays resulting from

this two-day meeting, *The Early Illustrated Book: Essays in Honor of Lessing J. Rosenwald* (1982). This conference was also the first of many Center endeavors to use the Library's rich collections as a springboard for studying the book and other material artifacts from the perspective of this new field.

True to the Center's commitment to outreach, it sponsored conferences and symposia not only at the Library of Congress but also at other institutions across the country. For the "Symposium on Publishing Archives," which brought together "publishers, book industry analysts, scholars, and librarians to examine the importance, collection, and use of publishing archives," held at Columbia University in October 1996, the Center joined forces with Columbia University's Rare Book and Manuscript Library, the Association of American Publishers, and the Book Industry Study Group.[18] It offered financial support for the interdisciplinary "Transactions of the Book" conference in November 2001 at the Folger Shakespeare Library, which attracted a host of scholars working within the parameters of book history. The conference's goals—"to investigate the histories of reading and writing and the ways in which texts were transmitted and knowledge circulated . . . in the early modern period" and "to disrupt easy divisions, such as those between individual disciplinary or cultural histories, or between scribal and print modes of production and reception"—resonate with concerns characteristic of the field as it moved into the new millennium.[19]

Another key engine of the Center's support for book history and print culture studies has been its publishing projects as well as its role in copublishing works with academic and independent presses. These projects, in Cole's eyes, are where the scholarship is embodied.[20] From 1978 to 2008 the Center for the Book sponsored or assisted with the publication of 110 books and pamphlets, some resulting from events sponsored by the Center, at times in conjunction with another division within the Library.[21] Born of a 1998 conference in Paris and featuring essays on China, Germany, the United States, Poland, Russia, France, Romania, and other nations, *Books, Libraries, Reading and Publishing in the Cold War* (2002), edited by Hermina G. B. Anghelescu and Martine Poulain, offers one example of a Center for the Book publication and illustrates the promotion of studies devoted to examining books within a particular historical condition—here the cold war—and their subsequent role across cultures. Between 1977 and 1987 the Center cosponsored (with the Library's Rare Book and Special Collections Division) the Engelhard Lectures on the Book, most of which were subsequently published.[22] Many are notable contributions to book history, including

David L. Vander Meulen's *Where Angels Fear to Tread: Descriptive Bibliography and Alexander Pope* (1987), which demonstrated the merging of traditional bibliography with the fresh perspective of book history.

To advance the study of the history of the book in the United States, the Center for the Book has published or copublished a number of significant volumes. Aimed at disseminating knowledge about resources as well as developing ideas for new projects, the Center commissioned two research guides indispensable to the study of American book history: Alice D. Schreyer's *The History of Books: A Guide to Selected Resources in the Library of Congress* (1987) and *A Handbook for the Study of Book History in the United States* by Ronald J. Zboray and Mary Saracino Zboray (2000). An important primary source for American book historians is *Federal Copyright Records, 1790–1800* (1987), edited by Elizabeth Carter Wills. Works of scholarship published or copublished by the Center have ranged widely over the entire field of the history of the American book—from the rare and expensive to the cheap and ephemeral. Several publications have focused on fine books and printing, including James D. Hart's *Fine Printing: The San Francisco Tradition* (1985); Ward Ritchie's *Fine Printing: The Los Angeles Tradition* (1987); and Claire Badaracco's *American Culture and the Marketplace: R. R. Donnelley's Four American Books Campaign* (1992). The last work recounts an attempt in the 1920s to promote American book design by publishing fine editions of some American literary classics. In a different vein, another Center publication, *Books in Action: The Armed Services Editions* (1984), edited by Cole and featuring an essay by him, focuses on the inexpensive paperbacks distributed in huge numbers (123 million copies in all) to American men and women serving abroad during World War II. *Books in Action* relates a remarkable undertaking in American publishing history, one that helped set the stage for the postwar paperback revolution. Other Center publications have focused on the history of other kinds of more popular or widely distributed books, including *The Textbook in American Society* (1981), edited by Cole and Thomas G. Sticht, and *Stepping Away from Tradition: Children's Books from the Twenties and Thirties* (1988), edited by Sybille Jagusch.

In 1985 the Center cosponsored with the Graduate Library School of the University of Chicago and the Illinois Center for the Book a pioneering conference on the nineteenth-century book in America. Held in Chicago, this venture was the Center's first cooperative book history conference to take place outside the Library of Congress. The resulting publication, *Getting the Books Out: Papers of the Chicago Conference on the Book in 19th-Century America* (1987), edited by Michael Hackenberg, included essays by many leading historians of the book in America. In 2002 the Center copublished *Perspectives on American Book History: Artifacts and Commentary*, edited by Scott E. Casper, Joanne D. Chaison, and Jeffrey D. Groves, the first major text covering topics spanning the entire history of the book in the United States and designed to bring the field and its archives to the undergraduate classroom through an accompanying CD-ROM of more than two hundred digital images. To celebrate its publication the Center held a symposium featuring many of the contributors. Through such events the Center has found a way to promote both the history of the book and the books that advance that history. By this point multivolume national histories of the book were under way in many countries, including the United States, another milestone marking the coming of age of the field.[23] In the United States the lead was taken by the American Antiquarian Society, but the Center contributed financially to the enterprise. More important, its longstanding commitment to promoting American book history had helped nurture a generation of scholars to undertake the project.

Although John Cole and the Center for the Book have naturally been greatly interested in the book in the United States, their interests also have had an international cast. According to Cole, the "founding impulses" of its international program stemmed from the Library of Congress's status as a "world library" and the significant interest in "the international flow of books," especially among publishers and librarians, when the Center was established.[24] That nearly half of its conferences and symposia held in 1979 were focused on either international or transatlantic issues highlights the broad and comparative approach taken by the Center from the very start. Although the need to approach book history from an international perspective was often stressed in initial formulations of the field, it is only recently, with the completion of many national histories of the book, that attention has been directed to comparative and global projects. The Center, in contrast, has always sought to advance such work through programs it has either organized or supported. One of its earliest conferences focused on the history of literacy from an international and comparative perspective. Cosponsored by the U.S. National Institute of Education, "Literacy in Historical Perspective" was held in July 1980 and featured papers on literacy in medieval continental Europe, early modern Britain, New England, and nineteenth-century America, China, and Russia.[25] In these efforts the Center has often drawn from the Library's own collections and its specialists' expertise. The two-day symposium "Publishing and Readership in Revolutionary France and America," held in 1989 in conjunction with the European Division and organized by Carol Armbruster, French specialist at the Library, and the two-day international conference "The Book in the Islamic World," held in November 1990 in conjunction with the Near East Division and organized by George Atiyeh, the head of that division, are two examples. The conference convened by Armbruster featured luminaries such as Roger Chartier, Henri-Jean Martin, Robert Darnton, and David Hall as well as important new voices in the field like Carla Hesse and Michael Warner. The November 1990 conference, a pioneering effort in the English-speaking world to study the history of the book in the Middle East, addressed a range of topics, from oral and scribal cultures' relationship with print to the book in the modern Arab world. Like other events cosponsored by the Center, both conferences yielded publications.[26]

The Center for the Book has likewise been active in promoting the history of both U.S. and international libraries. The history of libraries could be regarded as a species of book history, but the history of libraries predates the history of the book and has continued to be pursued independently.[27] A number of the Center's talks have been concerned with library history, including "On the History of Libraries and Scholarship" by I. R. Willison, then head of the rare book collections at the British Library; "The Limits of Library History" by David McKitterick, then curator of rare books at Cambridge University Library; "Readers & Libraries: Toward a History of Libraries and Culture in America" by library historian Kenneth Carpenter; and "The Ubiquitous American Library: A Look at an Understudied yet Essential Reading Institution in the 20th Century" by Wayne Wiegand, another noted American library historian.[28]

In 1998 the Center hosted a conference on library history to mark the fiftieth anniversary of the Library History Round Table. The proceedings, *Library History Research in America: Essays Commemorating the Fiftieth Anniversary of the Library History Round Table*, edited by Andrew B. Wertheimer and Donald G. Davis, Jr., were published as a special issue of *Libraries & Culture* (vol. 35, no. 1, 2000). The next year the Center published the proceedings as a separate volume. The Center once again demonstrated its international embrace in October 2000 by hosting "National Libraries of the World: Interpreting the Past, Shaping the Future," a conference in which more than twenty-five library historians from twelve countries and no fewer than thirty-two national library directors participated. By that time, as with the history of the book, multivolume national histories of libraries were under way in many countries. The three-volume *Cambridge History of Libraries in Britain and Ireland* appeared in 2006. A similar project is being planned for American libraries, with

Carpenter and Wiegand serving as general editors and with the Center for the Book and Cole playing a more direct and visible role than with *A History of the Book in America.* In 1996, in his preface to the published version of Carpenter's *Readers and Libraries,* Cole noted that the Center is "serving as the focal point for the development" of a "collaborative history of libraries in American culture," a history that "will examine the cultural role of libraries in the U.S. from a fresh and interdisciplinary point of view."[29]

By 1991 the field of book history had reached such maturity that its own scholarly society seemed to be called for. That year American scholar Jonathan Rose and British scholar Simon Eliot were the main figures behind the founding of the Society for the History of Authorship, Reading & Publishing, an international, interdisciplinary scholarly organization devoted to the history of the book. SHARP, as it is known for short, quickly grew into a large, flourishing organization with members from all over the world in many different fields and professions— "professors of literature, historians, librarians, publishing professionals, sociologists, bibliophiles, classicists, booksellers, art historians, reading instructors, and independent scholars."[30] In 1998 SHARP began publishing its own journal, *Book History,* a hardcover annual that the Council of Editors of Learned Journals deemed the year's "best new journal" in 1999.[31] The Center for the Book lent its support and in doing so contributed in noteworthy ways to the society's early growth.

The first SHARP conference was held in New York City in 1993; the second was at the Center for the Book, July 14–16, 1994, with Cole acting as host and chair of the planning committee. More than two hundred book historians attended, and eighty-two papers were presented on subjects ranging from almanacs to lending libraries, from titling practices and footnotes to marginalia, from French diaspora publishing to iconography and texts, from copyright to book reviews. James Billington, Librarian of Congress, announced to the gathering that "in all likelihood this was the largest scholarly meeting ever held at the Library."[32] Six years later Cole served on the planning committee for the 2001 SHARP conference held in Williamsburg, Virginia, and organized by Robert Gross. That same year the American Printing History Association (APHA) awarded SHARP its 2001 Institutional Award for "distinguished contributions to the study, recording, preservation, or dissemination of printing history."[33] Fittingly, the Center for the Book had been the recipient of the APHA Institutional Award for its distinguished contributions to printing history in 1994, the year it hosted the second annual SHARP conference.

To conclude this survey of the contributions that John Cole and the Center for the Book have made to promoting book history, the authors would like to acknowledge their personal experiences of this commitment. In the fall of 1999 we participated in a semester-long seminar on printing in the age of the hand press led by Elizabeth Eisenstein at the Folger Shakespeare Library. Inspired by the seminar, we, along with another participant, Sabrina Alcorn Baron, resolved to establish a scholarly forum devoted to the subject of print culture. We approached Cole and won the crucial support of the Center for the Book. His endorsement gained us a place to meet and the cosponsorship of the Office of Scholarly Programs at the Library of Congress. Launched in the spring of 2000, the Washington Area Group for Print Culture Studies has met regularly since, usually in the Wilson Room in the Library's Jefferson Building, an enviable setting for any group of its kind. Nearly eighty scholars have addressed the group, many prominent book historians among them, including Roger Chartier, Elizabeth Eisenstein, Robert Gross, Peter Stallybrass, Wayne Wiegand, Michael Winship, and Ronald Zboray and Mary Zboray. The forum would not have enjoyed the success that it has without Cole's initial and continued support. Cole and the Center again lent their assistance when the three of us undertook to edit a volume of essays exploring the legacy of Elizabeth Eisenstein's *The Printing Press as an Agent of Change* in the fields of print culture studies and book history. The Center for the Book joined with the University of Massachusetts Press to publish *Agent of Change: Print Culture Studies after Elizabeth L. Eisenstein* (2007), a collection of twenty essays covering topics from the early modern period through the digital age and concluding with a conversation with Eisenstein. To mark its publication the Center sponsored a symposium at the Library of Congress featuring presentations by several contributors, followed by a roundtable composed of other contributors and Eisenstein herself. Our experience offers just one more instance among so many of the significant roles John Cole and the Center for the Book have played in promoting the study of the history of the book.

Notes

1. For a recent overview of the field of book history see David Finkelstein and Alistair McCleery, *An Introduction to Book History* (New York: Routledge, 2005), esp. 1–27.

2. Both analytical bibliography and descriptive bibliography are concerned with the book as a physical object, but the former examines the book as evidence to recover the processes that created it, while the latter details the physical properties of the book that resulted from the process and any variations in that process.

See G. Thomas Tanselle, *A Description of Descriptive Bibliography* (Washington, D.C.: Library of Congress, 1992), a Center for the Book publication.

3. G. Thomas Tanselle, introduction to *Books and Society in History: Papers of the Association of College and Research Libraries Rare Books and Manuscripts Preconference, 24–28 June, 1980, Boston, Massachusetts,* ed. Kenneth E. Carpenter (New York: R. R. Bowker, 1983), xvii.

4. Book historians generally take a broad view of "book" and include under its umbrella artifacts such as ephemera, newspapers, periodicals, manuscripts, and the like.

5. Public Law 95-129, 95th Cong., 1st sess. (October 13, 1977), *An Act to Provide for the Establishment of a Center for the Book in the Library of Congress, and for Other Purposes,* reprinted in John Y. Cole, *The Center for the Book in the Library of Congress: The Planning Year* (Washington, D.C.: Library of Congress, 1978), [33].

6. John Y. Cole, "The Library of Congress Becomes a World Library, 1815–2005," *Libraries & Culture* 40, no. 3 (2005): 387.

7. "A Statement on the History of the Book," in Carpenter, *Books and Society,* xi.

8. John Y. Cole, "New Center for the Book at LC," *AB Bookman's Weekly* 61, March 13, 1978, 1763–64.

9. John Y. Cole, *The Center for the Book in the Library of Congress* (Washington, D.C.: Library of Congress, 1979), reprint of "The Center for the Book in the Library of Congress," *Quarterly Journal of the Library of Congress* 36 (Spring 1979): 178–88.

10. Ibid., [5].

11. Many state centers are dedicated to public outreach, literacy, and reading promotion. Some state centers on university campuses combine these roles with scholarly agendas. The Pennsylvania Center for the Book, housed at Penn State University, University Park, offers an example. Cole also supported the establishment of centers dedicated specifically to scholarship on the book such as the Center for the History of Print Culture in Modern America in Madison, Wisconsin, and the Penn State Center for the History of the Book at University Park.

12. Public Law 95-129, [34], 2 U.S.C. 175, sec. 5, pp. 2, 3.

13. John Y. Cole, "Promoting Books and Reading in the Electronic Age: The Center for the Book at 25," *Publishing Research Quarterly* 19, no. 1 (2003): 4.

14. Center for the Book, "Book and Library History Highlights, 1978–2001," *Book and Library History Update: News from the Center for the Book,* http://www.loc .gov/loc/lcib/0111/cfb.html; Carpenter, *Books and Society,* ix.

15. Robert A. Gross, "Communications Revolutions: Writing a History of the Book for an Electronic Age," *Rare Books & Manuscripts Librarianship* 13, no. 1 (1998): 9.

16. Carpenter, *Books and Society,* xi.

17. Cole, "Promoting Books and Reading," 5. For an account of the conference see John Y. Cole and William Matheson, "The Rosenwald Symposium on the Illustrated Book: A Report on a Symposium Honoring Lessing J. Rosenwald, Library of Congress, May 30–31, 1980," *Library of Congress Information Bulletin* 39 (August 1, 1980): 271–76.

18. Craig D'Ooge, "Robert Giroux to Present Keynote Talk at October 3–5 Symposium on Publishing Archives," press release, July 13, 1996, Public Relations

Office, *The Library Today*, Library of Congress Web site, http://www.loc.gov/today/pr/1996/96-101.html.

19. "Transactions of the Book: A Fall 2001 Conference Held on 2–3 November 2001," 2001–2 Program Archive, Folger Shakespeare Library Web site, http://www.folger.edu/template.cfm?cid=399.

20. John Y. Cole, interview, Center for the Book, Library of Congress, December 18, 2008.

21. For a continually updated list of publications sponsored by the Center for the Book see http://www.read.gov/cfb/publications.html.

22. The lectures were funded by a gift from Mrs. Charles Engelhard, Jr.

23. As of May 2009 three volumes of A History of the Book in America have been published: vol. 1, *The Colonial Book in the Atlantic World*, ed. Hugh Amory and David D. Hall (Worcester, Mass.: American Antiquarian Society; Cambridge: Cambridge University Press, 2000); vol. 3, *The Industrial Book, 1840–1880*, ed. Scott E. Casper, Jeffrey D. Groves, Stephen W. Nissenbaum, and Michael Winship (Chapel Hill: University of North Carolina Press in association with the American Antiquarian Society, 2007); and vol. 4, *Print in Motion: The Expansion of Publishing and Reading in the United States, 1880–1940*, ed. Carl F. Kaestle and Janice A. Radway (Chapel Hill: University of North Carolina Press in association with the American Antiquarian Society, 2009). Vol. 2, *An Extensive Republic: Print, Culture, and Society in the New Nation, 1790–1840*, ed. Robert A. Gross and Mary Kelley, and vol. 5, *The Enduring Book: Print Culture in Postwar America*, ed. Joan Shelley Rubin, David Paul Nord, and Michael Schudson, were both slated for publication in late 2009. For the inception of the series A History of the Book in America see John B. Hench, "Toward a History of the Book in America," *Publishing Research Quarterly* 10, no. 3 (1994): 9–21. For other national book history projects see Henri-Jean Martin and Roger Chartier, eds., *Histoire de l'édition française*, 4 vols. (Paris: Promodis, 1982–86); *The Cambridge History of the Book in Britain*, 6 vols. to date (Cambridge: Cambridge University Press, 1997–); Marieke van Delft and Clemens de Wolf, eds., *Bibliopolis: History of the Printed Book in the Netherlands* (Zwolle: Waanders; The Hague: Koninklijke Bibliotheek, 2003); Patricia Lockhart Fleming, Gilles Gallichan, Yvan Lamonde, Fiona A. Black, Carole Gerson, and Jacques Michon, eds., *The History of the Book in Canada/Histoire du livre et de l'imprimé au Canada*, 3 vols. to date (Toronto: University of Toronto Press; Montreal: University of Montreal Press, 2004–); *The Oxford History of the Irish Book*, 1 vol. to date (Oxford: Oxford University Press, 2006–); and *The Edinburgh History of the Book in Scotland*, 2 vols. to date (Edinburgh: Edinburgh University Press, 2007–).

24. Cole, "Promoting Books and Reading," 5–6.

25. For an account of the conference see John Y. Cole, "Literacy in Historical Perspective: A Conference Sponsored by the Center for the Book and the U.S. National Institute of Education, Library of Congress, July 14–15, 1980," *Library of Congress Information Bulletin* 39 (October 10, 1980): 406–12. Cole notes that the conference organizers were interested in how "historical research about literacy" might "help contemporary policymakers." The papers were later published in Daniel P. Resnick, ed., *Literacy in Historical Perspective* (Washington, D.C.: Library of Congress, 1983).

26. Carol Armbruster, ed., *Publishing and Readership in Revolutionary France and America* (Westport, Conn.: Greenwood Press, 1993); George N. Atiyeh, ed.,

The Book in the Islamic World: The Written Word and Communication in the Middle East (Albany: State University of New York Press; Washington, D.C.: Center for the Book, Library of Congress, 1995).

27. The ongoing national histories of the book generally only touch upon library history. For a discussion of library history that considers its relationship to book history see Donald G. Davis, Jr., and Jon Arvid Aho, "Whither Library History? A Critical Essay on Black's Model for the Future of Library History, with Some Additional Options," *Library History* 17, no. 1 (2001): 21–39.

28. The first three were published in the Center for the Book's Viewpoint series.

29. John Y. Cole, preface to Kenneth E. Carpenter, *Readers & Libraries: Toward a History of Libraries and Culture in America* (Washington, D.C.: Library of Congress, 1996), [6].

30. "About SHARP: Introduction," Society for the History of Authorship, Reading & Publishing (SHARP) Web site, http://www.sharpweb.org/intro.html.

31. "Book History," SHARP Web site, http://www.sharpweb.org/bookhist.html.

32. "News from the Center for the Book: Book Historians Gather for SHARP Conference," *Library of Congress Information Bulletin* 53 (September 19, 1994): 354–57.

33. "About SHARP: A Global Scholarly Network," SHARP Web site, http://www.sharpweb.org/intro.html.

"The Choice of Books": Ainsworth Rand Spofford, the Ideology of Reading, and Literary Collections at the Library of Congress in the 1870s

Carl Ostrowski

Ainsworth Rand Spofford was no fan of what he called the "grassy incubations" of Walt Whitman. As a thirty-five-year-old newspaper editor in Cincinnati in 1860, Spofford criticized Whitman's poetry on various grounds, including incoherence and indecency: "What we complain of in Walt Whitman, aside from that gross and obtrusive animalism which disgusts all intellectual men, is his utter contempt for expression, and the formless and apparently aimless character of his productions."[1] With these comments in mind, it is surprising to find Librarian of Congress Spofford writing to Whitman sixteen years later, asking him to confirm that the six editions of *Leaves of Grass* held by the Library of Congress were indeed all of the authorized editions.[2] Though Whitman's reputation steadily rose through the late nineteenth century, Spofford had not changed his opinion of the poet's work: he pointedly left Whitman's name out of some original verses celebrating American literary authors in 1900.[3] The narrative that emerges from these events would tend to valorize Spofford as a visionary librarian who put aside his personal taste in the interest of establishing the Library of Congress as a national library with comprehensive collections. The centerpiece of his collection-building efforts, of course, was the copyright deposit law of 1870, which secured for the Library all publications of the American press submitted for copyright protection.

My intention in this essay is not to challenge this narrative but to complicate it. Spofford deserves immense credit for the copyright deposit law as well as for his long campaign for a building whose grandeur would be commensurate with the institution's status as a de facto national library. But Spofford was, inevitably, a product of the culture of Victorian America. The growth of professional librarianship in the late nineteenth century took place alongside challenging developments in literary publishing in the United States, and Spofford's career must be understood within these contexts. While arguing passionately for wide inclusion as the guiding principle of collection development at the

Library of Congress, Spofford retained a paternalistic ethic of exclusion when it came to personal reading habits and public library selection practices. Moreover, for all of Spofford's eloquence on the principle of inclusion at the Library of Congress, his adverse judgments about the cultural value of popular literature were somewhat reflected in the Library's literary collections and cataloging practices. An analysis of post-1870 Library catalogs along with works Spofford published outside of his official duties as Librarian reveals his ambivalence about the very collections his efforts made possible.

The Fiction Question

Spofford expressed his philosophy regarding reading practices and library collection policies in *A Book for All Readers*, published in 1900. In the first chapter, "The Choice of Books," he offered guidelines to librarians and individual readers about the most important subject areas to collect, including bibliographical resources to help them make selections. Spofford advised readers to begin with biographies and histories before proceeding to essays, poetry, travel literature, science, fiction, literary history, and classical literature. His advice on reading in *A Book for All Readers* squared perfectly with the ideology of reading that drove the library profession in the late nineteenth century. The ideology included several tenets: "read with a purpose," "read systematically and widely," "digest what you read," and read with discrimination.[4] Similar sentiments are found in other influential guides to book collecting, such as Frederic B. Perkins's *The Best Reading* (first published in 1872), which provided a bibliography of titles along with "Readings on Reading" and "Suggestions for Courses of Reading."[5] Spofford endorsed the principle of literary selectivity in the eight-volume anthology *The Library of Choice Literature*, which he coedited with Charles Gibbon in 1883, and in a pamphlet entitled *What to Read; When to Read; How to Read*, published the same year. Spofford's *A Book for All Readers* was therefore part of a larger effort among librarians and self-appointed cultural arbiters of the period to shape the reading habits of Americans.

Coming as it did after his official retirement as Librarian of Congress, *A Book for All Readers* represented a capstone to Spofford's long career. By then freer to express his personal views on reading, Spofford warned against small-town public libraries spending limited funds on popular fiction: "Why should library guides put in circulation such stuff as the dime novels, or 'Old Sleuth' stories, or the slip-slop novels of 'The Duchess,' when the great masters of romantic fiction have endowed us with so many books replete with intellectual and moral power?" Spofford went on to quote a newspaper account of the case of Boston teenage killer Jesse Pomeroy, who "confessed that he had always been a great reader of 'blood and thunder' stories, having read probably sixty dime novels, all treating of scalping and deeds of violence." To counter the pernicious influence of cheap popular literature, Spofford argued that public librarians should steer readers away from morally questionable or aesthetically inferior books and toward "other and improving reading, thus fulfilling the true function of the library as an educator."[6] In this respect Spofford was a perfect exemplar of the "apostle of culture" model of the profession that Dee Garrison describes, citing the characteristics of Victorian-era librarians, many of whom shared Spofford's New England background and prudish cultural standards.[7]

Although distaste for popular literature was widespread within the profession during the late nineteenth century, in Spofford's case it probably also had roots in the Transcendentalist movement. As a New England transplant and bookseller in Cincinnati in the 1840s and 1850s, Spofford played a leading role in spreading the Transcendentalists' ideas to the Midwest.[8] The Transcendentalists often wrote about the need for discrimination in reading. Henry David Thoreau had anticipated late-nineteenth-century attitudes about literary selectivity in his first book, *A Week on the Concord and Merrimack Rivers*, advising readers to "read the best books first, or you may not have a chance to read them at all."[9] He attacked popular literature and its readers in a chapter of *Walden* entitled "Reading."[10] Spofford was no doubt also aware of Emerson's influential late essay, "Books." On the subject of fiction, Emerson conceded that novels may inspire noble behavior among readers, and he praised them for confronting pressing social issues, but on the whole he condemned novels for "the poverty of their inventions."[11]

Librarians of the late nineteenth century struggled restlessly with what was called "the fiction question," a topic they debated at meetings of the American Library Association (ALA).[12] One notable artifact of the librarians' sense of cultural mission and their disdain for popular fiction is an 1881 ALA list of twenty-eight authors whose works were considered of dubious value for collection in a public library due either to suspect moral principles or to inferior literary quality. Covering American and British writers, the list focused on authors of juvenile literature (Horatio Alger, Oliver Optic) and novelists who specialized in adventure, sensation, and mystery (Edward Bulwer-Lytton, Wilkie Collins, Mayne Reid). As Garrison has pointed out, a number of the authors on the list were women whose fiction violated Victorian ideals of feminine propriety

(M. E. Braddon, Rhoda Broughton).[13] The ALA stopped short of any specific recommendations, but in *A Book for All Readers* Spofford cites this so-called black list somewhat approvingly, referring to it as "one of many endeavors constantly being made . . . to stem the ever increasing flood of poor fiction which threatens to submerge the better class of books in our public libraries."[14] Few librarians were better positioned to understand the dimensions and implications of this deluge than Spofford himself.

Spofford and the Copyright Deposit Law

Spofford achieved his bird's-eye view of the output of the American press at the Library of Congress, which was entitled to deposit copies of every American book registered for copyright protection. Spofford's vigorous advocacy of a copyright deposit law has been thoroughly documented by John Y. Cole. Within months of his promotion from assistant librarian in December 1864, Spofford convinced Congress to pass a law restoring the Library's right to deposit copies of newly published books. When the law's enforcement provisions proved inadequate, Spofford tracked down copyright records from U.S. district courts to claim the books of publishers who had not sent copies to the Library. Eventually, Spofford lobbied the congressional Joint Committee on the Library and the Commissioner of Patents to back legislation moving all copyright deposit activities from the Patent Office, where they had been carried out since 1859, to the Library of Congress. Congress enacted a copyright law along the lines Spofford proposed on July 8, 1870.[15] According to the law, the Library of Congress would receive "two complete printed copies" of every "book, map, chart, dramatic or musical composition, engraving, cut, print, or photograph or negative thereof" submitted for copyright protection in the United States.[16]

Spofford's eloquent arguments on behalf of the principle of near-universal inclusion through copyright deposit were all the more remarkable given his personal views on popular fiction. Recapitulating these arguments in an 1897 essay, "The Function of a National Library," Spofford wrote that a national library was bound to collect "the entire product of the American press, irrespective of intrinsic value." Spofford saw this partly as a means of assessing American literature; the collections would provide "perpetual evidence of [the nation's] literary history and progress—or retrogression, as the case may be." Spofford also kept in mind the needs of historians, arguing forcibly that "what is pronounced trash today may have an unexpected value hereafter, and the unconsidered trifles of the press of the nineteenth century may prove highly curious and interesting to the twentieth, as examples of what the[ir] ancestors . . . wrote and thought about."[17] Allowing for the condescension with which Spofford describes nineteenth-century American literature, no contemporary historian could state the principle with more conviction.

Looking closely at the 1870 copyright deposit law and Spofford's arguments in support of it, however, one finds that certain apparently straightforward terms turn out to be more complicated than they seem. For example, in the American literary publishing industry of the 1860s and 1870s, the definition of the word "book" may not have been entirely self-evident.[18] These decades were the heyday of the dime novels, whose influence over impressionable readers Spofford found so troubling. In 1860 Beadle & Adams began to issue its Dime Novels series as "small, sextodecimo booklets of approximately 100 pages, with clear type and with orange wrappers upon which was printed a stirring woodcut in black." The cheap novels evolved both in format and content over time, and the nickel novels that appeared later were "without outside wrappers but with a black line illustration on the front page; . . . the quartos with 16 or 32 pages, the octavos with 32."[19] Published serially in paper covers, dime or nickel novels looked more like pamphlets than books, straddling a line between book and periodical that can be fuzzier than the 1870 copyright deposit law acknowledges.[20]

The very first novel in Beadle & Adams's series was *Malaeska* by Ann Sophia Stephens, who originally published the work as a serial in the *Ladies' Companion* in 1839; she sold the rights to reprint it to Irwin Beadle in 1860 for $250. This work was eligible for copyright, apparently on the grounds that it had not been copyrighted in its original periodical format, and was registered by Beadle & Co. in 1860.[21] Most of Beadle's Dime Novels were original works and therefore eligible for copyright protection, but some had been previously published. Books whose eligibility for copyright protection was in doubt suddenly dominated the marketplace in the 1870s in a way that Spofford could not have anticipated when he supported the 1870 deposit law.

The middle to late 1870s witnessed the rise of what established publishers referred to as the "cheap libraries." In the absence of an international copyright law, American firms could publish popular foreign novels at low cost, since no payments were legally due to the authors. In fact, section 103 of the 1870 copyright law had explicitly protected the rights of American publishers to reprint such works, stipulating that "nothing herein contained shall be construed to prohibit the printing, publishing, importation, or sale of any book . . . written, composed, or made by any person not a citizen of the United States nor resident therein."[22] Such books had traditionally been regulated within the publishing industry by means of "trade courtesy" conventions. A publisher who announced an intention to publish a foreign novel was allowed to do so without other reputable firms infringing on his edition. This publisher thereafter enjoyed an informally observed "association" with the foreign author in question.[23] This courtesy, which had no legal authority, sometimes involved the American publisher compensating the foreign author voluntarily in order to receive advance sheets. Reprints had always been part of American literary publishing, but their production skyrocketed in the 1870s. In 1874 Donnelley, Lloyd & Company of Chicago began to publish well-known British novels at cut-rate prices of ten to twenty cents, ignoring trade courtesy practices. In a short time Beadle & Adams responded with the Fireside Library, and Harper & Brothers established its own cheap library series, the Franklin Square Library. Soon cheap reprints of foreign novels and public domain works flooded the market in numbers that threatened to "wreck the country's established book business."[24]

The most famous (or notorious) of the cheap libraries was the Seaside Library, published by George Munro. In 1878 Munro began to issue novels at the rate of one a day, including the Old Sleuth series and works by Margaret Wolfe Hungerford (better known by her pen name, "Old Duchess"), upon both of whom Spofford would eventually cast opprobrium in *A Book for All Readers*. Specializing in reprints of British and French novels, the Seaside Library sold an astonishing five million books in its first two years.[25] Munro's entrepreneurship dovetailed with the popularity of the "sensation novel" of the 1860s and 1870s, whose main practitioners included Wilkie Collins and Mary Elizabeth Braddon, among others.[26] Dwelling on themes of crime, murder, bigamy, and adultery, these British novels were prominently featured in the Seaside Library. In *A Book for All Readers* Spofford takes special note of this series as he reflects on the value of the 1891 international copyright agreement:

> The Seaside and other libraries, with their miserable type, flimsy paper, and ugly form, were an injury alike to the eyesight, to the taste, and in many cases, to the morals of the community. More than ninety per cent. of these wretched "Libraries" were foreign novels. An avalanche of English and translated French novels of the "bigamy school" of fiction swept over the land. . . . Having at last got rid of this unclean brood, (it is hoped forever) we now

have better books, produced on good paper and type, and worth preserving, at prices not much above those of the trash formerly offered us.[27]

The popularity of cheap reprints complicates another apparently self-evident term that Spofford used in justifying the 1870 copyright deposit law: "the product of the American press." The American press produced millions of books by British and French novelists in the 1870s to satisfy the demands of American readers. But many of these pirated works, not being eligible for copyright, were not subject to copyright deposit provisions. In light of these developments in the publishing industry, the question arises whether books whose eligibility for copyright protection might be doubtful due to the terms of the 1870 law nevertheless made their way into Library of Congress collections. What was eligible for copyright deposit, what was not, and what literary works were purchased when they could not be collected via deposit? Catalog records for the 1870s are incomplete, as Spofford and his staff were far too busy with copyright deposits to pay sufficient attention to cataloging. Extant records show that the Library's collections absorbed some but not all of these books that flourished around the margins of the new copyright law.

Popular Fiction in the Library of Congress Catalogs

The Library of Congress issued four printed catalogs in the 1870s, of which the first three were supplemental to the preexisting printed catalog: a catalog of books added to the library in 1871, a catalog of books added during 1872, and a catalog of the "principal accessions" of 1873–75. In 1878 and 1880 the Library published the first two volumes of a projected complete alphabetical catalog; these volumes covered "A" to "Braidwood" (1878) and "Brailsford" to "Cragin" (1880), at which point the project fell victim to the Library's chronic staffing deficit.[28] One way to gauge collection practices in the 1870s is to check the 1881 ALA list of questionable authors against Library of Congress catalogs of the period. The Library was bound by the copyright law to collect American authors on the list, and the catalogs suggest it succeeded. Horatio Alger, for example, published three novels in 1871, *Tattered Tom, Strong and Steady,* and *Paul, the Peddler,* and all three books appear in the 1871 supplemental catalog. The prolific juvenile author Oliver Optic published five novels in 1871, only three of which appear in the 1871 supplemental catalog. By the time of the 1878 complete catalog, however, the two overlooked novels appear, along with no fewer than sixty-one additional titles. Popular novelist E. D. E. N. Southworth, who was also on the ALA list, published two novels in 1871 and three in 1872; all five novels appear in the respective supplemental catalogs. These results come as no surprise, since these works were unambiguously covered by the law, and publishers had an incentive to protect the works of popular writers by complying with the deposit law.

British sensation novelists who appeared on the ALA list included Mary Elizabeth Braddon, Rhoda Broughton, and Wilkie Collins. Their novels, though ineligible for copyright protection (and therefore not subject to deposit), were routinely purchased for the Library. The 1873–75 catalog of principal accessions lists twelve newly acquired novels by Collins, two in original British editions and most of the rest in editions by Collins's authorized U.S. publishers, Harper & Brothers.[29] Although Rhoda Broughton's novels were criticized for "her frankness about female sexuality and her want of propriety," the 1880 catalog shows that the Library held seven of them—four American reprints and three London editions.[30] In the case of Mary Elizabeth Braddon, who earned notoriety early in her career as the author of *Lady Audley's Secret*, the Library collected five novels between 1873 and 1875, all in London editions.[31] Purchase of British sensation novels is best explained by the Library's informal function as a source of light reading for members of Congress and their families. However, it is unclear why some novels were collected in British and others in American editions. If the Library sometimes purchased American reprints of popular British novels, this would represent no departure from longstanding practice.[32] With the Library's annual Book Fund static in the early 1870s at $8,000, Spofford probably economized wherever possible, and despite the well-founded grievances of British authors, these editions were perfectly legal.[33]

Although reprints occasionally show up in Library catalogs, the majority of them apparently eluded collection. One of the country's leading literary publishers was T. B. Peterson & Brothers of Philadelphia, which had long specialized in reprints of British works. A publishing list indicates that in 1873 the company offered editions of four novels by Bulwer and eleven by Collins; none of these show up in the Library's *Alphabetical Catalogue* of 1880. The American News Company offered seven titles by British novelist W. H. G. Kingston in 1873, but none were listed among principal accessions in the *Catalogue of Recently Added Books* from 1873–75.[34] The 1880 catalog lists several novels by Wilkie Collins in cheap library editions, including *After Dark* (Union Square Library), *The Fallen Leaves* (Seaside Library), and *The Law & the Lady* (Fireside

Library), but other Seaside editions of Collins's novels are missing. One interpretation of such inconsistent results is that Library staff cataloged anything received from the publishers of cheap libraries but did not attempt to ensure complete collections. Some of these novels may indeed have arrived at the Library as copyright deposits, though their eligibility would have been questionable at best.[35]

Popular foreign novels, even sensational ones, were collected at the Library of Congress. But Braddon, Broughton, and Collins were well-known novelists reviewed in major literary periodicals. In contrast, Beadle's Dime Novels were not regarded as serious literature, and cataloging them at the Library of Congress can best be described as belated. Beadle authors often made it into the catalogs even when their Beadle novels did not. For example, the aforementioned Ann Sophia Stephens was a well-known novelist outside of the numerous books she wrote for Beadle. The 1871 and 1872 catalogs list several new accessions from Stephens, mostly published by T. B. Peterson & Brothers, but none of the works she concurrently published with Beadle. Her fellow Beadle author, the Irish-born adventure novelist Mayne Reid, presents a more complicated picture. Reid was active in the early 1870s, and the supplemental catalogs from 1871 and 1872 include some of his books. The 1871 catalog lists four newly acquired titles by Reid, but all of them are books he published in the 1850s and 1860s. The catalog does not include the five Beadle's Dime Novels he published in 1868 and 1869. By the time of publication of the 1872 supplemental catalog, however, the Library had acquired five more novels by Reid, two in editions published by Ticknor and Fields in 1855 and 1861 and three from Beadle's Dime Novels series from the late 1860s that had not been acquired by 1871 (but this was not Reid's entire Beadle output during the late 1860s). Despite occasional examples such as this one that defy easy explanation, Beadle's Dime Novels are almost entirely absent from the three supplemental catalogs of 1871, 1872, and 1873–75.

The 1878 *Alphabetical Catalogue* presents a new and revealing picture. All of the dime novels by Reid and everyone else in Beadle's stable of authors are listed in the 1878 catalog. Unlike other works of fiction, however, the Beadle publications are listed under their *publisher's* name, mostly by series. The catalog lists such series as Beadle's Dime Biographical Library, Beadle's Dime Song Books, and a complete run of Beadle's Dime Novels, listed alphabetically by author's name in small type under the Beadle heading. Their belated appearance probably indicates that the novels were submitted to the Library in accordance with copyright deposit law throughout the 1870s but put aside so that Spofford's overworked staff could catalog books that were considered either more reputable or more useful to Congress.[36] Spofford aspired to produce a complete list with the 1878 *Alphabetical Catalogue*, at which point the Beadle publications were no longer overlooked.

It turns out, however, that cataloging practices have an unexpected capacity to encode cultural value judgments. Not only was cataloging of Beadle's Dime Novels delayed, but even upon inclusion the novels were treated differently from more mainstream works. Their listing by publisher and then by series rather than by author implies that such novels were regarded as an undifferentiated mass of formula fiction, in contrast to full-fledged works of the imagination by authors who occupied a higher position in the literary hierarchy. The example of authors such as Reid and Stephens, who straddled the line between pulp novelist and mainstream author by writing for both types of publishing firm, underscores what appears to be an arbitrariness in such designations. Whereas modern readers tend to identify the status or quality of a literary work primarily by reference to its author, a publisher's imprimatur apparently carried more classificatory weight with Spofford, at least in the case of Beadle publications. A Beadle & Adams Dime Novel was by definition a certain kind of book, regardless of the identity of its author.

Spofford occupied a vexing position among American librarians in the late nineteenth century and faced unique challenges in regard to conflicting ideals of professional responsibility. As a young editor for the *Cincinnati Daily Commercial* Spofford had gravitated toward the role of cultural arbiter when he attempted to educate his readers on the proper judgment of modern literature. As a founding trustee of the Public Library of the District of Columbia Spofford chaired the Committee on Books, where he exercised "a strong influence in determining the character of the book collection as an agent of public education . . . by drawing up lists for purchase and by almost daily counter-signature of book orders."[37] In contrast, all he could do at the Library of Congress was try to process an unprecedented boom of sensational, cheaply produced fiction aimed unapologetically at working-class readers. The solution to his dilemma was to publish works unrelated to his official duties as Librarian, in which he aimed to shape the reading choices of the American public. The very titles of his works in the 1880s, *What to Read; When to Read; How to Read* and *The Library of Choice Literature*, convey this intention to help readers make choices from a bewildering cultural landscape. That so much of this landscape fell short of his literary standards helps to explain the hostile tone of some of his remarks in *A Book for All Readers*. Also contributing to these sentiments, perhaps, was a strange mixture of professional authority and helplessness that Spofford experienced as he tried to balance his personal views against the kind of neutrality required by his role in building a comprehensive collection of American imprints at the Library of Congress.

I find especially notable Spofford's efforts to shape what we would today regard as a canon of great American authors. After all, while the novels of British and French sensationalists put out by reprint publishers proved all too appealing to American readers, these works were not thought to represent the American character. Spofford could fulfill his professional role as an apostle of culture by guiding present and future readers toward those nineteenth-century American authors who, by his lights, deserved serious attention. He hints toward his vision of this group in scattered passages throughout *A Book for All Readers*, but his most direct assessment of American literature appears in the poem "The Librarian's Dream," in which the luminaries of world literature appear. Stanzas sixteen and seventeen merit quotation:

> Then followed a group of America's best,
> With Irving, and Bryant, and Holmes,
> While Bancroft and Motley unite with the rest,
> And Thoreau with Whittier comes.
>
> With his Raven in hand dreamed on Edgar Poe,
> And Longfellow sweet and serene,
> While Prescott, and Ticknor, and Emerson too,
> And Hawthorne and Lowell were seen.[38]

It may not be entirely fair to regard this poem as a serious intervention in canon construction, given its light tone and the constraints of meter and rhyme. Nonetheless, an observation or two might be ventured. A product of regional chauvinism, Spofford gives pride of place to the writers of his native New England. The New Yorkers Irving, Bryant, and the peripatetic Poe serve as the only exceptions. The West and the South are unrepresented, as Spofford promotes a New England–centric view of American culture that prevailed well into the twentieth century. Spofford champions the claims of poets, essayists, and historians over fiction writers. The only novelist in the poem is Hawthorne; Spofford overlooks Herman Melville, Harriet Beecher Stowe, Henry James, William Dean Howells, Stephen Crane, and Mark Twain.[39] Whitman's omission is to be expected, despite Spofford's noteworthy gesture of making sure the Library of Congress held all of the poet's works. It was one thing to collect an author's works in their entirety in a national library but another thing altogether to use one's cultural authority to push that author's claims on posterity. The grouping together of American authors reveals that Spofford, like others of his generation, subscribed to a nationalist paradigm of literary history. In the poem America's best take their place on the world stage, following in the wake of Homer, Dante, Shakespeare, and so on, thereby signaling the nation's cultural maturity. From a twenty-first-century perspective such a paradigm can be seen to have ignored the purchasing choices of ordinary readers and the international character of Anglo-American publishing. This is why Spofford could unselfconsciously argue on behalf of a copyright deposit law that purported to collect the "annual product of the American press," while in fact the law let a large quantity of books published (i.e., reprinted) in America fall outside of its purview.

The ironies that emerge from consideration of Spofford's career make him a more representative and more compelling figure than an assessment of him as a visionary. Spofford was, if not a victim, at least a chagrined observer of his own success at the Library of Congress. Lacking the power that even a small-town public librarian maintained regarding the character of the collections over which he presided, Spofford turned to outside publishing ventures to exercise his professional authority. But when the perpetually overworked Librarian finally found time to publish *A Book for All Readers* in 1900, the library profession was moving away from the genteel reading standards that he advocated with such force. Lindsay Swift had published his influential essay "Paternalism in Public Libraries" in the *Library Journal* in 1899, arguing against the puritanical censoring of fiction enacted by timid selection committees.[40] The trend in coming decades would be for the profession to abandon its concept of librarians as cultural gatekeepers in favor of a more bureaucratized, service-oriented mission.

Another irony attends the concept of canonization of American letters. While Spofford argued for a limited canon of great New England–based American authors, his institution collected via copyright deposits the same popular novelists he sought to exclude from the attention of readers. When late-twentieth-century scholars began to promote the literary merit of nineteenth-century works that had long been excluded from academic attention, the wide inclusion policy that Spofford had ushered into existence ensured that copies of these texts would be available for study. Modern students, therefore, have Spofford to thank for a choice of books wider in scope than at any time since American literature became a field of academic study. Although we might make choices different from those Spofford anticipated, this in no way diminishes our debt.

Notes

1. Both quotations are from "The 'Poetry' of Mr. Walt Whitman," *Cincinnati Daily Commercial,* January 19, 1860.

2. John Y. Cole, *For Congress and the Nation: A Chronological History of the Library of Congress* (Washington, D.C.: Library of Congress, 1979), 40.

3. The poets included are Bryant, Holmes, Whittier, Poe, and Longfellow in Ainsworth R. Spofford, *A Book for All Readers: Designed as an Aid to the Collection, Use, and Preservation of Books and the Formation of Public and Private Libraries,* 2nd ed. (New York: G. P. Putnam's Sons, 1900), 419.

4. Wayne A. Wiegand, "Research Libraries, the Ideology of Reading, and Scholarly Communication, 1876–1900," in *Libraries and Scholarly Communication in the United States: The Historical Dimension,* ed. Phyllis Dain and John Y. Cole (New York: Greenwood Press, 1990), 72.

5. Frederic Beecher Perkins, *The Best Reading,* 4th ed. (New York: G. P. Putnam's Sons, 1886).

6. Spofford, *A Book for All Readers,* 19, 21, 22.

7. Dee Garrison, *Apostles of Culture: The Public Librarian and American Society, 1876–1920* (New York: Free Press, 1979).

8. Louise Hastings, "Emerson in Cincinnati," *New England Quarterly* 11, no. 3 (1938): 443–69.

9. Henry David Thoreau, *A Week on the Concord and Merrimack Rivers* (Princeton, N.J.: Princeton University Press, 1980), 96.

10. Henry David Thoreau, *Walden* (New Haven, Conn.: Yale University Press, 2004), 103.

11. Ralph Waldo Emerson, *Society and Solitude. Twelve Chapters* (Boston: Fields, Osgood & Co., 1870), 175–76, 193.

12. Garrison, *Apostles of Culture,* 68.

13. Garrison notes that "feminine discontent, vaguely defined but deeply felt, permeates the domestic fiction judged 'immoral' by leading librarians and literary conservatives" ("Immoral Fiction in the Late Victorian Library," in *Victorian America,* ed. Daniel Walker Howe [Philadelphia: University of Pennsylvania Press, 1976], 154).

14. Spofford, *A Book for All Readers,* 23. Spofford included the term "black list" in quotation marks.

15. All of the information in this paragraph is from John Y. Cole, *Copyright in the Library of Congress: 125th Anniversary* (Washington, D.C.: Library of Congress, 1995). This is a reprint of Cole's article on the subject, which originally appeared in the *Quarterly Journal of the Library of Congress* in April 1971.

16. *Statutes at Large of the United States of America* (Boston: Little, Brown and Company, 1871), 16:212–13.

17. *Handbook of the New Library of Congress with Essays on the Architecture, Sculpture, and Painting and on the Function of a National Library* (Boston: Curtis & Cameron, 1897), 125 (first two quotations), 126, http://hdl.loc.gov/loc.gdc/

scd0001.20056413001ha.1.

18. Spofford acknowledged exactly this point in a letter he wrote to Harper & Brothers on May 18, 1877: "The statutes regulating copyright have never defined the meaning of the word 'book' as used repeatedly by the law, nor do they afford any answer to the query as to what or how much is protected or may be covered by the entry of a book" (Library of Congress Archives, Manuscript Division).

19. Albert Johannsen, *The House of Beadle & Adams and Its Dime and Nickel Novels: The Story of a Vanished Literature* (Norman: University of Oklahoma Press, 1950), chap. 1, http://www.ulib.niu.edu/badndp/chap1.html.

20. Publishers of cheap libraries used this paper-covered format to take advantage of lower postal rates for periodicals. Spofford lobbied the Senate unsuccessfully in 1888 to amend postal rates on the grounds that they were subsidizing the distribution of what he called "the 'bigamy' school of fiction" (Lydia Cushman Schurman, "The Librarian of Congress Argues against Cheap Novels Getting Low Postal Rates," in *Pioneers, Passionate Ladies, and Private Eyes: Dime Novels, Series Books, and Paperbacks*, ed. Larry E. Sullivan and Lydia Cushman Schurman [New York: Haworth Press, 1996], 66).

21. Johannsen, *The House of Beadle & Adams*, chap. 6, http://www.ulib.niu.edu/badndp/chap6.html.

22. *Statutes at Large*, 16:215.

23. Jeffrey D. Groves, "Courtesy of the Trade," in *A History of the Book in America*, vol. 3, *The Industrial Book 1840–1880*, ed. Scott E. Casper, Jeffrey D. Groves, Stephen W. Nissenbaum, and Michael Winship (Chapel Hill: University of North Carolina Press, 2007), 140.

24. Frank Luther Mott, *Golden Multitudes: The Story of Best Sellers in the United States* (New York: R. R. Bowker Company, 1947), 151.

25. David Dzwonkoski, "George Munro"; "George Munro and Company"; "George Munro's Sons"; "George Munro Publishing House," all in *Dictionary of Literary Biography*, vol. 49, *American Literary Publishing Houses, 1638–1899, Part 1: A–M*, ed. Peter Dzwonkoski (Detroit: Gale Research Company, 1986), 315.

26. Patrick Brantlinger, "What Is 'Sensational' about the Sensation Novel?" *Nineteenth-Century Fiction* 37, no. 1 (1982): 1.

27. Spofford, *A Book for All Readers*, 415–16.

28. *Catalogue of Books Added to the Library of Congress during the Year 1871* (Washington, D.C.: Government Printing Office, 1872); *Catalogue of Books Added to the Library of Congress during the Year 1872* (Washington, D.C.: Government Printing Office, 1874); *Catalogue of Recently Added Books, Library of Congress, 1873–75* (Washington, D.C.: Government Printing Office, 1876); *Alphabetical Catalogue of the Library of Congress*, vol. 1, *A–Braidwood* (Washington, D.C.: Government Printing Office, 1878); *Alphabetical Catalogue of the Library of Congress*, vol. 2, *Brailsford–Cragin* (Washington, D.C.: Government Printing Office, 1880).

29. Harper & Brothers might have submitted deposit copies of Collins's novels as a gesture toward solidifying its trade courtesy claim on the author, whose relations with his American publisher were "remarkably cordial" (William M. Clarke, *The Secret Life of Wilkie Collins* [London: Allison & Busby, 1988], 140).

30. R. C. Terry, "Rhoda Broughton," in *Dictionary of Literary Biography*, vol. 18, *Victorian Novelists after 1885*, ed. Ira B. Nadel and William E. Freedman (Detroit: Gale Research Company, 1983), 16.

31. Winifred Hughes, "Mary Elizabeth Braddon," in Nadel and Freedman,

Victorian Novelists, 8.

32. Catalogs indicate that the Library of Congress collected pirated American editions of British novels in the 1830s and 1840s (Carl Ostrowski, *Books, Maps, and Politics: A Cultural History of the Library of Congress, 1783–1861* [Amherst: University of Massachusetts Press, 2004], 128).

33. Annual budgets for the Library are listed in the *Library of Congress Journal,* vol. 1, 1861–91, Library of Congress Archives, Manuscript Division.

34. Complete publishing catalogs from 1873 by T. B. Peterson & Brothers and the American News Company are reproduced in the *Dictionary of Literary Biography,* vol. 49, *American Literary Publishing Houses, 1638–1899, Part 2: N–Z,* ed. Peter Dzwonkoski (Detroit: Gale Research Company, 1986). Data concerning the authors Bulwer, Collins, and Kingston come from pages 649 (Bulwer), 643 (Collins), and 596 (Kingston).

35. By adding some element to the original work, such as illustrations or a preface, a publisher could evidently attempt to secure a copyright on a pirated novel. According to the General Index of Copyright Records, 1870–97, Munro submitted hundreds of books from the Seaside Library series for copyright protection. I am indebted to Rosemary Kelly of the Copyright Office in the Library of Congress for this information.

36. Beadle's Dime Novels were probably among the seventy thousand books "piled on the floor in all directions" in 1877, as Spofford and his staff struggled to keep up with the pace of deposits (Cole, *Copyright,* 22).

37. From a memorial to Spofford composed by the trustees of the Public Library of the District of Columbia and sent to his family after Spofford's death in 1908 (Ainsworth Rand Spofford Papers, Manuscript Division, Library of Congress).

38. Spofford, *A Book for All Readers,* 419. Motley is John Lothrop Motley, a New England Brahmin and historian. William Hickling Prescott and George Ticknor were also historians from prominent New England families.

39. James and Twain may have been omitted not because they were fiction writers but because they were still living in 1900. Spofford's list includes only dead writers. Crane died in June 1900.

40. Lindsay Swift, "Paternalism in Public Libraries," *Library Journal* 24 (1899): 609–18.

The Library of Congress in 1892: Ainsworth Spofford, Houghton, Mifflin and Company, and *Uncle Tom's Cabin*

Michael Winship

On Wednesday, March 23, 1892, A. S. Wheeler, a clerk employed by the Boston publishing firm Houghton, Mifflin and Company, visited the Library of Congress at its location in the dome of the U.S. Capitol. He was there on secret business. Upon completing his consultations at the Library, Wheeler retired to his hotel, the Riggs House, and penned a thirteen-page letter (see below) to his employer in which he gave "full particulars" of his investigations.[1] It provides an interesting and colorful account of the Library of Congress and its operations only a few years before it moved in 1897 to a new, dedicated library building, now known as the Jefferson Building.

An explanation is in order. At the time of Wheeler's visit, questions had arisen concerning the legal status under copyright of Harriet Beecher Stowe's *Uncle Tom's Cabin*, one of the greatest publishing phenomena of the nineteenth century. The work originally had been published serially from June 5, 1851, to April 1, 1852, in the *National Era*, a Washington-based antislavery weekly edited by Gamaliel Bailey. At the time, Stowe was resident in Brunswick, Maine, and a regular contributor of sketches and stories to the *National Era*, though she had never attempted anything as ambitious or clearly political as *Uncle Tom's Cabin*. Perhaps this explains why she took the unusual step of arranging for the registration of the work for copyright in the U.S. District Court of Maine.

If *Uncle Tom's Cabin* attracted considerable attention in the *National Era*, it only became a true best seller with its publication in two volumes by John P. Jewett and Company of Boston on March 20, 1852: an unprecedented 310,000 copies were produced during its first year of book publication. In 1860 the rights passed to another Boston firm, Ticknor and Fields, and then eventually to the Houghton firm, which in 1878 acquired the rights of the many classic works by New England authors originally published by Ticknor and Fields. When the original copyright term of twenty-eight years expired in 1879, Stowe and her new publisher were careful to file for a renewal of an additional fourteen years: *Uncle Tom's Cabin* would finally enter the public domain only in 1893.

If sales of *Uncle Tom's Cabin* as a book were initially spectacular, by mid-1853 sales had come to a near halt and continued to be slack during the 1850s and 1860s, when only about 8,000 additional copies were produced. During the 1870s sales began to pick up, and the original 1852 plates were used to produce just under 20,000 further copies. In 1879, the same year that copyright was renewed, the Houghton firm reissued the text, printed from newly manufactured plates, in an expensive "red-line" and a cheaper "library" edition. During the 1880s, as the firm continued to issue it in a variety of new forms and editions, the work became a dependable, steady seller on Houghton, Mifflin and Company's backlist, contributing to the solid financial foundation on which any established publisher relies. In the five-year period from 1886 to 1890 nearly 110,000 copies were sold.[2]

Thus, it is hardly surprising that Houghton, Mifflin and Company was alarmed in 1892, when the copyright status of *Uncle Tom's Cabin* was questioned, even if it had only just over a year of copyright protection remaining. On March 1, 1892, an obscure advertising industry periodical, the *National Advertiser*, announced "A Remarkable Discovery" that, according to the technicalities of copyright law, *Uncle Tom's Cabin* "was not, and never has been, legally copyrighted."[3] As the article pointed out, the 1880s had seen the rise of an increasing number of "pirates," publishing firms that made a business of reprinting foreign and non-copyrighted works in inexpensive, shabby editions, issued in series that qualified for distribution through the mails as second-class matter. If the "discovery" were correct, any publisher would be free to issue *Uncle Tom's Cabin* in its own edition. Houghton, Mifflin and Company quickly sought legal advice and within weeks sent Wheeler to Washington, D.C., to investigate.

The results of Wheeler's consultation with Librarian of Congress Ainsworth Rand Spofford are reported in full in his letter. The copyright records showed that, in general, the legal requirements had been met for establishing and renewing the copyright of *Uncle Tom's Cabin*, but there were areas of concern—as Spofford remarked, the final determination of its copyright status was a matter for the courts.[4] Putting a bold face on the matter, in mid-April Houghton, Mifflin and Company placed a full-page notice in *Publishers Weekly* denying the truth of the claims made by the *National Advertiser* and stating: "Any attempt to reprint 'UNCLE TOM'S CABIN' before the expiration of copyright will be illegal and an infringement on the rights of Mrs. Stowe and ourselves, and will be promptly prosecuted by us." A second "Note to the Trade" in mid-May warned that the facts in the matter would enable the firm "to obtain an injunction against any person who shall . . . print, publish, sell or expose for sale any copy" of *Uncle Tom's Cabin* without authorization.[5] Apparently, this bluster worked, for no record survives that the courts were called on to establish the firm's rights as publishers of the work before its copyright finally expired on May 12, 1893.

This minor incident in the publishing history of *Uncle Tom's Cabin* provides us with a vivid depiction of conditions at the Library of Congress in 1892. In his letter Wheeler gives a good sense of the clutter and press of business at the Library as well as an interesting insight into the personality of its librarian, Ainsworth Rand Spofford. In his sixty-seventh year at the time of Wheeler's visit, Spofford served as Librarian of Congress from 1864 to 1897 and by 1870 had orchestrated the centralization of copyright activities at the Library, a step vital to its development into a truly national library.[6] His command of the niceties of copyright law is evident from Wheeler's report, though he quite rightly refused to offer a final opinion on the copyright status of *Uncle Tom's Cabin*. He emerges as cool, precise, and knowledgeable, in marked contrast to the "apparent disorder" of the collections and the "heavy plodding" nature of his clerks. Firsthand accounts of the Library of Congress from this period are unusual, and thus I offer here an annotated transcription of this remarkable survival.

Letter from A. S. Wheeler to Houghton, Mifflin and Company, March 23, 1892

Note: The letter was written on thirteen leaves of stationery from the Riggs House, Washington, D.C. In this transcription I have silently regularized interlineations, casual corrections, and end-line hyphenations and replaced underlining with italics; spelling and punctuation errors in the original have been retained.

March 23rd 1892
Messrs H. M. & Co.
Boston

Gentlemen:—
I reached here at 10:45 this morning and at 11:30 I was in Mr. Spofford's room at the Capitol. At one oclock I telegraphed you as follows; "Allen cat money but book deposited April 1, 1852. Steep on Dec. 9, 1878.

Poor Wire me at Riggs House whether intelligable. Letter by mail."[7] In explanation of this message here are the full particulars of my call on Mr. Spofford.—The Library of Congress is a medium sized room (for such a large building) just off from the Dome. Mr. S's desk is a large standing one in the centre of the room and its overloaded condition (I thought of Mr. F. J. G's!) shows what a heavy pressure of work he must be under.[8] His room was filled with a number of persons coming and going and with a number of clerks at desks and about the alcoves. The condition of the room, as regards the piles of books, magazines, papers etc lying around in apparent disorder, was dreadful. The whole place is overcrowded and the clerical force seems entirely inadequate. When I first went in I stood around with something of the air of a sightseer, (the Capitol seemed full of them) & took note of the clerks & tried to pick out Mr. S. from the rest. The clerks struck me as being for the most part rather heavy plodding sort of men, most of them between 25 & 35 and their appearance was quite the reverse of "spruce." They somehow seemed to me to look like less *intelligent* men than I expected to find. Mr. S. was very much engrossed in making an examination of a pile of books on his desk but when a clerk (I think it was Mr. Stockins friend Mr. Strout, tho' I didn't introduce myself to him) asked what he could do for me and I said I wished to see Mr. Spofford, Mr. S. left his work and came at once to where I stood.[9] I gave him my letter and we sat down at one side of the room while he read it. As soon as he had finished it I said that if he wished I would come in later as I saw he was extremely busy and that perhaps then we could talk with less likelihood of my business being known. He replied that he had as much time then as he ever had and that he would show me right away all the records they had. As our conversation was in low tones I thought it best to sit right down and get all the information I could at once. I could not see that during the whole time I sat there (over an hour) that it attracted *any* attention from the persons in the room or from the clerks. He first sent a messenger for one of the clerks (a rather old man who seemed to be a sort of porter or helper) who had charge of the keys. The old records are kept locked up. Mr. S. directed him to get a certain volume of Maine records and then showed me in it an entry in the name of Mrs H. B. Stowe under date of May 12, 1851. As a sort of postscript under the entry, was a memo that a copy was deposited April 1, *1852.* I afterwards handed Mr. S. half a dollar and he promised to mail you a copy of that entry to-night. I could not get one made out while I was there. He said he had no records to show that any copies of the Nat'l Era were deposited with the Maine clerk. He had a file in the Lib. Of Cong. but it was a file that he had bought.

In the Mass. records he showed me an entry dated Nov. 1, 1852 in the name of John P. Jewett & Co. as proprietors and the record of the deposit of a copy on Dec. 27, 1852. But that entry was not renewed. That was for the edition with Illustrations by Billings.[10] He then showed me the entry of the receipt of two copies received Dec. 9, 1878 sent to perfect the entry made Nov. 13, 1878 for the renewal from May 12, 1879. I asked him if it mattered because the copies were received before the copyright expired and he said that the law didn't forbid their being too *early*. He carefully avoided in his conversation, as he does in his correspondence, expressing any *opinion*. I once or twice asked him what he thought of such and such things and he said "That's a matter for the courts to settle." He said when I mentioned what Alfred Hurd said to A. F. H. that he never had and would not give such a thing as a certificate that a copyright had expired.[11] He said "The law don't provide for such a thing." Here is an important fact. He said, a few months ago Mr. *J. S. Ogilvie*, representing the U.S. Book Co. he believed, came there and consulted the D.C. and the Mass. Records and finding no entry in either in 1851, jumped at the conclusion that no entry had been *made*.[12]

It never seemed to occur to him, so Mr. S. says, to look in the Maine or any other records. He further said that about a month ago a N.Y. lawyer had been there looking for information regarding the book but he didn't know what he had found out. As regards the form of wording of the notice Mr. S. said that *that* was a matter for the courts and that some courts *had decided* that it must be the exact form prescribed by law while other courts, on the grounds of equity, had decided that if sufficient notice were given the exact wording was not essential.[13] He seemed to carry a great deal of information in his head and while speaking of the deposit of copies of the Nat'l Era in 1851 I said I understood that only one copy was required by the law of that time. He replied that under an act of 1846, 9 U.S. statutes, page 106 (he said, "write that down") the law called for a copy to be deposited at the Smithsonian Inst. and another in the Liby of Congress. But, he added, there was no penalty, neither fine nor vitiation of copyright, because of failure to do this. As he spoke I understood him to mean no penalty in case of failure to deposit in either or both places, but as I write, it occurs to me he may have referred only to the Smith. Inst. I presume you can find out about this statute from Judge Bennett.[14]

After all points had been gone over I brought up the question of the faithfullness of his clerks. He said there was no one in his office who would, unasked, volunteer information without asking his permission. He thinks Ogilvie inspired that article in the Nat'l Adv's. The writer of the article evidently knew nothing of the Maine record and probably didn't look for a *renewal* in *1879* (recorded of course in 1878).

Mr. S. says his office is one of public records & the information it contains is open to the public upon application. But he doesn't, unasked, give out knowledge that comes to him in consequence of his position and would not allow his clerks to nor does he believe that they do.

I tried to be diplomatic when talking on this point and do not think I offended him in the least.

As regards Griswold's publication he didn't know of *that* until after G. had left his office & he thinks that but two numbers were ever issued. He regards him as a schemer.[15]

I have endeavored in this letter, to err if at all, on the side of fullness rather than brevity. It seems to me wisest for me to remain here until you shall have received this letter and telegraphed me either that my work on this matter is finished or else that you have other instructions for me. I think I ought to receive word from you by Thursday night in which case, if all is O.K., I will go to Baltimore for Friday, Phila Saturday and spend Sunday & the first of next week in N.Y.

If everything is all right I will return my papers etc by mail.

Yours very truly

A S Wheeler

P.S. This might be the means of saving us. Everything else, save the wording of the notice, seems perfect.

P.S. #2, I shall post this about 5.30 P.M. As yet, no ans. to my telegram of one oclock.

Supplement.

Would it not be well to write the Nat'l Advs that we hold the certificate from the Librarian of Congress (after getting it) of the entry of May 12, 1851, and also a certificate of renewal *from* May 12, 1879. That *might* prevent the pirates from making any further search. You could send on copies for them to print if thought best, though might show we had been scared.

Notes

1. This letter and the earlier telegram (see note 7) are now at the Houghton Library, shelved as MS Am 2346 (2725), folder 5, and are printed here by permission of the Houghton Library, Harvard University.

2. For a more complete account of the work's publishing history see Michael Winship, "'The Greatest Book of Its Kind': A Publishing History of *Uncle Tom's Cabin*," *Proceedings of the American Antiquarian Society* 109 (2002): 309–32; and

Claire Parfait, *The Publishing History of "Uncle Tom's Cabin," 1852–2002* (Aldershot: Ashgate, 2007).

3. "A Remarkable Discovery," *National Advertiser* 3 (March 1, 1892): 227.

4. The chief concerns were that, although Stowe had arranged for registration of the title of the work in Maine, the *National Era*, published in Washington, D.C., had never perfected the copyright by depositing copies of published issues and that Bailey had been inconsistent in printing copyright notices.

5. *Publishers Weekly*, April 16, 1892, 602, and May 14, 1892, 753.

6. John Y. Cole, "Of Copyright, Men & a National Library," *Quarterly Journal of the Library of Congress* 28 (1971): 114–36.

7. The original of this coded telegram survives in the Houghton, Mifflin archives together with Wheeler's letter with an attached slip that translates the message as follows: "Entry of May 12th is made in name of Mrs Stowe Entry of May 12th was made in district of Maine Entry of May 12th was not perfected as no copies of National Era were deposited but book deposited April 1st 1852—Renewal in 1879 was perfected by deposit of two copies with proper title and copyright pages on December 9th 1878. Records seem to have been carefully kept Wire me at Riggs House if intelligible letter by mail. A. S. Wheeler"

8. Francis Jackson Garrison, son of the abolitionist William Lloyd Garrison, worked in the editorial office of the firm.

9. Both Mr. Stockins and his friend Mr. Strout are unidentified.

10. Jewett published an expensive, illustrated gift edition of *Uncle Tom's Cabin* in December 1852 for the holiday season.

11. Albert Flyer Houghton, nephew of the firm's founder, Henry Oscar Houghton; Alfred Hurd (possibly "Hard") may have been related to Melanchthon Montgomery Hurd, a partner in the firm since 1864, though the context suggests that he was an employee of the U.S. District Court.

12. J. S. Ogilvie, publisher of inexpensive reprints of noncopyrighted works in series; the United States Book Company was a trust formed in 1890 as a combination of many of the publishers of these reprints.

13. This sentence is preceded and followed by a large space and bracketed in blue pencil in the margins with "*See below*" written at the top of the page.

14. Edmund Hatch Bennett, partner in and legal advisor to the firm. The final two lines of this paragraph are bracketed off, with "See P. S." written in the margin.

15. William McCrillis Griswold, indexer and bibliographer, worked as a clerk in the copyright office from 1882 to 1888 and compiled *A Synopsis of Copyright Decisions* (Bangor, Maine: Q. P. Index, 1883), though the reference here seems to be to a different publication.

"Wake Up and Read!" Book Promotion and National Library Week, 1958

Jean Preer

In the early 1950s publishers and librarians shared an array of intersecting interests. Ranging from copyright and postal rates to intellectual freedom, these challenges grew out of the desire of both professional communities to expand the availability of books and to enlarge the audience of readers. Throughout the early 1950s the American Book Publishers Council and the American Library Association targeted specific legislative goals and responded to immediate threats. But in a communications environment transformed by television, book clubs, and cheap paperbacks, publishers and librarians also sought to proclaim more broadly the central role of books and reading. Spearheaded by the National Book Committee, the observance of National Library Week (NLW), March 16–22, 1958, brought together publishers, librarians, civic leaders, and local volunteers and employed all the tools of mass communication to call upon Americans to "Wake Up and Read!" In the process NLW organizers established a model of private-public partnership and multilayered leadership that was continued with the creation of the Center for the Book in the Library of Congress in 1977.

Intersecting Interests

To gain the benefits of joint action, major publishing houses had formed the American Book Publishers Council (ABPC) in 1946. Working in the for-profit sector, publishers in the 1950s felt more threatened by the changing environment than did librarians. Seeing the traditional literary values of old family firms succumb to the pressures of commercialization, publishers like Alfred A. Knopf feared for the future of the "good" book.[1] Editors, Knopf lamented, no longer worked with authors but with manuscripts; book clubs, movie adaptations, and paperback reprints determined what books would reach the most readers. On the other hand, ABPC economist Robert Frase calculated that publishers barely broke even on their core business and depended on book club contracts and reprint rights to make a modest profit.[2] In an article entitled "Publishing and Social Responsibility" Hiram Haydn, editor-in-chief at Random House, highlighted shortcomings in the book distribution system. As evidence, he noted that the ten thousand new books and twenty-five hundred reprints issued a year reached only 1 percent of the population; smaller communities lacked bookstores, thirty million Americans lacked library service, and many public libraries had book budgets that "permit the purchase of no more than a few dozen titles a year."[3]

Both publishers and librarians saw the potential for reaching new readers in rural areas. The ABPC, through its Committee on Reading Development, and the American Library Association (ALA) had already collaborated with the U.S. Department of Agriculture Extension Service in sponsoring a conference on rural reading in 1951. With support from Sears Roebuck, the conference proceedings were transformed into the best-selling anthology *The Wonderful World of Books*, the culmination of what Theodore Waller of Grolier Publishing Company described as "perhaps the most ambitious promotion program for any book of general interest in recent years."[4] Librarians had somewhat more reason for optimism as they sought to expand the community of readers. After a sustained legislative campaign lasting more than a decade and with the support of publishers, women's clubs, and national civic and educational organizations, librarians had secured passage of the Library Services Act in 1956. The appropriation of federal funds to states for demonstrations of public library service meant that books would reach previously unserved and underserved areas. To qualify for the new funding, states had to formulate plans for library service, elevating book distribution from a community-based model to larger units of library service. In anticipation, a committee of the ALA Public Libraries Division in 1954 began to revise the association's standards for public library service, which had last been issued in 1943. With funding from the Carnegie Corporation and working with Robert D. Leigh, director of the ALA-commissioned Public Library Inquiry of the late 1940s, the committee in 1956 issued general guidelines and two hundred specific standards for library facilities and services. The new standards stressed a cooperative approach and called on librarians and officials to work jointly, lest readers in their locality suffer.[5] Publishers, again identifying their common interest with librarians, supported these new standards.[6]

Intellectual freedom remained a shared concern of publishers and librarians. Censorship threats growing out of cold war anti-Communist hysteria had prompted the issuance of the Freedom to Read Statement by the ABPC and the ALA in 1953.[7] Publishers who were, according to Waller, "concerned with any trespass on the right freely to write, publish, sell, lend, or read" joined librarians in opposing congressional bills to control comic books and to require labels on allegedly subversive works in the Library of Congress.[8] Although these concerns had modulated somewhat following Senator Joseph McCarthy's death, a succession of new challenges infused a new sense of urgency into concerns about books and reading. In 1955 Rudolf Flesch's best-selling book, *Why Johnny Can't Read*, catapulted phonics from education journals to *Time* magazine, and in 1957 the successful launch of *Sputnik* by the Soviet Union put the failure of American schools at the heart of a global scientific and technical competition.[9]

The impetus to organize a broad campaign to promote libraries, books, and reading emerged from these intertwined concerns. One strand was prompted by the belief that Americans were not up to the intellectual issues of the postwar world. In his introduction to the new library standards, journalist Gerald W. Johnson declared that in the "moment of crisis upon us" people had to broaden their intellectual horizons. He wrote: "If the United States is to continue to lead the world, the people of the United States must continue to expand their mental horizon; and their best means of doing so is by constant, intelligent use of the public library."[10] Biographer Marchette Chute observed that Americans were living in a complicated time "when we must be well informed if we are to survive, and as a democratic nation we depend on knowledge as we never have before. . . . We cannot afford a nation of non-readers." This emphasis on the nation's interest in reading recalled the traditional role of the library in fostering an informed citizenry. The other strand, however, reflected the new era of postwar prosperity and concerns that this new affluence and sophistication had not translated into an increased interest in books and reading. As Chute observed, a shorter work week, electrical appliances, and a longer life expectancy meant that Americans had plenty of time for reading but had "not yet learned what can be done with it."[11]

Writing in 1957, ABPC executive director Dan Lacy recalled that a decade earlier the Public Library Inquiry found that only 10–15 percent of the adult population were active library users. Since the 1940s adult circulation had remained static and on a per capita basis might have declined.[12] Lacy distinguished "pastime use" of libraries, that is, for entertainment and leisure reading, which had lost ground, from "purposive use" or information seeking, which had held its own. He attributed the decline in pastime use to four factors, starting with the pervasive attraction of television. (Studies showed that in the late 1950s five out of six families owned sets, with each set turned on for an estimated five hours a day.)[13] Other factors included greater prosperity, with discretionary income spent on cars, sports, and travel; the move to the suburbs, with the attendant burdens of homeownership; and a new propensity for group activities. Referring to David Riesman's *The Lonely Crowd,* Lacy contrasted the "inner-directed, purposeful character of an earlier day—associated with the lonely practice of reading—with the other-directed character of today" and concluded, "The whole tenor of our time seems to call for active, participant, and gregarious pastimes."[14]

Private-Public Partnership

With changing currents in the market for trade books, the ABPC Committee on Reading Development sought allies in its efforts to expand the audience for books. In cooperation with radio station WNYC in New York, it planned a weeklong "Festival of Books" with program tapes available through the National Association of Educational Broadcasters. In 1950, in what Waller called its greatest achievement, the ABPC established the National Book Awards in cooperation with the American Booksellers Association and the Book Manufacturers Institute.[15] The highly regarded prizes honored such distinguished and sometimes controversial writers as Rachel Carson and Ralph Ellison and in the process put books in the news.

In 1954, after consulting leaders in various fields, the ABPC organized a citizens' committee to concern itself "with the large social and cultural implications of books, as distinct from the solely professional and commercial problems of libraries and publishers." An organizing committee, chaired by George N. Schuster, president of Hunter College, and including Douglas Black of Doubleday, Gardner Cowles of *Look* magazine, Flora Belle Ludington, president of the ALA, and Whitney North Seymour, past president of the Association of the Bar of the City of New York, drafted a statement of purpose:

> The National Book Committee is a society of citizens devoted to the use of books. Its purpose is to keep books free, make them widely available, and encourage people to read them. It is independent and non–profit making. Its membership includes professional bookmen, but it does not concern itself with the private interest of the book community except where that interest is demonstrably and unequivocally identical to the public interest. . . . It is clearly within the public interest to expand the reading audience, to

encourage the wiser and wider distribution and use of books, and to nourish the freedom to read.[16]

With bylaws in place, the new National Book Committee (NBC) organized an executive committee with a membership mix representing corporate, mass media, and not-for-profit organizations that would henceforth characterize NBC book promotion efforts. Its chair, Gilbert W. Chapman, was president of Yale & Towne Manufacturing, a Tennessee company whose successful Read Aloud Bookshelf project had been featured in *Harper's* magazine.[17] Membership on the national board was limited to 150, with the president and president-elect of the ALA and the president of the ABPC serving during their elective terms.[18]

While librarians and publishers shared common concerns and values, they moved in different circles. Working with and within the NBC linked librarians to this expanded network of contacts. Publicity specialist Marie Loizeaux noted that "librarians talk mostly to themselves" but do not "command a wide audience of non-readers or even of non-library-users." She continued: "But the National Book Committee does, and we salute this dedicated group of laymen—'laymen' only as far as professional librarianship is concerned—who, as leaders in their various fields, command attention and respect and who are so devoted to the encouragement of the development of the reading habit. They have an audience we are unlikely to reach."[19] The NBC adopted four priority areas representing the intersecting interests of various constituencies within the community of the book: protection of intellectual freedom, development of lifelong reading habits, promotion of library services, and distribution of American books abroad.[20] The committee regularly reported on them in the *National Book Committee Quarterly*.

In their 1973 review of the work of the National Book Committee, Virginia Mathews and John Frantz stressed its important role in bringing the different sectors of the community of the book together. They wrote that in the 1950s

> consumers of books and users of libraries seemed to have little awareness of each other or self-identity as readers; the public was not in touch with the professionals responsible for planning or providing for their needs; professionals involved in reading and libraries had little voice in policy making or funding decisions; people were hesitant to adopt the out-of-step 'egghead' image of the reader. . . . The school too often destroyed reading enjoyment by concentrating too relentlessly on skills.[21]

Seeing the need for a "massive frontal attack" to shake an indifferent public from its apathy, an NBC subcommittee proposed an "appreciation week" focused on reading, books, and libraries.

From the start, planners envisioned the effort as a public relations campaign. As NBC chair and Viking publisher Harold Guinzburg reported to the ABPC board, the committee variously considered weeks celebrating reading, books, and culture before deciding to celebrate National Library Week.[22] In this the NBC was influenced by the report and recommendations of its public relations consultant, Lynn Farnol. Drawing on public opinion polls and his own mail survey of community leaders, librarians, booksellers, book reviewers, and editors, Farnol documented the need for such a campaign and a rationale for focusing on libraries. His major findings, which appeared in numerous articles and presentations before and during the first National Library Week, revealed that the United States had the lowest proportion of book readers of any major English-speaking country. A 1955 Gallup poll found that 61 percent had not read any book except the Bible in the previous year and that 26 percent of college graduates and 82 percent of those who had attended only elementary school could not remember reading a single book in the past twelve months. An earlier poll showed that only 17 percent were reading a book at the time, while another revealed that though more than half the adults surveyed lived within a mile of a public library, only one-fifth had visited the library during the year preceding the survey.[23]

Farnol's report indicated a wide-open market for books and widespread support for such a promotional effort, but, just as important, it recommended a focus on libraries for their symbolic importance and operational advantages. Libraries, he observed, "are symbols of importance in all communities, library organizations constitute the machinery that form a nucleus for the project, down to the local level in every community where a public library exists."[24] Thanks to Andrew Carnegie, libraries had what publishers and booksellers lacked—a presence in nearly every community of any size across the country.

And although Farnol did not mention it, librarians also had professional organizations in every state and extensive experience in organizing promotional campaigns celebrating libraries, books, and reading. As the National Library Week campaign geared up, the American Library Association was concluding its American Heritage Project, organized in 1951 with Ford Foundation funding. Part of ALA's seventy-fifth anniversary celebration, the project was directed from ALA headquarters, but national leaders had worked through state-level offices to organize local reading and discussion groups on the meaning of American democracy in crisis times. ALA had cooperated with publishers on the project, particularly Cass Canfield of Harper & Brothers, which published three American Heritage Project books, and Gardner Cowles of *Look* magazine, who provided financial support.[25]

Multilayered Leadership

In April 1957 NBC chair Guinzburg announced that the ABPC board had approved plans for National Library Week, a two-year appropriation, the support of ABPC staff, and use of ABPC offices. John Robling, former advertising director for magazine publisher *McCall's* and public relations director of the National Book Committee, was appointed National Library Week director.[26] He was joined later by Virginia Mathews, editor and director of publicity at Longmans, Green & Co., who became assistant director in charge of field organization.[27]

The scheme involved both top-down and bottom-up initiatives along the lines of the American Heritage Project. The big difference was that this program celebrating libraries was initiated and largely conceived by publishers with the approval and participation of librarians. Responsibilities of all the players were clearly laid out: National Library Week headquarters in New York was to develop a common theme, prepare materials, and coordinate national publicity. According to executive director Lacy, the role of the ABPC was to help make things happen. "Relatively small though it is, the book industry can play 'a catalytic role' through NLW, in bringing to bear on behalf of books the great number of agencies that use and need books." A national NLW steering committee included Douglas Black and Marchette Chute from the NBC national board; Theodore Waller; Louis Cowan, vice president of the Columbia Broadcasting System; John Fischer, editor of *Harper's* magazine; William Nichols, publisher of *This Week* magazine; David Clift, executive secretary of the ALA; and Guinzburg and Ward Cheney of the National Book Committee.[28] The ALA was to establish NLW committees in each state. A committee of civic leaders would oversee the state observance, while a committee of librarians would provide advice and support. Local librarians would organize local activities using NLW materials.

Although the ALA did not control the organization or funding of the 1958 National Library Week, it took full advantage of the opportunity NLW presented. Writing in the *ALA Bulletin*, Clift explained this opportunity to the library community in an article entitled "What National Library Week Can Mean": "It can mean a nationwide emphasis on the values of reading—

reading for education—for pleasure—to help with the day's work—to be a better citizen. It can mean more public awareness of the values to be found in books. It can mean more perceptive attention to libraries of all kinds—their place in the life of the community—the services they offer to everyone."[29] Len Arnold, a PR consultant for the ALA who had overseen American Heritage Project publicity, believed that National Library Week would put a spotlight on libraries as never before, combining "a strong idea, able leadership, financial wherewithal, and a working organization of willing and enthusiastic citizens." ALA would have its own Committee on National Library Week headed by ALA president Lucile Morsch. Since librarians had worked with community groups on other library campaigns, Arnold urged them to adapt the NLW framework to "fit the public relations problems which are peculiar to each library situation."[30]

On its part, NLW staff in New York devised the theme "Wake Up and Read!" as well as its eagle emblem and its slogan, "For a Better-Read, Better-Informed America." Promotional ideas drawn from real-life successes were compiled in an *NLW Organization Handbook* and made widely available in library publications. The book emphasized using volunteer help to build awareness of the importance of reading, books, and libraries and included such tried-and-true activities as library open houses, exhibits, special events, reader surveys, contests, reading nights, and panel discussions. Local publicity efforts were to be bolstered with national media coverage arranged by the National Book Committee.[31] An NLW promotional kit included a poster, streamers with the NLW logo, bookmarks, table tents, advertising mats for local merchants, and suggestions for window displays in local stores.[32]

The first National Library Week put lay leadership center stage while librarians worked behind the scenes. Identification and recruitment of the chairs of state citizens' committees were the key to stimulating interest in libraries and books among those who might provide crucial future support. While some chairs came from nonprofit organizations, education, and foundations, many came from the corporate world, including executives from department stores, newspapers, utilities, and banks.[33] Field representative Virginia Mathews stressed that the membership of a citizens' committee should represent a state's diverse geographical, industrial, business, education, cultural, and civic interests.

The *NLW Handbook* included a sample talk that librarians could use to recruit civic leaders, who could in turn enlist volunteers from their own organizations.[34] Based on an address by NLW director John Robling, it supplied a litany of answers to the question "Who is affected by reading in every community?"

[Reading] matters to parents—mothers and fathers who see their children bored with easy entertainment, but unable to supply their own. . . . It matters to businessmen—who need employees who are able to read and absorb material intelligently. . . . It matters to the community leaders among you. . . . It matters to teachers terribly . . . . It matters to doctors, to social workers, to ministers—all those who deal with human suffering. Every day they see people with desperate problems and lacking the inner resources to face them.[35]

With its theme in place, committees organized, materials distributed, and allies enlisted in the cause, National Library Week began on March 16, 1958, with a proclamation from President Dwight D. Eisenhower and a statement supporting libraries from former presidents Herbert Hoover and Harry S. Truman.[36] The NLW emblem had a semiofficial and patriotic look: an eagle holding festive ribbons declaring "Wake Up and Read."[37] Continuing the patriotic theme, a *New York Times* editorial at the beginning of the week emphasized the civic importance of libraries.[38]

Mass Audience

From the outset, organizers of National Library Week sought to employ all communications media and "refused to allow the Library Week Program to denigrate television or any other medium in its efforts on behalf of reading, books and libraries. The theme was coordination, not competition."[39] Lined up well in advance, coverage of National Library Week appeared in print and nonprint media, appealing to readers and nonreaders across a broad demographic. In its spring catalog sent to eight million homes Sears, Roebuck continued to offer biographies of great Americans (as part of the American Heritage Project) and called on customers to become better acquainted with their local libraries during National Library Week.[40] Steering committee member William Nichols arranged to have a "Wake Up and Read" feature appear prominently in *This Week* magazine, the Sunday newspaper supplement with a circulation of twelve million.[41]

During the entire month of March 1958 major magazines with circulation totaling more than eighty million featured articles on the NLW theme.[42] There seemed to be no subject, from interior decorating to gardening and travel, that was not connected to libraries, books, and reading. In *McCall's* an illustrated article showed how books could improve a living space; in *Better Homes & Gardens* Bergen Evans praised the value of home libraries; in *Holiday* magazine Marchette Chute celebrated the New York Public Library; while in the *Atlantic Monthly* National Book Award winner Catherine Drinker Bowen praised librarians.[43] Many articles featured the National Library Week eagle emblem and slogan.

Much of the media coverage addressed two concerns that had troubled the National Book Committee and led to its national book promotion. One was the perceived threat to books by the new media of mass communication, particularly television. The other was the perceived challenge to high quality works posed by book clubs and cheap paperback editions. For its National Library Week issue *Reader's Digest* offered a contrary view in C. Lester Walker's article, which recounted the amazing and unexpected success of Professor Floyd Zulli, Jr.'s early morning program, *Sunrise Semester*, on WCBS-TV in New York. A specialist in comparative literature, Zulli lectured for a half-hour, starting at 6:30 a.m., five mornings a week in a no-frills, no-nonsense style on works by such authors as Balzac, Dostoyevsky, Proust, and Gide. His debut lecture on Stendahl's novel *The Red and the Black* triggered such a run on libraries and bookstores that virtually overnight the book became unobtainable. Although few signed up to get course credit through New York University, an estimated 150,000 viewers tuned in.[44] In an article entitled "Books Are Here to Stay" appearing in the *Saturday Evening Post* during National Library Week, Bennett Cerf noted that more copies of the Modern Library edition of *The Red and the Black* sold in nine days following the broadcast than had sold in the previous four years. He concluded, "I am one book publisher, in short, who is convinced that far from hindering the reading of good books, television definitely has encouraged it."[45] Articles about National Library Week in the *New York Times* noted that eggheads were in style. Lucile Morsch observed that carrying a book now marked a man of distinction.[46]

The presentation of the National Book Awards during National Library Week reaffirmed the commitment of major publishers to works of the highest quality. Winners for 1958 were John Cheever for *The Wapshot Chronicle*, Catherine Drinker Bowen for *The Lion and the Throne*, and Robert Penn Warren for *Promises: Poems 1954–1956*.[47] In his address at the award ceremony poet Randall Jarrell warned about the impact of mass media and popular culture, which, he said, veil the perception of reality, "diverts from it and becomes an obstacle to experiencing it." In response, the *Times* Books and Culture columnist observed that Jarrell might be too pessimistic. With most classics available in inexpensive paperback formats, "Americans do not read only tawdry and trivial works." Readers need to read new books, the columnist pointed out, to keep in touch with the age as well as great books "to understand the essential dignity and beauty of living."[48] In contrast to the National Book Awards, advertising by major publishers during National Library Week sent confusing signals about their commitment to quality versus their need to appeal to a mass market. Doubleday and World Publishing ads, which included the NLW slogan and emblem, featured swashbuckling adventures and potboiler romances rather than serious nonfiction and literature. Macmillan ran the most intriguing series of ads, using the NLW theme to suggest that the transformative powers of reading could influence personal, family, and community change. On March 2, "The Day America Decided to 'Wake Up and Read,'" its ad showed how reading influenced the lives of a commuter, a housewife, a public figure, a student, a working man, two women at a social gathering, and a family.[49]

What did libraries and librarians gain from National Library Week? Journals of state library associations over the next year reported success stories about local observances. The celebration seems to have been the catalyst that National Book Committee members had envisioned. NLW director Robling tallied activities in more than five thousand cities, villages, and towns that "succeeded in arousing a sense of personal need as well as a deeper responsibility for the status of reading in the community and in the nation." Of 40 states reporting, he noted 969 members on state committees; in 22 states, 1,783 members served on local committees. A total of 22 states reported 2,826 in-library events; 20 states reported 1,484 ceremonies held outside libraries; 21 states reported 5,086 window displays; 20 states reported 2,826 in-school events; while 15 states reported 612 community events put on by schools. Dramatic increases in usage were reported in Iowa, with 50 percent of libraries showing a circulation increase over March of the previous year. Many libraries reported their single highest monthly circulation ever.[50]

Louisiana state librarian Sallie Farrell, a veteran of the American Heritage Project, reported that beyond the things that could be counted, the most valuable parts of National Library Week were opportunities for citizens and librarians to work together, participation of all types of libraries, and publicity that magnified the impact of the many disparate activities.[51] Inspired by the Macmillan advertising series, the *Mississippi Library News* published its own "The Day Mississippi Decided to Wake Up and Read," which noted the opening of new library buildings, the initiation of the first ever library service in several communities, and the awakening of Mississippians to the value of books.[52] But the piece ended with a question: "After National Library Week—What?" "In the near term, librarians and publishers agreed on the success of their joint promotion effort and continued it with ABPC funding and the same theme during the next year. By the early 1960s, however, administration of the week had tilted further toward librarians with state library associations assuming responsibility for statewide committees."[53]

When the National Book Committee ceased operation in 1974, National Library Week became an ALA event.[54] The idea of a national promotion of reading, books, and libraries remained, however, along with the essential elements put in place during the first National Library Week: a partnership between private organizations and public institutions; national inspiration, state coordination, and local activity; use of all the tools of mass communication to reach the broadest possible audience; and honoring quality works while expanding the audience for books and reading of all kinds. Not long after the National Book Committee closed shop, Librarian of Congress Daniel Boorstin created a Center for the Book within the Library of Congress to promote libraries, books, and reading using all the methods of mass communication and eventually working through state centers.[55] In 1978, when Virginia Mathews began her thirty-year career as a consultant working with John Y. Cole, the Center's director, the past of the National Book Committee joined the future of the Library of Congress and its Center for the Book in carrying on the tradition of promoting books and reading nationally on the behalf of the community of the book and citizens everywhere.

Notes

I would like to thank Indiana University's School of Library and Information Science graduate assistant Meredith Albertin for her outstanding help in tracking down material for this article and Virginia Mathews for several most enjoyable conversations about her work with the National Book Committee and the Center for the Book.

1. Alfred A. Knopf, "Book Publishing: The Changes I've Seen," *Atlantic Monthly* 200 (December 1957): 155.

2. Robert W. Frase, "Economic Trends in Book Publishing," in *Books and the Mass Market*, ed. Harold K. Guinzburg, Robert W. Frase, and Theodore Waller (Urbana: University of Illinois Press, 1953), 26.

3. Hiram Haydn, "Publishing and Social Responsibility," *National Book Committee Quarterly* 3, nos. 2–3 (1959): 7.

4. Theodore Waller, "Expanding the Book Audience," in Guinzburg, Frase, and Waller, *Books and the Mass Market*, 56; Jean L. Preer, "The Wonderful World of Books: Librarians, Publishers, and Rural Readers," *Libraries & Culture* 32 (Fall 1997): 403–26.

5. American Library Association, Public Libraries Division, Co-ordinating Committee on Revision of Public Library Standards, *Public Library Service: A*

Guide to Evaluation, with Minimum Standards (Chicago: American Library Association, 1956), 65, 7.

6. "American Library Association Sets New Goals for Public Libraries," *National Book Committee Quarterly* 1, no. 3 (1957): 3.

7. "Text of Librarians' Manifesto and Resolution on Book Curbs," *New York Times*, June 26, 1953, 8.

8. Waller, "Expanding the Book Audience," 62.

9. National Book Committee, "Purpose and Performance: A Review and Evaluation of the Work of the National Book Committee," report, National Book Committee, New York, 1973, 10.

10. ALA, *Public Library Service*, x.

11. Marchette Chute, "The Aims of National Library Week," *National Book Committee Quarterly* 2, no. 1 (1957): 1.

12. Dan Lacy, "The Adult in a Changing Society: Implications for the Public Library," *Library Quarterly* 27, no. 4 (1957): 281.

13. In this Lacy shared the later view of Robert Putnam in *Bowling Alone: The Collapse and Revival of American Community* (New York: Simon & Schuster, 2000).

14. Lacy, "The Adult in a Changing Society," 282–83.

15. Waller, "Expanding the Book Audience," 64.

16. "How the National Book Committee Was Formed," *National Book Committee Quarterly* 1, no. 4 (1957): 1; also National Book Committee, "Purpose and Performance," 2.

17. Gilbert W. Chapman, "An Experiment in Reading," *Harper's* 23 (December 1956): 73–75. See also "Reading Aloud Bookshelves Prove Successful in Tennessee," *National Book Committee Quarterly* 1, no. 1 (1956): 1–2.

18. "How the National Book Committee Was Formed," 1.

19. Marie D. Loizeaux, "Talking Shop [National Library Week]," *Wilson Library Bulletin* 31 (May 1957): 735.

20. National Book Committee, "Purpose and Performance," 7–8. For more on American books abroad see Louise B. Robbins, "Publishing American Values: The Franklin Book Programs as Cold War Cultural Diplomacy," *Library Trends* 55 (Winter 2007): 638–50.

21. National Book Committee, "Purpose and Performance," 8–9.

22. "Publishers and Booksellers Discuss Plans for National Library Week," *Publishers Weekly*, June 17, 1957, 34–35.

23. Loizeaux, "Talking Shop," 735; National Book Committee, "Purpose and Performance," 8.

24. "Publishers and Booksellers Discuss Plans," 34.

25. Jean L. Preer, "The American Heritage Project: Librarians and the Democratic Tradition in the Early Cold War," *Libraries & Culture* 28 (Spring 1993): 165–88.

26. "Sponsorship of NLW," *Library Journal* 83 (January 1, 1958): 16–17.

27. "Virginia Mathews Joins NLW Staff," *ALA Bulletin* 51 (November 1957): 750.

28. "Library Week Scheduled for March 16–22, 1958," *National Book Committee Quarterly* 1 (Spring 1957): 4–7.

29. David H. Clift, "What National Library Week Can Mean," *ALA Bulletin* 51 (November 1957): 751.

30. Len Arnold, "Materials, Ideas, Areas of Action for National Library Week," *ALA Bulletin* 51 (November 1957): 751–755, 802, quote at 751.

31. "NLW Promotion Ideas," *Library Journal* 83 (January 1, 1958): 18–27.

32. Virginia H. Mathews, "Some Notes and Suggestions for National Library Week," *Wilson Library Bulletin* 32 (January 1958): 367–69, 409–11.

33. Ibid.

34. "Sample Talk—Recruiting Citizens for NLW Service," *Library Journal* 83 (January 1, 1958): 24–26. For an example of how a state chairman used the same talk see H. Eugene Miles, "Let's Wake Up and Read," *Montana Libraries* 11 (April 1958): 4–15.

35. John S. Robling, "Wake Up and Read!" *California Librarian* 19 (January 1958): 49–50, 61–62; "NLW Promotion Ideas," 24–25.

36. Herbert Hoover and Harry S. Truman, "A Statement from Two Presidents on the Occasion of the First Observance of National Library Week March 16–22, 1958," *Texas Libraries* 20, no. 2 (1958): 25. The full text also appeared in "Week-Long Event Honors Libraries. Institutions' Resources and Reading at Home to Be Promoted Nationally," *New York Times*, March 16, 1958, 70.

37. See, for example, its use in "McCall's List of 100 Best Books for Children," *McCall's* 85 (March 1958): 56, as well as in many other articles and advertisements.

38. "Wake Up and Read" (editorial), *New York Times*, March 16, 1958, 28.

39. National Book Committee, "Purpose and Performance," 10.

40. "Sears Continues Library and Reading Promotion," *Library Journal* 83 (March 1, 1958): 718.

41. Arnold, "Materials, Ideas, Areas of Action," 751.

42. "Major Magazines Using Library Week Themes," *Library Journal* 83 (March 1, 1958): 719.

43. "Plan a Place for Books," *McCall's* 85 (April 1958): 138–39; Bergen Evans, "You Can Start a Good Home Library on a Budget," *Better Homes & Gardens* 36 (March 1958): 34, 37; Marchette Chute, "America's Finest Library," *Holiday* 23 (March 1958): 39–40, 42, 45–47, 49, 129; Catherine Drinker Bowen, "My Friends, the Librarians," *Atlantic Monthly* 201 (March 1958): 48–52.

44. C. Lester Walker, "The Big Boom in Good Books," *Reader's Digest* 72 (March 1958): 150–52.

45. Bennett Cerf, "Books Are Here to Stay," *Saturday Evening Post*, March 22, 1958, 80.

46. Austin C. Wehrwein, "Needs Stressed in Library Week. Appeals Note Shortages of Books and Services, with Emphasis on Schools," *New York Times*, March 16, 1958, 71.

47. Topics of the Times, *New York Times*, March 14, 1958, 24.

48. Books and Culture, *New York Times*, March 15, 1958, 16.

49. "The Day America Decided to 'Wake Up and Read'" (Macmillan Company ad), *New York Times*, March 2, 1958, BR11.

50. John S. Robling, "National Library Week April 12–18, 1959," in *American Library Annual 1959*, ed. Wyllis E. Wright, 160–62 (New York: R. R. Bowker, 1958).

51. Sallie Farrell, "'Wake Up and Read!'" *Louisiana Library Association Bulletin* 21 (Fall 1958): 97–99.

52. "The Day Mississippi Decided to Wake Up and Read," *Mississippi Library News* 22 (March 1958): 4–5.

53. Virginia H. Mathews, "Editorial: In the Spotlight," *ALA Bulletin* 54 (January 1960): 7, 36. The article was accompanied by a photo of an NLW workshop for state executive directors presented by Grace T. Stevenson, former director of the American Heritage Project.

54. John C. Frantz, "A Death in the Family," *American Libraries* 6 (April 1975): 206–7.

55. Daniel J. Boorstin, "A Center for the Book in the Library of Congress," in *The Republic of Letters* (Washington, D.C.: Library of Congress, 1989), 40–42. For a charming tribute to the book see Daniel J. Boorstin, "A Design for an Any-time, Do-It-Yourself, Energy-Free Communication Device," *Harper's* 248 (January 1974): 83–86. See also John Y. Cole, "The US's Center for the Book: An Alliance between Public and Private Interests," *Logos* 3, no. 1 (1992): 34–40.

The Library of Congress, the Smithsonian Institution, and the Global Exchange of Government Documents, 1834–1889

Nancy E. Gwinn

In the United States support for international agreements regarding the official exchange of publications came from those who needed the information published by foreign learned societies and academies. Learned and scientific societies were the most active participants in exchanges of transactions and proceedings, and such exchange programs clearly reflected the growth of American cultural and scientific nationalism during the nineteenth century. In addition, exchange of scientific publications provided a mechanism that helped give America a visible identity within the world cultural community.

One of the first acts of America's earliest scientific society, the American Philosophical Society, founded in Philadelphia in 1743, for example, was to ask its founder, Benjamin Franklin, to distribute volume 1 of its *Transactions* to institutions in England, Russia, and Italy. By this means the United States began to enter into scientific correspondence, manifested in the exchange of publications.[1] Over time, as governments published growing amounts of information important to scientists, educators, and legislators, two key institutional players began to promote the international exchange of government publications. Although the Library of Congress initiated the first exchange of publications in the 1830s, it was a partnership between the Library and the Smithsonian Institution that resulted, by the end of the nineteenth century, in an international convention for an official worldwide system of publications exchange.

Alexandre Vattemare

Congressional interest in disseminating official government publications began in 1834, when Congress passed a resolution providing twenty-five copies of every U.S.-funded work for the Joint Committee on the Library of Congress to use in return for donations to the Library. Later, on January 10, 1837, the joint committee specifically authorized the Library of Congress to exchange public documents with the French government.[2] Interest in exchanges with France solidified around a scheme proposed later by the Frenchman Alexandre Vattemare (1796–1864), a gifted ventriloquist and actor known as Monsieur Alexandre who came to the United States in 1839 to perform in a New York theater.[3] Vattemare's ulterior motive was to gain the support and participation of Americans in his Central Agency for International Exchange, headquartered in Paris. While visiting libraries and museums throughout Europe, he had developed a compelling, enthusiastic vision for the exchange of publications and cultural artifacts—and he believed that such exchanges would promote mutual understanding among nations and improve chances for a peaceful negotiation of differences.[4] In two trips to the United States that bracketed the decade of the 1840s, Vattemare managed to persuade many governmental bodies and learned societies to appoint him their official exchange agent and/or pass legislation supporting exchanges with foreign countries.[5] In addition to the U.S. Congress, his list of exchange partners included seventeen state legislatures and seven federal government departments; city corporations; colleges and universities; and historical, natural history, and other learned societies.

American political rationale for support of Vattemare's system reflected the scientific and cultural nationalism of the first half of the nineteenth century, intensified by the War of 1812, which stimulated the emergence of a number of American scientific and learned societies.[6] By exchanging their transactions and proceedings for those of European societies, American scientific societies such as the American Philosophical Society, the Academy of Natural Sciences of Philadelphia, and the Western Academy of Natural Sciences in Cincinnati hoped to demonstrate the validity of American research efforts and to enter into the global scientific communication network. These aims were articulated as early as 1771, when the American Philosophical Society produced the first volume of its *Transactions*, in an enclosure to each member of the Pennsylvania assembly that read:

> As the various societies which have of late years been instituted in Europe have confessedly contributed much to the more general propagation of knowledge and useful arts, it is hoped it will give satisfaction to the members of the honorable house to find that the province which they represent can boast of the first society and the first publication of a volume of Transactions for the advancement of the useful knowledge of this side of the Atlantic—a volume which is wholly American in composition, printing, and paper,

and which, we flatter ourselves, may not be thought altogether unworthy of the attention of men of letters in the most improved parts of the world.[7]

These early societies focused largely on natural history (the identification of the distinctive American plants, animals, fossils, and minerals), spurring patriotic feelings that helped engender financial support from various levels of government.[8] Thus, it was not an unusual circumstance for Vattemare to seek government support for his enterprise.

In December 1839 Vattemare requested that the U.S. Congress pass legislation allowing for the exchange of government and other publications and appointing him as the official agent. He envisioned that the Library of Congress would be the vehicle through which Congress and its Joint Committee on the Library of Congress would manage such a national program. Following Vattemare's aggressive and exhausting lobbying effort, Congress unanimously adopted the bill, which President John Tyler signed into law on July 20, 1840. The act authorized the Librarian of Congress to exchange the Library's duplicates and other documents for books or works from foreign nations; further, fifty extra copies of documents printed by either house were to be made available to the Librarian for that purpose. When Vattemare returned to France in 1841, the Librarian of Congress furnished him with seven hundred volumes of congressional documents, a collection said to be twice as large as any in Washington.[9] Although Congress did not pass an appropriation to support the new law, it corrected this oversight when Vattemare returned to Washington in 1848 with a new petition.

On June 26, 1848, Congress passed the authorizing act that empowered the joint committee to carry out an exchange of U.S. public documents, "appoint such agents as they may from time to time deem requisite," and use $2,000 from the U.S. Treasury to pay expenses of "the agency, donation, and exchange," even those expenses that had already occurred. Furthermore, all books transmitted through the agent would be admitted duty free if they were for the use of any unit of federal or state government "or of the Academy at West Point, or of the National Institute." A month later the joint committee appointed Vattemare its agent for international exchanges between the U.S. and foreign governments and allowed him $1,500 to cover his personal expenses and that of his agency up to June 30, 1849.[10] The joint committee's chairman, Senator James Alfred Pearce of Maryland, pleased that the still-young nation had taken this step toward joining the world's cultural community, wrote to Vattemare: "The scientific and literary union of nations which your efforts have effected will consolidate 'the Republic of Letters.'"[11]

To solidify further Vattemare's official position, the secretary of the treasury issued a circular to all collectors and customs agents instructing them that in order to guard against fraud, all documents and other publications sent to the United States from Vattemare's agency must bear its stamp. In addition, Congress nearly gave Vattemare the franking privilege, but the bill passed only the Senate and went no farther.[12] Enthusiastic legislators authorized other gifts, including one hundred copies of William Hickey's compilation of documents entitled *The Constitution of the United States*, a complete series of the weights and measures of the United States, Little, Brown's edition of *American Laws*, and four copies of the narrative of the United States Exploring Expedition.[13] Small wonder that Senator Thomas Hart Benton gushed, "You are truly, what you have been called, the *hyphen* of the Old & of the New World, and may it be adamantine."[14] Congress hailed Vattemare's plans for exchanging government publications as a method for showing off to the world the products of the new democracy while acknowledging the usefulness to Congress of keeping up with legislative and other official activity abroad. Unfortunately, the plan was not firmly in place.

Vattemare's industry resulted in strong French and European collections at the Boston Public Library, the New York State Library, the Library of Congress, and countless other smaller American libraries. According to one French statesman, through Vattemare's agency Americans had sent more than 70,000 volumes to public establishments in France, and more than 100,000 French volumes had been taken to America.[15] More than 130 public libraries and other establishments benefited from his exchange system, ranging from the 50 volumes sent to St. John's College in Annapolis, Maryland, to nearly 1,000 books, maps, and charts sent to the New York State Library.[16] In 1883 the New York State Library estimated the total value of gifts from Vattemare at $50,000.[17] Vattemare had a catalytic influence on American society through his promotion of the establishment of free public libraries; the Boston Public Library considers him one of its founders.[18]

The reasons for Vattemare's ultimate failure lay partially in his initial success. The enthusiastic acceptance of his cause in the United States resulted in a flood of publications flowing into and out of his Parisian apartments. He was unable to manage the enterprise efficiently, and, despite receiving subsidies in the United States, he also invested much of his personal fortune. The financial drain on his resources worsened, and despite constant petitioning, Vattemare was unsuccessful in convincing the

French government to support his enterprise. In fact, representatives of the French Legation in Washington disavowed him to Librarian of Congress John Silva Meehan, who had become unhappy with the condition of shipments from the Vattemare enterprise. In 1853 Meehan informed Vattemare that Congress had rescinded the law that had appointed him its agent for exchanges.[19] Perhaps more important, the 1840s marked a period of decline for American scientific societies as the center of scientific activity began to move to Washington under the influence of the federal government and the newly created Smithsonian Institution.

The Smithsonian Institution

In 1846 the Smithsonian's board of regents hired as its first secretary Joseph Henry (1797–1878), the nation's foremost scientist known especially for his work on electricity and magnetism. Secretary Henry quickly established a publications series, *Smithsonian Contributions to Knowledge*, and offered it for exchange to a broad range of domestic and foreign scientific and learned societies. Henry and his two assistant secretaries, Charles Coffin Jewett (1816–68) and later Spencer Fullerton Baird (1823–87), put into place a grand scheme that would assist communication among individual scientists, societies, libraries, universities, and other educational bodies all over the world.[20] By appointing forwarding agents in key foreign cities and arranging for free shipping with freight companies, the Smithsonian quickly became a successful middleman in the exchange of publications between American scientists and scientific and educational institutions and like bodies in Europe and other parts of the world.

Henry and Baird were also keenly interested in the distribution and exchange of government publications, which contained much of interest to the scientific world. As a result, from its earliest years the Smithsonian sought to include government publications in its exchange operations, and Henry and Baird worked directly with federal agencies. In 1852 the U.S. Patent Office provided four hundred copies of its 1847 annual report for distribution abroad, and the commissioner of Indian Affairs forwarded to the Smithsonian copies of the first volume of Henry Rowe Schoolcraft's pioneering work on the history, condition, and prospects of Indian tribes, which had been privately published but prepared under the direction of the Bureau of Indian Affairs.[21] The postmaster general, Census Office, surgeon general, and Coast Survey were other early participants in the distribution plan. Also in 1852 the Senate cooperated by ordering quantities of other publications, such as

Howard Stansbury's report of the exploration of Utah, to be printed for the purposes of exchange.[22] By this time the Smithsonian had acquired valuable government publications from abroad; among the 4,745 items received for the Smithsonian library in 1852 were 1,547 charts from the British Admiralty and expedition reports of several French voyages.[23]

Delighted with the success of his early solicitations to government bureaus for documents to send abroad, Baird sought to establish a more systematic method of government document exchange. In 1852 he requested that Congress make available at least thirty copies of a complete series of congressional publications for European libraries. He estimated that the Congress could authorize the automatic printing of at least one hundred to three hundred copies of all works of scientific interest for distribution by the Smithsonian "at modest cost to government," with return donations sent to the Library of Congress to enhance its collections. The State Department was authorized to distribute copies of government documents to U.S. colleges or lyceums but not to public libraries or individuals. Baird proposed that the Smithsonian be the distributor and even suggested that copies might be given to individual scientists whose names could be kept on a special list for the purpose. "It is . . . a matter of complaint with men having special objects of research that public documents relating to their investigations are not assigned to them," he reported.[24]

Baird's timing was not good, however, for at this time the Joint Committee on the Library of Congress was still committed to Vattemare as its agent for foreign exchange and was apparently unwilling to make a change on the domestic side. Even after Congress rescinded the law that authorized Vattemare to serve as agent, arrangements for government document distribution and exchange continued, but only on an ad hoc basis.[25] Nevertheless, the Smithsonian continued to assist individual government bureaus with their exchange efforts, and by 1867 the exchange service had handled more than twenty thousand government publications for individual bureaus at a cost to the Smithson endowment of more than $8,000.[26]

Baird's suggestion of establishing exchanges to benefit the Library of Congress was in keeping with Secretary Henry's views. In 1851 Henry had made clear to Congress that the Smithsonian fund would never be large enough to support book purchases "sufficient to meet the needs of the American scholar." He suggested that the Library of Congress was a much more appropriate place for "a collection of books worthy of a Government whose perpetuity principally depends upon the intelligence of the people," an idea that had also begun to receive the support of the joint committee.[27] However, after the failure of the earlier Vattemare exchange scheme, neither the Librarian, John Silva Meehan, nor his successor, physician John G. Stephenson, seemed eager to initiate another. So uninterested were they that in 1857 Congress transferred to the Department of State the responsibility for international exchange of government documents and designated the Department of the Interior as the federal agency responsible for distribution.[28]

Such was not the case with Ainsworth Rand Spofford (1835–1908), who was appointed Librarian of Congress in 1864. Three years earlier, when Spofford first arrived as assistant librarian, he was dismayed at the condition of the Library and the deficiencies in its collections. In the 1861 annual report he wrote for his superior Spofford decried the lack of nearly all publications of the U.S. government in the collection, including, for example, the vastly important accounts of coastal, railroad, and geological surveys. Most important, Spofford exhorted the congressional members: "This Library, it is to be remembered, is the only one commonly visited by travellers and by the American people. It is in some sense the Library of the Government; and that no copies of the great national works published by order of the government are to be found in its Catalogue or upon its shelves may well surprise and disappoint visitors, from among our own citizens or from abroad."[29]

Spofford was prepared to use any legitimate means to begin his conversion of the small, sleepy legislative library into an institution of national stature. In addition to supporting Henry's ideas for helping the Library of Congress build a comprehensive national collection, Spofford also attempted to rekindle interest in the exchange of government publications. In 1864, six months before his promotion to Librarian, Spofford contacted Secretary of State William Seward, urging that systematic exchanges be established with various European governments. He concluded: "The Vattemare Agency . . . was long ago proved to be a failure and a successful exchange must . . . be made in some other way."[30]

The Smithsonian provided the "other way." Following a disastrous fire in the Smithsonian's "Castle" building in 1865, the next year Spofford and Secretary Henry arranged for the Smithsonian's library to be moved to the Library of Congress's fireproof quarters in the U.S. Capitol. Shortly afterward, Spofford approached Henry with another idea of mutual benefit. Since the Smithsonian's exchange system would continue to feed its growing collection of scientific transactions and proceedings, now housed in the Library of Congress as the Smithsonian Deposit, why not use the Smithsonian system for the exchange of official publications between governments, with the foreign documents also going to America's national library? Henry readily agreed.

Moving with surprising swiftness, Congress passed a supporting resolution on March 2, 1867.[31] The resolution ordered that the joint committee be given disposition of fifty copies of all House and Senate documents and all publications issued by any department or bureau of the government so that they could be exchanged through the Smithsonian agency for similar works published in foreign countries. Publications received in return were to be deposited in the Library of Congress.

Unfortunately, implementation was not as swift. Although Congress had made no appropriation to underwrite the program, two months after passage of the act Henry sent a circular via the Department of State to foreign ministers in the United States and to U.S. ministers stationed abroad. At a minimum he wanted to determine how many and which governments would be interested in such an enterprise. The circular detailed the kinds of publications foreign governments could expect from the United States: not only would the reports and proceedings of Congress and presidential messages be sent but also the annual reports and other publications of departments and bureaus. The topics covered would concern legislation, jurisprudence, foreign relations, commerce, statistics, arts, manufactures, agriculture, geography, and hydrography, just for a start. Henry warned potential recipients that they would "embrace a large number of volumes each year, the most of which are bound."[32]

Just as with donations to scientific societies, Henry wanted significant returns from foreign governments. He knew that in some countries, government publications were not actually printed by the government, and he wanted to make absolutely clear that he expected a comprehensive response. Returns should include all documents printed at public expense as well as those "published by booksellers with the aid of grants or subscriptions from governments."[33]

Once the substance of the exchange was laid out, Henry turned to the mechanics. He and Baird both knew that success would rely on each government clearly assigning the responsibility for carrying out the exchange to a single centralized agency, whether one bureau of government or a public library. Henry was willing to negotiate with individual offices, but he knew the considerable labor involved. As a carrot, Henry offered delivery of U.S. publications free of freight charges, and, since the Smithsonian already had an extensive network of agents, he could promise that there would be someone in each country to collect the publications for the United States and transmit them to the Smithsonian. Henry was also willing to send duplicate copies of U.S. documents directly to the appropriate government bureau abroad to reduce the labor on the receiving end.[34]

The response to the circular was favorable: eighteen countries quickly indicated an interest in the exchange. Norway, Victoria (Australia), and the Republic of Chile immediately proceeded to send boxes of their government documents to the United States.[35] To the frustration of both Spofford and Henry, however, the joint committee was unable to secure the fifty sets of U.S. publications to send abroad in order to inaugurate the expanded service.

"The Public Printer does not consider himself authorized to furnish [the fifty sets] without further legislation," Henry bemoaned in his annual report for 1867. Apparently, the distribution of the regular edition of government publications was already directed by the law, and the public printer thought the new legislation failed to make sufficiently clear that this regular edition should be increased in number.[36] Librarian Spofford was even more vexed at the delay, since he knew that the Library was particularly deficient in foreign documents.[37] Both Spofford and Henry urged the passage of supplementary legislation, and they worked together to find a resolution. In January 1868 Henry secured the promise of one of the Smithsonian's regents, J. V. L. Pruyn, who was also on the joint committee, to push for the needed resolution.[38] On June 8 Spofford took the matter up with the joint committee. Spofford and Henry were embarrassed that a few eager foreign governments had already sent shipments of documents to the United States. Henry lent his voice to Spofford's, detailing the many queries received from foreign governments and reminding the Librarian of the importance of prompt congressional action.[39]

Congress responded on July 25 by passing another resolution, this time specifically directing the public printer to print fifty copies "in addition to the regular number" of all congressional documents and one hundred copies "in excess of the usual number" of all other government publications whenever the joint committee directed the printer to do so. This time the resolution specifically said the documents should be delivered to the Librarian of Congress to be exchanged and that all government publications be included under this resolution whether they were printed by the Government Printing Office or elsewhere.[40]

But still nothing happened, even though Russia, Sweden, Spain, and the free city of Hamburg joined the earlier foreign governments in forwarding documents to the United States.[41] In reply to another query from Henry in February 1869, Spofford optimistically responded that although it was still too soon for action, he had been told that the first document to be supplied would be the *Agricultural Report* for 1867.[42] The Department of State was also receiving queries, and in the fall of 1869 Henry reassured Secretary of State Hamilton Fish to expect the exchange to start "during the present year."[43] By the close of 1869 eighteen governments had responded favorably to Henry's circular and appointed official exchange agents for the purpose.[44] Still Henry received no U.S. government publications to transmit abroad.

With the shipment numbers growing, Henry grew apprehensive about the rising cost of the exchange system. The Smithsonian had always subsidized much of the freight and extra charges in order to ensure that recipients received materials free or at low cost. But by 1870 he noted that the total system was costing about $5,000 per annum. Postage charges were one substantial component of the costs of domestic distribution: packages too small to be handled by shippers were mailed through the post office. In early days Henry had persuaded members of Congress to use their franking privileges for some of the domestic transmissions, but the Smithsonian had not had postal concessions in its own name since 1870.[45] In 1872 the postal code was amended to give free postage to any package marked "Smithsonian Exchange," but this privilege was soon rescinded.[46] The Smithsonian did not receive full franking privileges until 1879.[47]

Nevertheless, the prospect of adding official government publications in quantity to the system, no matter how important, was certainly a matter of fiscal concern. Yet it also represented an opportunity. If Congress could be persuaded to subsidize the system to support the exchange of government documents, the whole system would benefit.

Progress continued at a snail's pace, and Henry became annoyed with the continual queries received from foreign governments through the Department of State. The Smithsonian was filling a crowded basement with copies of government publications from various agencies, but, absent an official order from Spofford, Baird could only make ad hoc shipments.[48] In March 1872 Henry again raised the matter of the government document exchange with Spofford, who promised he would "attend to the international exchange as soon as the list of the works to be sent is finished."[49] Without official notice from the Library of Congress to begin, Henry was unable to make a case for a congressional subsidy, and the costs of the ad hoc shipments were beginning to mount. He noted in his desk diary that he could not get Congress to reimburse the Library for $700 expended for government exchanges because "Mr. Howe the chairman . . . [of the Joint Committee on the Library of Congress] thought the [recipients] ought to pay the cost of exchange at least one way. I informed him that in no other country was there a system of exchange."[50] In his 1874 annual report Henry stated that the exchange service was now costing one-seventh of the institution's annual income.[51]

Finally the logjam was broken: in October 1874 Librarian Spofford ordered that documents be shipped to Canada, Japan, and Germany.[52] A year later, in order to clear out the Smithsonian's basement, Henry ordered boxes of documents stored there to be sent to the Smithsonian's agents abroad to await further instructions. He then issued a second circular, repeating all of the guidelines and requests of the first circular of seven years earlier. "We have concluded to act in regard to them [public documents] ourselves," he noted; soon shipments of documents were sent to Turkey, France, Portugal, Sweden, Brazil, Argentina, Belgium, Chile, and Mexico.[53] But Spofford requested a halt until the joint committee could issue further instructions.[54]

After receiving instructions to proceed, in March 1876 Henry accelerated the schedule for exchange shipments to Europe so that England and France received monthly shipments and Germany, Russia, and Italy bimonthly or quarterly shipments as needed, depending on the quantity of material to be sent. Henry then moved to intertwine inextricably the exchange of government documents with the traditional scientific material flowing through the system. On April 13 he received Spofford's blessing to exchange the documents with universities and societies as well as with governments.[55] This step gave the Smithsonian more flexibility in disposing of the quantities of documents received for exchange purposes, regardless of the source or number.

The First International Convention

For over a quarter of a century the Smithsonian Institution had provided a model to the world of how a centralized exchange operation could employ economies of scale in the service of international scientific communication. Henry's two circulars to the international diplomatic community in 1867 and 1874 announced that the institution was officially adding government publications to its operations and suggested that other nations adopt the same pattern of centralized operations. Belgium and the Netherlands were the first to follow the Smithsonian's suggestion when they established central exchange bureaus in the early 1870s.[56]

The growth of exchange operations and the pressure for governments to take responsibility for them made clear the need to establish a formal diplomatic structure in the form of an official international convention. In 1875 at the Paris meeting of the International Congress of Geographical Sciences representatives of seventeen countries, including the United States, passed a resolution to call on their governments "to organize in each country a central bureau whose duty it shall be to collect such cartographic, geographic, and other publications as may be issued at the expense of the state, and to distribute the same among the various nations which adopt the present programme."[57]

The drive toward an international convention moved slowly, and Henry was not to see the result. On May 13, 1878, Joseph Henry died, and less than a week later the board of regents unanimously elected Spencer Fullerton Baird as the second secretary of the Smithsonian Institution. Baird assured a colleague that he intended to carry on Henry's policies and traditions, including the international exchange activity.

In April 1883 the International Conference on Exchanges convened in Brussels for the purpose of finalizing a treaty that had been first proposed at the 1875 Geographical Sciences meeting.[58] Such a convention would regulate the process by determining which countries and organizations could participate in the exchange system, what publications could be exchanged, who would pay the costs, and how the exchange would be conducted. Two separate documents addressed different aspects of the exchange service.

Ratification of the 1883 convention was delayed until a diplomatic conference for the signing of the conventions was called in 1886. The Smithsonian was not notified in time to comment further on the conventions, but Baird signified his willingness to follow the stipulations, and Lambert Tree, U.S. minister to Belgium, signed for the United States.[59] Not until June 18, 1888, did the Senate recommend ratification. President Grover Cleveland signed the document on July 19, and the treaty was finally proclaimed on January 15, 1889.[60] Spencer Fullerton Baird, architect of the international system of exchanges, died almost a year before the ratification was finally completed.

Fourteen years passed between the initial proposal in 1875 and the final proclamation of the international convention that would establish an official, government-supported, worldwide system of international publication exchange. Although many countries participated in the exchange discussions, some of them (including major powers like France, Germany, and Great Britain) did not sign the convention once the actual obligations were clearly understood. A total of twenty-one countries had signed the treaty by the end of World War II.[61]

As disappointing as this outcome may have been, the convention did establish a sense of order and uniformity in exchange efforts. It stimulated the establishment of centralized bureaus of exchange, even in countries that did not sign the treaty. It also laid the basis worldwide for publication exchange, which carried on well into the twentieth century.

The legislated addition of government documents to the Smithsonian's exchange system in 1867 was a key facet of the development of international publication exchange, for the combined initiative of key individuals at the Smithsonian and the Library of Congress helped raise the matter of exchange to a national level in many countries and stimulated the establishment of national coordinating bodies. Most important, the Smithsonian system became the model for an evolving worldwide system of publication exchange—and therefore a foundation for scholarly communication that greatly enhanced the prestige of both American science and government. When the first international treaty concerning publication exchange was finally proclaimed in 1889, the Smithsonian was confirmed as America's official international exchange agent, a role that it had already played for nearly forty years.

Somewhat ironically, the system of international exchanges that had evolved by 1889 in many ways represented the ideals expressed by Alexandre Vattemare when he was at the height of his influence forty years earlier. Vattemare envisioned a central agency in Paris that would operate through similar agencies in the United States and other countries. He solicited government support and expected that the agencies would receive it. Although the successful model of a central agency came to be located in Washington, D.C., rather than in Paris, it was nevertheless at the hub of a communication network that included other government-supported agencies. Vattemare hoped such a system would reduce isolation and promote greater understanding among the countries of the world; certainly, it helped the United States enhance both official and unofficial contacts between Americans and citizens of other nations. If Vattemare's spirit was present in the room that housed the official signing of the convention, he must indeed have been gratified to see how his obsession had come to fruition.

Notes

1. Nancy E. Gwinn, "The Origins and Development of International Publications Exchange in Nineteenth Century America," Ph.D. diss., George Washington University, 1996, 48. See also James E. McClellan III, *Science Reorganized: Scientific Societies in the Eighteenth Century* (New York: Columbia University Press, 1985).

2. William Dawson Johnston, *History of the Library of Congress, vol. 1, 1800–1864* (Washington, D.C.: Government Printing Office, 1904), 253–54.

3. The most recent account of Alexandre Vattemare's life is in *The Extravagant Ambassador: The True Story of Alexandre Vattemare, the French Ventriloquist Who Changed the World*, ed. Earle Havens and Pierre-Alain Tilliette (Boston: Boston Public Library; Paris: Paris bibliothèques, 2007).

4. Ibid., 74, 80.

5. Alexandre Vattemare, "Rapport de M. Alex. Vattemare à M. le Ministre de l'instruction publique et des cultes," extrait du *Moniteur Universel*, November 1, 1851, 5–9, Alexandre Vattemare Papers, Rare Books and Manuscripts Division, New York Public Library, Astor, Lenox and Tilden Foundations, New York (hereafter cited as Vattemare Papers, NYPL).

6. Alexandra Oleson and Sanborn C. Brown, eds., *The Pursuit of Knowledge in the Early American Republic: American Scientific and Learned Societies from Colonial Times to the Civil War* (Baltimore, Md.: Johns Hopkins University Press, 1976), xvi.

7. George Brown Goode, *The Origins of Natural Science in America*, ed. Sally Gregory Kohlstedt (Washington, D.C.: Smithsonian Institution Press, 1991), 367–68 n. 7.

8. Oleson and Brown, *Pursuit of Knowledge*, xvii–xix.

9. Johnston, *History of the Library of Congress*, 256–57.

10. Ibid., 260–61; James Alfred Pearce to Michael Nourse, July 28, 1848, Librarian's Letterbooks, Manuscript Division, Library of Congress (hereafter cited as LC).

11. Pearce to Vattemare, July 11, 1848, Vattemare Papers, NYPL.

12. Johnston, *History of the Library of Congress*, 261–62.

13. Vattemare, "Rapport," 2–3.

14. Benton to Vattemare, September 27, 1848, Vattemare Papers, NYPL.

15. *M. Guizot on the System of International Exchanges and on the Actual State of Letters in the United States* (Paris: Paul Dupont, 1855), 13–19.

16. Charlotte Fletcher, "The Reverend Thomas Bray, M. Alexandre Vattemare, and Library Science," *Library Quarterly* 27 (April 1957): 98; Elisabeth Revai, *Alexandre Vattemare, Trait d'union entre deux mondes* (Montreal: Bellarmin, 1975), 126.

17. Cecil R. Roseberry, *A History of the New York State Library* (Albany: State Education Department, University of the State of New York, New York State Library, 1970), 23.

18. "'Free to All': Alexandre Vattemare, the Boston Public Library and the Beginnings of the Public Library Movement in America," in Havens and Tilliette, *Extravagant Ambassador*, 239–67.

19. John Silva Meehan to Pearce, November 26, 1849, Librarian's Letterbooks, LC; Meehan to Vattemare, June 16, 1853, Vattemare Papers, NYPL.

20. As Henry's first assistant, Jewett laid the groundwork for the exchange system, but Henry fired Jewett in 1854.

21. Henry Rowe Schoolcraft, *Historical and Statistical Information Regarding the History, Condition, and Prospects of the Indian Tribes of the United States* (Philadelphia: Lippincott, Grambo, 1851–57).

22. Howard Stansbury, *Exploration and Survey of the Valley of the Great Salt Lake of Utah; Including a Reconnaissance of a New Route through the Rocky Mountains*, 31st Cong., special sess. no. 3, S. Doc. (Philadelphia: Lippincott, Grambo, 1852).

23. Smithsonian Institution, *Annual Report*, 1852, 47, 50–51. (Annual reports of the Smithsonian board of regents to the Congress hereafter cited as SI, *Annual Report* plus the year date.)

24. SI, *Annual Report*, 1852, 52; George H. Boehmer, "History of the Smithsonian Exchanges," in SI, *Annual Report*, 1881, 745–46.

25. For example, in 1856 the secretary of state was authorized to purchase one hundred copies each of Audubon's *Birds of America* and *Quadrupeds of North America* to exchange with foreign governments (Boehmer, "History," 746).

26. William Crawford Winlock, "The International Exchange System," in George Brown Goode, *The Smithsonian Institution, 1846–1896: The History of Its First Half Century* (Washington, D.C., 1897), 406.

27. SI, *Annual Report*, 1851, 22; John Y. Cole, *For Congress and the Nation: A Chronological History of the Library of Congress* (Washington, D.C.: Library of Congress, 1979), 23.

28. Joint Resolution 5, January 28, 1857, *U.S. Statutes at Large* 11 (1855–59): 253.

29. John Young Cole, Jr., "Ainsworth Spofford and the 'National Library,'" Ph.D. diss., George Washington University, 1971, 74.

30. Spofford to Seward, June 13, 1864, Librarian's Letterbooks, No. 6, LC.

31. *A Resolution to Provide for the Exchange of Certain Public Documents, U.S. Statutes at Large* 14 (1867): 573.

32. "Circular Relative to Exchanges of Government Documents," May 16, 1867, in Boehmer, "History," 746–48.

33. Ibid., 747.

34. Ibid., 747–48.

35. Ibid., 748–49; Chr. Holst, Sec. Norwegian University to Henry, February 22, 1868, Incoming Correspondence, Office of the Secretary, 1863–79, Record Unit 26, Smithsonian Institution Archives (hereafter cited as RU [number], SIA); Spofford to Henry, June 18, 1868, Librarian's Letterbooks, No. 7, LC.

36. SI, *Annual Report*, 1867, 40.

37. Library of Congress, *Annual Report*, 1867, 5.

38. William J. Rhees, ed., *The Smithsonian Institution; Journals of the Board of Regents . . .*, Smithsonian *Miscellaneous Collections* 18, no. 329 (1880): 317.

39. Cole, "Ainsworth Spofford," 116.

40. SI, *Annual Report*, 1875, 31–32.

41. Library of Congress, *Annual Report*, 1868, 6.

42. Henry to Ainsworth Spofford, February 17, 1869, Ainsworth Spofford Papers, Library of Congress, Washington, D.C.; Spofford to Henry, February 19, 1869, Librarian's Letterbooks, No. 7, LC.

43. Henry to Hamilton Fish, Secretary of State, November 4, 1869, Record Group 59, General Records of the Department of State, Miscellaneous Records Received, Domestic Letters Sent, National Archives and Records Administration (hereafter cited as RG 59, NARA).

44. The countries were Argentine Republic, Baden, Belgium, Chile, Colombia, Costa Rica, Denmark, Finland, France, Great Britain and Ireland, Hamburg, the Netherlands, Norway, Spain, Sweden, Switzerland, Victoria (Australia), and Württemberg (Boehmer, "History," 748).

45. Publishers were able to send volumes to the Smithsonian free of postage from 1855 until the copyright deposit requirement was repealed in 1859. See William J. Rhees, ed., *The Smithsonian Institution: Documents Relative to Its Origin and History, 1835–1899*, 2 vols. (Washington, D.C.: Government Printing Office, 1901), 1:500–501, 608.

46. Rhees, *Journals*, 389.

47. Rhees, *Documents*, 1:818–19.

48. Joseph Henry, Desk Diary, July 15, 1871, Henry Collection, RU 7001, Box 15, SIA; Henry to Hamilton Fish, Secretary of State, July 17, 1870, RG 59, NARA.

49. Henry, Desk Diary, March 7, 1872.

50. Henry, Desk Diary, January 2, 1874.

51. SI, *Annual Report*, 1874, 23.

52. Two boxes of documents were shipped to Norway on June 18, 1873, and were counted as part of the official transmissions, but the circumstances for this shipment are unclear (Robert D. Stevens, *The Role of the Library of Congress in the International Exchange of Publications: A Brief History* [Washington, D.C.: Library of Congress, 1953], 12; Boehmer, "History," 774).

53. Henry, Desk Diary, October 30 and November 18, 1875; SI, *Annual Report*, 1875, 33.

54. Spofford may have been concerned that the return shipments would put even more pressure on the available shelf space in the Capitol; because of the influx of copyright deposits, by 1875 Spofford had reported that he had completely run out of shelf space (Cole, *For Congress and the Nation*, 34–36).

55. Henry, Desk Diary, April 13, 1876.

56. Leendert Brummel, *The Netherlands and the International Exchange of Publications* (The Hague: Royal Library, 1957), 16–21.

57. Other delegates represented Austria-Hungary, Belgium, Chile, Dominican Republic, France, Germany, Italy, Hungary, Norway, Portugal, Romania, Russia, Spain, Sweden, the Swiss Confederation, and Turkey (Boehmer, "History," 776).

58. Copies of the proposed and final conventions and correspondence relating to the conference are printed in SI, *Annual Report*, 1883, 120–49.

59. SI, *Annual Report*, 1886, 105.

60. A copy of the official convention is contained in Rhees, *Documents*, 2:1139–44.

61. Brummel, *The Netherlands*, 25–26.

International Trends in Library History

Donald G. Davis, Jr.

In 1998 Mary Niles Maack, faculty member at UCLA and longtime colleague in the Library History Round Table (LHRT) of the American Library Association, presented a paper entitled "International Dimensions of Library History: Leadership and Scholarship, 1978–1998." Her brief survey reviewed the progress and significance of three types of conference initiatives: awards and programs within the American Library Association, the Library History Seminars held every five years, and the number of international conferences—all of which had grown in their inclusion of international topics and speakers.

Maack closed by suggesting two ongoing complementary trends— the expansion of interest in international topics by American scholars and the broadening scope for library historians, one that embraces the history of books, publishing, reading, and scholarship. In addition to covering the activities of the LHRT, Maack also noted the founding of the Society for the History of Authorship, Reading, and Publishing (SHARP) in 1991 as evidence for these trends. She closed her survey by reminding her readers of the impact of electronic communication technology on libraries as they have been known historically. This, she says, has

> significant implications for the library, which, as a social agency, has for almost all its history been associated with a place, a building, and a collection of physical materials. As we enter the twenty-first century, we are already experiencing the issue of dealing with digital records that can be simultaneously accessed from many locations, and we are being forced to ask some deep questions about what libraries have been in the past, what they have done for us, and what profound effects they have had on scholarship and on society.[1]

More than a decade later, what are the identifiable trends in the international world of library history? The three types of program events that Maack pointed out have continued with ripples, if not tidal waves, across our subdiscipline, although they seem to have declined in attendance. The two complementary developments—more interest in international topics and the coupling of library history with book history and reading history—also continue, though they have taken a slightly different direction than she might have envisioned. Moreover, there are new trends that warrant notice that are a consequence of earlier developments. Without striving to be comprehensive, this article seeks to outline with a broad brush the evolution and current status of international library history as we move into the new century's second decade. It is not intended to be a bibliographical review.

In preparation for this review I queried several international colleagues.[2] Together we identified four trends that have resulted from the efforts put forward in the twentieth century. With regard to library history, they are 1) a broader base of scholarship that incorporates new approaches, 2) a wider scope of related research and publishing that reaches special groups of readers, 3) a greater appreciation of the role of libraries that considers varying audiences, and 4) more pragmatic considerations that make for new challenges.

A Broader Base of Scholarship That Incorporates New Approaches

Library history writing in the United States has exhibited an international emphasis to a greater degree than in the past, possibly because international graduate students have been attracted to researching the history of libraries in their homelands.[3] Another part of this picture is the number of substantial national histories of libraries that have appeared, are in progress, or are projected.[4] These endeavors, supported by a number of scholars within and outside the profession, have codified the library history of a nation or region in an encyclopedic form. Finally, there is evidence that more and more trained library historians are utilizing primary source materials more extensively in their research, resulting in more analytical approaches and treatments, in contrast to progressive and celebratory treatments.[5]

A Wider Scope of Research and Publishing That Reaches Special Groups of Readers

The production of library history has always appealed to a certain literary elite and to antiquarians in the library profession. The result has been a relatively narrow scope of types of history: biographical and institutional as well as histories that focus on special events. In the past decade the social history of books and book collections (libraries) has attracted the interest of scholars in the humane social sciences; several studies have dealt with nations outside the United States.[6] The continuing enthusiasm for book history on an international scale also has fueled interdisciplinary research that draws bibliophiles together with those concerned with the sociology of readers and users. Indeed, the whole process of creating, publishing, distributing, and consuming printed material has been the subject of much study.[7] Another evidence of this widening scope of library history is its inclusion under a broader umbrella of information history, surely an international theme. The argument for doing so is that if "information," however defined, is more encompassing and less concrete than libraries per se, then it should have "primacy of continuous theme," with libraries subsumed.[8]

This wider scope is evident too in the broader range of topics pursued by library history units in national library associations and the International Federation of Library Associations and Institutions (IFLA).[9] These groups have suffered, however, from the absence of a pool from which to draw leaders. This is part of the library history units' constant struggle to achieve a critical mass within their professional organizations. But they still represent the most broadly based, continuing groups within the library history community. Meanwhile, cooperation among those passionate about broad book history has encouraged the rise and growth of the Society for the History of Authorship, Reading and Publishing. This body has been operating for nearly two decades and has now gained strength through its annual conferences (held outside North America in alternate years), its newsletter, and its annual volume, *Book History*, published since 1998 by Pennsylvania State University Press. It has been a rallying point for those interested in the environment of libraries and their history from around the world. Library historians have found a hospitable home here.

A Greater Appreciation of the Role of Libraries That Considers Varying Audiences

As the culture that supports libraries and their patrons—books and their readers and information and its users—has embraced the electronic and digital revolution, a new appreciation has arisen of just what libraries meant, and can mean, to changing societies. The role of popular information for the masses has invited research as scholars have begun to realize that mass consumption of ideas did not begin with television or the Internet. A new interest in and respect for the impact on individuals and communities of social libraries, public libraries, and school libraries is apparent.[10] The irony is that this is occurring just as many libraries that serve the general populace are turning more and more to the World Wide Web to secure both ready reference information sources and more lengthy texts—many of which can be accessed beyond the library's walls. The result of these developments has been a return to praising the role of libraries, going beyond their conventional benefits to the symbols they have become. The library as building, place, physical collections, and knowledgeable people has continued to attract historical interest.[11] Some say this frequently happens when an institution is undergoing a serious transformation in which its inherited position is being severely challenged. But is this nostalgia directed to a dying institution to give it a decent burial, or does the renewed interest remind folk of the foundations of a type of human activity that can be experienced only in some kind of library? What, then, is the significance of the changing role of libraries?

More Pragmatic Considerations That Make for New Challenges

All of the considerations mentioned above exist in an environment that seems hostile to continued library development. Currently, whole subject fields depend on information sources that come via the home computer, perhaps linked into a library's site somewhere. We library historians often do not realize the extent of this, because for all the right reasons we are enamored with archival and often obscure or unique items. But special libraries as well as academic, school, and public libraries all are faced with having to justify print materials and to provide electronic sources. Yes, we can cite statistics that show library usage in innovative ways. But many professionals and students remember the library as a place alone and not simply as a source of material. Funding authorities and the general tax-paying public cannot ignore the dwindling numbers of serious patrons, as opposed to those seeking light entertainment and casual Internet users. Here the ALA has been aggressively innovative in promoting libraries to the public, while at one time their value might have been self-evident. Surely libraries are foundational institutions like banks, courts, and churches. When all these are changing, too, where does the library stand in a culture's priorities?[12] If cultures can move so swiftly to the cell phone age without developing serious literacy, what does that tell us about the presumed value of collected materials called libraries?

In summary, the achievements of library historians of national stature in Europe and North America and in those nations under their cultural influence have been magnificent. The encyclopedic, multivolume works no doubt codify important knowledge. But will they be foundations and encouragement for further work, or will they simply crown the achievements of a generation or two of serious library historians and discourage others from moving beyond them? Squeezed out of the mainstream of their profession and often seen as preoccupied antiquarians, the number of participants in national and international groups for library historians does not seem to have increased appreciably. Thankfully, cultural historians beyond the library profession have taken an interest in the treasures of research materials that we utilize. Does the prodigious output of the past two decades bring an era to an end—or initiate a new renaissance in the history of libraries, internationally or nationally?

One polar star for the promotion of the value of books and libraries, past and present, has been the Center for the Book at the Library of Congress, established under Librarian Daniel Boorstin in 1977. He had the great wisdom to appoint American cultural historian John Y. Cole as its executive director, a position he has occupied ever since. Through its publications, programs, and initiatives the Center has been truly international in scope without slighting the nation that supports it. Its network of state centers for the book and its allied centers for the book in many nations of the world have served to recognize authors, to stimulate publication, to promote reading, and to raise the consciousness of those who would recognize the value of libraries within the human community. The Center has been host to numerous national and international conferences dealing with the history of books and libraries. Book festivals, both state and federal, are logical extensions of these activities. John Cole has been the key player in all this.[13]

The library history world may seem to be fading in some quarters, but bright spots remain in the Center for the Book, the Library History Seminars, the health of our internationally read journals—and that small cadre of committed scholars and supporters in many countries of the world. Let's hope that this will suffice.

Notes

1. Mary Niles Maack, "International Dimensions of Library History: Leadership and Scholarship, 1978–1998," in *Library History Research in America: Essays Commemorating the Fiftieth Anniversary of the Library History Round Table, American Library Association,* ed. Andrew B. Wertheimer and Donald G. Davis, Jr., 66–76 (Washington, D.C.: Library of Congress, Center for the Book, 2000). This article assumes that international interests are represented by any research and

publication that deal comprehensively with national topics or comparatively with those beyond national confines.

2. These included Alistair Black, Peter Hoare, and Wayne A. Wiegand.

3. Library History Seminar XI convened at Allerton Park, Illinois, October 27–30, 2005. Of the twenty-five contributed papers included in the published proceedings, sixteen concerned topics beyond North American library history. See "Libraries in Times of War, Revolution, and Social Change," ed. W. Boyd Rayward and Christine Jenkins, special issue, *Library Trends* 55, no. 3 (2007).

4. The four-volume series, André Vernet and Claude Jolly, eds., *Histoire des bibliothèques françaises* (Paris: Promidis–Éditions du Cercle du librairie, 1988–92), was an early leader in this recent phenomenon. Library historians in several other countries in the Atlantic community and those influenced by it have considered similar projects. Two that have materialized include Peter Hoare, ed., *The Cambridge History of Libraries in Britain and Ireland*, 3 vols. (New York: Cambridge University Press, 2006) and Patricia Lockhart Fleming et al., eds., *History of the Book in Canada/Histoire du livre et de l'imprimé au Canada*, 3 vols. (Toronto: University of Toronto Press, 2004, 2005, 2007). A major reference work that deals with worldwide libraries is David H. Stam, ed., *International Dictionary of Library Histories*, 2 vols. (Chicago: Fitzroy Dearborn Publishers, 2001). Another international contribution is the projected five-volume history of libraries in Western civilization by Konstantinos Sp. Staikos. (Three volumes have been published by Oak Knoll Press as of the summer of 2009.) The foremost library historian in China is Cheng Huanwen of Sun Yat-Sen University in Guangzhou, who has written numerous books, some of which have touched on international themes. Adding to the several brief surveys in print, the IFLA Library History Section has projected a one-volume history of libraries with chapters by scholars from a number of continents.

5. This is the observation of several contributors of the biennial review essays of American library history research that have appeared in *Libraries & Culture* and *Libraries & the Cultural Record* beginning in the mid-1960s. As *Libraries & Culture* editor from 1976 to 2005, my impression is that this is true for articles dealing with American topics but perhaps less so for themes explored in other countries, where, in general, secondary materials are used more or less exclusively.

6. Examples include Lauren Amtower, *Engaging Words: The Culture of Reading in the Later Middle Ages* (New York: Palgrave, 2000); Steven Kale, *French Salons: High Society and Political Sociability from the Old Regime to the Revolution of 1848* (Baltimore, Md.: Johns Hopkins University Press, 2004); and Martyn Lyons, *Readers and Society in Nineteenth-Century France: Workers, Women, Peasants* (New York: Palgrave, 2001).

7. Examples include Jennifer Anderson and Elizabeth Sauer, eds., *Books and Readers in Early Modern England* (Philadelphia: University of Pennsylvania Press, 2002) and Christine Pawley, *Reading on the Middle Border: The Culture of Print in Late-Nineteenth-Century Osage, Iowa* (Amherst: University of Massachusetts Press, 2001).

8. Examples include Alistair Black, David Muddiman, and Helen Plant, *The Early Information Society: Information Management in Britain before the Computer* (Burlington, Vt.: Ashgate, 2007) and Lawrence J. McCrank, *Historical Information Science: An Emerging Unidiscipline* (Medford, N.J.: Information Today, 2001).

9. While it is true that national associations focus on the library history of their own cultures, increasing attention is being paid to libraries in other countries and international themes. This is nearly always the case at meetings of the Library History Section of IFLA, though even here the host country usually has one or two of the usual three annual papers. Two notable recent exceptions were the 2001 conference in Boston and the 2002 conference in Glasgow, both of which concentrated on national themes. The first resulted in Donald G. Davis, Jr., ed., *Winsor, Dewey, and Putnam: The Boston Experience*, Occasional Papers, No. 212 (Champaign: Graduate School of Library and Information Science, University of Illinois at Urbana-Champaign, 2002), featuring papers by Kenneth E. Carpenter, Wayne A. Wiegand, and Jane Aikin, all notable American library historians.

10. Though institutional histories appear, particularly at anniversaries or commemorative occasions, there seems to be a renewed focus on the "social" library that serves the general population and thus provides popular materials for the nonelites in society. Wayne Wiegand is fond of a phrase of Doug Zwiezig that there should be less focus on the "user in the life of the library" and more on the "library in the life of the user." This ties libraries to their publics and popular culture.

11. In the resurgent interest in the library as place, scholars and popular writers are intrigued again by library architecture and the contributions of libraries that are not specifically tied to bookish activities. National, university, and major public libraries have attracted the most attention. The interest in Carnegie library buildings worldwide since the Carnegie centennial is one example of this.

12. The research, historical and current, is there, but with electronic innovation seeming to trump everything in the historic domain of libraries, the contest can be discouraging. One library historian says, "If only we could get the hyperventilating ahistorical evangelists of information technology to read the stuff we're writing for some historical ballast, perhaps our profession would not be obsessing so much on technique." In the end, although good feelings are important, the number of political allies and the amount of financial support have become a kind of report card on how well libraries are getting their message across.

13. The Web site of the Center for the Book at the Library of Congress provides a good overview of the Center's activities (http://www.read.gov/cfb) and John Cole's work as the Center's director (http://www.read.gov/cfb/staff.html).

Contributors

Jane Aikin received a master's degree in library science from Indiana University, Bloomington; a master's degree in history from Kent State University, Ohio; and a doctorate in U.S. history from the University of Michigan, Ann Arbor. She was a faculty member at Indiana University and at Kent State University and later served as a program staff member at the Council on Library Resources, Inc., and the Association of Research Libraries. Since 1986 she has been associated with the National Endowment for the Humanities, where in 2010 she became Director of the Division of Research Programs. Aikin's research interests are the history of cultural institutions, professions, public policy, and scholarly communication. She is the author of numerous publications on the Library of Congress and coeditor with John Cole of *For Congress, the Nation, and the World: The Encyclopedia of the Library of Congress* (2005).

Donald G. Davis, Jr., is professor emeritus of library history at the University of Texas at Austin, where he served in the School of Information and the Department of History for thirty-five years. He holds degrees from UCLA, UC Berkeley, the University of Illinois at Urbana-Champaign, and Austin Seminary. Davis has authored and coedited numerous conference proceedings and reference works, among them *American Library History: A Bibliography* (1989), *Encyclopedia of Library History* (1994), and *Dictionary of American Library Biography, 2nd Supplement* (2003). In addition to his passion for writing book reviews and bibliographical essays, he has served in the library history units of the American Library Association and the International Federation of Library Associations and Institutions.

Nancy E. Gwinn, director, Smithsonian Institution Libraries, has previously held positions with the Library of Congress, the Council on Library Resources, and the Research Libraries Group. She holds an A.M.L.S. degree from the University of Michigan and a Ph.D. from George Washington University. Her research interests include nineteenth-century American cultural history and the history of the Smithsonian Institution as well as current issues involving collaborations among libraries, archives, and museums in the digital era.

Guy Lamolinara is the communications officer for the Center for the Book in the Library of Congress. He has previously worked in the Library's Office of Strategic Initiatives and Public Affairs Office. Prior to coming to the Library in 1990 he worked for a variety of publications, including *Congressional Quarterly Weekly Report* and the *Kansas City Times*. He holds an M.A. in journalism from Ohio State University.

Eric N. Lindquist is a history librarian at the University of Maryland. In addition to having an M.L.S. degree, he holds a Ph.D. in British history. His research interests include the history of the book in early modern Britain and Parliament in the early seventeenth century. He is finishing a study of an early-seventeenth-century Member of Parliament that includes an edition of a parliamentary diary.

Mary Niles Maack is professor emerita at the University of California at Los Angeles where she served for 25 years in the Department of Information Studies. She is the associate editor of the *Encyclopedia of Library and Information Sciences*, 3rd. ed (2010). Maack has authored numerous historical and comparative studies that have appeared in major refereed journals in the field. Her publications also include two books as well as book chapters and contributions to several reference books. She has won both the Justin Winsor Award of the ALA Library History Round Table and the Jesse Shera Award of the ALA Library Research Round Table. Maack has taught courses on book history, library history, reference and information services, information institutions, public libraries, and comparative and international librarianship. In 2005 she received the Distinguished Teaching Award from the UCLA Department of Information Studies. She is a member of the editorial advisory board of *Libraries & the Cultural Record*.

Josephus Nelson is senior writer-editor in the Office of the Associate Librarian for Library Services, Library of Congress. He holds a master's degree in library science from the University of Michigan and a master's degree in history from the University of Oxford. His research interests include archives, reference service, and oral history.

Carl Ostrowski is professor of English at Middle Tennessee State University. His study of the early history of the Library of Congress, *Books, Maps, and Politics: A Cultural History of the Library of Congress, 1783–1861*, won the 2007 Eliza Atkins Gleason Book Award from the Library History Round Table of the American Library Association. He has published articles on American literature in *Studies in American Fiction, African American Review*, and *ESQ: A Journal of the American Renaissance*.

Jean Preer is a professor in the Indiana University School of Library and Information Science–Indianapolis. She has also taught at the library school of the Catholic University of America in Washington, D.C., where she served as associate dean. In 2006 she received the Association for Library and Information Science Education (ALISE) Award for Teaching Excellence. In 2007 her essay "Promoting Citizenship: Librarians Help Get out the Vote in the 1952 Presidential Election" was awarded the Justin Winsor Prize by the Library History Round Table of the American Library Association. She is the author of *Library Ethics* (2008), the 2009 winner of the Greenwood Publishing Group Award for Best Book in Library Literature. She holds an M.L.S. degree from the University of California–Berkeley and a J.D. and a Ph.D. in American civilization from George Washington University.

Eleanor F. Shevlin is an associate professor of English at West Chester University of Pennsylvania, where she teaches courses in eighteenth-century British literature and culture, book history, and postcolonial studies. Currently at work on the study of a late-eighteenth-century British publishing firm, she is the editor of the forthcoming *History of the Book in the West, Vol. 3, 1700–1800* (Ashgate).

Michael Winship is the Iris Howard Regents Professor of English II at the University of Texas at Austin. He has written widely on the history of publishing in the nineteenth-century United States and teaches regularly at the Rare Book School at the University of Virginia. He completed and edited the final three volumes of *Bibliography of American Literature* (1983–91) and was editor and contributor to *The Industrial Book, 1840–1880* (2007), the third volume of the series A History of the Book in America.

Chronology and Bibliography of John Y. Cole

The chronology below provides an overview of John Y. Cole's career and includes institutional, local, state, and national awards he has won for his leadership at the Library of Congress and for his book promotion activities carried out as director of the Center for the Book. Because Cole has published so extensively on the Library of Congress, the selected bibliography that follows will prove a valuable guide to scholars and students who can find information on every aspect of the Library, from scholarly studies of its history and beautifully illustrated publications on the art and architecture of the 1897 Jefferson Building to articles describing contemporary developments, such as activities of the Center for the Book and large-scale digitization projects instigated by Librarian of Congress James H. Billington.

Not included in the bibliography are sound recordings of early (1978-1990) Center for the Book programs and Library of Congress webcasts of more than 250 Center programs (1998-present) introduced or moderated by Cole. Also not included are more than 40 programs broadcast by C-SPAN (1996-present) at which Cole was the introducer, moderator, or a principal speaker. The sound recordings are in the collections of the Library of Congress; the webcasts are available at www. read.gov/webcasts, and the C-SPAN broadcasts at www.c-spanvideo. org/johnycole. In addition, as part of a 2008 Center for the Book pilot project, Cole presented anecdotes about the history of the Library of Congress and spoke about his personal love of books and reading in more than a dozen short videos; see www.redroom.com.

Finally, two of John Cole's books and a selection of his presentations about the history of the Library of Congress are available at www.loc.gov/ about/history.html. The books are *Jefferson's Legacy: A Brief History of the Library of Congress* (1993), and *On These Walls: Inscriptions and Quotations in the Buildings of the Library of Congress* (1995).

In addition to dozens of scholarly books and book chapters and articles in publications such as *Libraries & Culture* and the *Quarterly Journal of the Library of Congress,* Cole has edited numerous books and has contributed forewords, prefaces, and afterwords to many books dealing with the Library and with book and library history. He has written more than one hundred articles for the *Library of Congress Information*

Bulletin, and it is through these articles that one can trace the ongoing development of the Center for the Book and contemporary activities of the Library. Cole's numerous historical articles for the *Bulletin* include a series of brief studies published in honor of the Library's bicentennial, celebrated in 2000.

John Cole's bibliography, containing more than four hundred publications, is organized into six thematic sections, with a chronological sub-arrangement within each section: "The Library of Congress: History and Development" (page 170), *"Encyclopedia of the Library of Congress"* (page 176), "Librarians of Congress and Other Library Staff" (page 177), "The Center for the Book: History and Development" (page 180), "The Center for the Book Viewpoint Series" (page 189), and "Other Publications and Contributions" (page 190).

John Y. Cole Chronology

Education

University of Washington, Seattle, B.A., history, 1962
University of Washington, Seattle, School of Librarianship, M.Libr., 1963
Johns Hopkins University, Baltimore, Md., M.L.A., 1966
George Washington University, Washington, D.C., Ph.D., American civilization, 1971 (dissertation: "Ainsworth Rand Spofford and the 'National Library'")

Professional Experience

Chief, Library Branch, U.S. Army Intelligence School, Fort Holabird, Md., 1964–1966
Library of Congress, Washington, D.C.
    Librarian, Congressional Research Service, 1966–1968
    Technical officer, Reference Department, 1969–1972
    Coordinator, foreign newspaper microfilming, Reference Department, 1972–1975
    Coordinator, newspaper microfilming, Reference Department, 1975
    Chairman, Librarian's Task Force on Goals, Organization, and Planning, Office of the Librarian, 1976
    Assistant head, Planning Office, Office of the Librarian, 1977

Executive director, Center for the Book, Office of the Librarian, 1978–1986

Director, Center for the Book, Office of the Librarian, 1986–1988

Director, Center for the Book, Office of Associate Librarian for Cultural Affairs, 1989–1995

Director, Center for the Book, Office of Associate Librarian for Library Services, 1995–

Concurrent Professional Experience

Library of Congress, Washington, D.C.

Acting director, Office of Associate Librarian for Cultural Affairs, March 1990–February 1992

Acting director of publishing, Office of Associate Librarian for Cultural Affairs, September 1993–May 1995

Co-chair, steering committee, Library of Congress Bicentennial, Office of the Librarian, October 1997–December 2000

Acting director of publishing, Office of Associate Librarian for Library Services, January–July 2009

Author coordinator, annual National Book Festival, 2001–

Concurrent Teaching Experience

Associate professorial lecturer in American civilization, Library of Congress coordinator for the Library of Congress/George Washington University joint Ph.D. program in American civilization, and instructor, "Americana in the Library of Congress," George Washington University, Washington, D.C., 1975–1980

Instructor, "Libraries in American Society," School of Library and Information Science, Catholic University of America, Washington, D.C., summer 1981

Instructor, "The Library of Congress and American Librarianship," School of Library and Information Studies, University of California, Berkeley, winter quarter, 1981–82

Lecturer, "The Library of Congress and American Librarianship," Graduate School of Library and Information Science, University of California, Los Angeles, March 16 and 18, 1982

Instructor, "Books and Libraries in the Electronic Age," School of Librarianship, University of Washington, Seattle, summer quarter, 1982

Personal Awards and Honors

William A. Jump Meritorious Award for Exemplary Achievement in
Public Administration, for "outstanding leadership in directing the
Librarian's Task Force on Goals, Organization, and Planning," 1977
(first Library of Congress employee to be so honored)

Distinguished Alumnus Award, Graduate School of Library and Information Science, University of Washington, 1983

Invited Lecturer, Columbia University School of Library Service, Rare
Book School, "The Library of Congress in the 19th Century," July
12, 1984

Special Citation, White House Conference on Libraries and Information Services Task Force, for "commitment and special support
for the betterment of libraries and the improvement of library
services," 1989

Special Recognition Award, International Reading Association, Man-
hattan Council, for "exemplary efforts in furthering literacy and the
encouragement of reading," 1990

Invited Lecturer, Rudi Weiss Annual Memorial Lecture, Annual Conference of the New York State Library Association, Rochester, "The Open
Door: Books, Reading, and Libraries in the 1990s," Oct. 12, 1991

Special Achievement Award, National Commission on Libraries and
Information Science, for "strong and spirited leadership of the Center
for the Book, which has set a standard of excellence for the nation's
educational and cultural life that is an inspiration to all," 1992

President's Award, District of Columbia Library Association, "for
outstanding contributions to the Washington Metropolitan Area,"
including leadership of the Center for the Book, administrative
contributions to the Library of Congress, and authorship in 1994
of *Capital Libraries and Librarianship: A Brief History of the District of
Columbia Library Association, 1894–1994*, 1996

Historians James P. Danky and Wayne A. Wiegand dedicate their new
book, *Print Culture in a Diverse America* (Urbana: University of Illinois
Press, 1998): "For John Cole, friend, supporter, inspiration."

Oklahoma Book Award, for "distinguished service in support of the
Oklahoma Center for the Book," 1999

Invited Lecturer, Elizabeth W. Stone Annual Lecture, Catholic University
of America, "Libraries, Creativity, Liberty: The Library of Congress
and Its Bicentennial," March 30, 2000

Joseph A. Lippincott Award, American Library Association, "for distinguished service to the profession of librarianship," 2000

U.S. Poet Laureate Billy Collins writes and dedicates a poem, "Voyage," to John Cole to celebrate his 25th anniversary as director of the Center for the Book, 2003.

Center for the Book Awards and Honors

NEA Broadcasting Award, National Education Association, for the Library of Congress/Center for the Book/CBS "Read More About It" book promotion project, 1986

International Book Award, UNESCO-Affiliated International Book Committee, for the Center's "imaginative and practical campaigns on behalf of books and reading in all their diverse aspects, campaigns which have inspired similar efforts in the United States and internationally," 1987

Institutional Award, American Printing History Association, "in grateful recognition of the center's services in advancing understanding of the history of printing and its allied arts," 1994

Raven Award, Mystery Writers of America, in recognition of the Center's "support of and dedication to literacy education as a whole," including "the crucial role it has played in the National Book Festival since its origin in 2001," 2008

Professional Affiliations and Activities

American Library Association, International Relations Committee, 1974–1976, and Publishing Committee, 1979–1981 (chair, 1979)

Organization of American Historians, Bibliographical and Research Needs Committee, 1979–1981

International Federation of Library Associations and Institutions, Standing Committee, Literacy and Reading Section, 1997–present (chair, 1997–2001; editor of section *Newsletter*, 1997-2008)

Articles with Biographical Content

"Two LC Lads in London." *Library of Congress Information Bulletin* (hereafter *LCIB*) 26 (Mar. 30, 1967): 221–22.

"John Cole Named Director of the Center for the Book." *LCIB* 37 (Feb. 24, 1978): 126-127.

Beverly T. Watkins, "'To Keep the Book Flourishing': Center Extols the Printed Word." *Chronicle of Higher Education,* June 1, 1981, 13–14.

Robert A. Carter, "The Center for the Book: Seeking Outreach." *Publishers Weekly* 227 (Jan. 4, 1985): 30–34.

"John Y. Cole: Reaching Out with the Library of Congress." *Humanities Discourse* 2 (Sept.–Oct. 1988): 3–6.

"John Cole Receives 25-Year Pin." *LCIB* 48 (Apr. 17, 1989): 149–51.

Joseph Deitsch, "Portrait: John Y. Cole." *Wilson Library Bulletin* 64 (Apr. 1990): 49–51.

"A Conversation with John Y. Cole." Interview by Sheldon Hackney, chairman, National Endowment for the Humanities. *Humanities: The Magazine of the National Endowment for the Humanities*, Nov.–Dec. 1993, 4–7.

"Distinguished Service: Cole to Receive 2000 Lippincott Award." *LCIB* 59 (May 2000): 117.

Elizabeth Jacobsen, "Analytical Intellectual Biography of John Y. Cole." University of California at Los Angeles, Graduate School of Library and Information Studies, 2004. www.gseis.ucla.edu/faculty/maack/documents.JohnCole/doc.

"Volume Honors Cole's Contributions to the Library." *LCIB* 69 (Mar. 2010): 50-51.

Selected Writings of John Y. Cole, 1970–2010

Section I: The Library of Congress: History and Development

This section includes writings about the Library's administrative history and organization; the development of its collections and services; the construction, art, and architecture of its buildings; and its legislative, national, and international roles. The Bicentennial Background Series (1999–2001) was written while the author was co-chair of the Library's Bicentennial steering committee.

1970–1979

"Of Copyright, Men & a National Library." *Quarterly Journal of the Library of Congress* (hereafter *QJLC*) 28 (Apr. 1971): 114–36. Reprinted in *Library Lit. 2: The Best of 1971*, edited by Bill Katz, 325–59. Metuchen, N.J.: Scarecrow Press, 1972. Reprinted in *Copyright in the Library of Congress, 125th Anniversary*, 1–26. Washington, D.C.: Library of Congress, 1995.

"The Main Building of the Library of Congress: A Chronology, 1871–1980." *QJLC* 29 (Oct. 1972): 267–70. Reprinted in *Ten First Street,*

Southeast: Congress Builds a Library, 1886–1897, edited by Helen-Anne Hilker, 39–43. Washington, D.C.: Library of Congress, 1980.

"Smithmeyer & Pelz: Embattled Architects of the Library of Congress." *QJLC* 29 (Oct. 1972): 282–307.

"Library's Main Building Opened to the Public 75 Years Ago; Grandeur Heightens Enjoyment of Literary Feast." *Library of Congress Information Bulletin* (hereafter *LCIB*) 31 (Nov. 3, 1972): 466–67, 470.

"LC and ALA, 1876–1901." *Library Journal* 98 (Oct. 15, 1973): 2965–70. Reprinted in U.S. Senate, *Nomination of Daniel J. Boorstin of the District of Columbia to be Librarian of Congress, Hearings before the Committee on Rules and Administration, U.S. Senate, 94th Congress, 1st sess.*, July 30 and 31, Sept. 10, 1975, 132–37. Washington, D.C.: Government Printing Office, 1975.

"The Library of Congress: A List for Further Reading." In Charles A. Goodrum, *The Library of Congress*, 285–88. New York: Praeger, 1974.

"The Library of Congress in the 19th Century: An Informal Account." *Journal of Library History* 9 (July 1974): 222–40.

"WPA Research Materials at the Library of Congress." *LCIB* 33 (Nov. 29, 1974): A243–45.

"For Congress and the Nation: The Dual Nature of the Library of Congress." *QJLC* 32 (Apr. 1975): 118–38. Reprinted in U.S. Senate, *Nomination of Daniel J. Boorstin*, 87–107.

"'Wordy Outlets for Impracticables and Pretenders': The Librarian of Congress Balks at Attending ALA 1876." *American Libraries* 6 (May 1975): 283.

"The Librarian's Task Force on Goals, Organization, and Planning: A Report Covering the Period January 16–February 11, 1976." *LCIB* 35 (Feb. 20, 1976): 112–13. Additional Librarian's Task Force reports in *LCIB* 35 (Apr. 9, 1976): 232–35; (July 16, 1976): 417–18; (Aug. 13, 1976): 471–73; (Sept. 3, 1976): 521–24; (Sept. 24, 1976): 595–98; (Oct. 29, 1976): 672–74; and (Dec. 10, 1976): 765–68; and in *LCIB* 36 (Jan. 14, 1977): 23–24; (Feb. 4, 1977): 100–104.

"The Library of Congress in American Life." In *Advances in Librarianship*, vol. 8, edited by Michael H. Harris, 55–79. New York: Academic Press, 1978.

The Library of Congress in Perspective: A Volume Based on the Reports of the 1976 Librarian's Task Force and Advisory Groups (editor). New York: R. R. Bowker Co., 1978. 281 pp. Includes "The Library of Congress, 1800–1975," 5–83.

"Library of Congress." In *The Architecture of Washington, D.C.*, vol. 2, edited by Bates Lowry, [3–4]. Washington, D.C.: Dunlap Society, 1979. Includes five microfiche.

For Congress and the Nation: A Chronological History of the Library of Congress.
Washington, D.C.: Library of Congress, 1979. 196 pp.

1980–1989

"The Library of Congress and American Research Libraries." In *University Library History: An International Review*, edited by James Thompson, 187–208. New York: K. G. Saur, 1980.

Foreword to the *Early Illustrated Book: Essays in Honor of Lessing J. Rosenwald*, edited by Sandra Hindman. Washington, D.C.: Library of Congress, 1982.

"Cross-Currents: The British Library and the Library of Congress in Historical Perspective." *Library Review 32* (Winter 1983): 247–58.

"Amassing American 'Stuff': The Library of Congress and the Federal Arts Projects of the 1930s." *QJLC* 40 (Fall 1983): 356–89.

"The Library of Congress and the Presidential Parade." *LCIB* 43 (Oct. 15, 1984): 343–48.

The Library of Congress: A Documentary History on Microfiche. Bethesda, Md.: Congressional Information Service, Inc., 1987. Includes 499 microfiche.

The Library of Congress: A Documentary History. Guide to the Microfiche Collection (editor). Bethesda, Md.: Congressional Information Service, Inc., 1987. 86 pp. Includes "The Library of Congress and Its Multiple Missions," 1–16, and "Studying the Library of Congress: Resources and Research Opportunities," 17–20.

"The International Role of the Library of Congress: A Brief History." In *Alexandria: The Journal of National and International Library and Information Issues* 1, no. 3 (1989): 43–51. Reprinted in *LCIB* 49 (Jan. 15, 1990): 15–18, 45.

"Studying the Library of Congress: Resources and Research Opportunities." *Libraries & Culture* 24 (Summer 1989): 357–66.

1990–1999

Libraries and Scholarly Communication in the United States: The Historical Dimension (edited with Phyllis Dain). New York: Greenwood Press, 1990. 146 pp. Includes "The Library of Congress and American Scholarship, 1865–1939," 45–61.

"A Few Facts about the Library as It Turns 190." *LCIB* 49 (Apr. 9, 1990): 146–47.

Introduction to *A Literary Companion: 1992 Library of Congress Engagement Calendar*. Petaluma, Calif.: Pomegranate Calendars & Books, 1991. Introductions were written for this annual Library of Congress literary engagement calendar until the series ended in 1999.

"Library of Congress." In *The Reader's Companion to American History*, edited by Eric Foner and John A. Garraty, 660–62. Boston: Houghton Mifflin Co., 1991.

Preface to *Full Circle: Ninety Years of Service in the Main Reading Room*, by Josephus Nelson and Judith Farley. Washington, D.C.: Library of Congress, 1991.

"Jefferson's Legacy: A Brief History of the Library." *LCIB* 50 (Apr. 8, 1991): 124–30.

Jefferson's Legacy: A Brief History of the Library of Congress. Washington, D.C.: Library of Congress, 1993. 103 pp.

"Thomas Jefferson and the Library of Congress." In *Jefferson the Man: In His Own Words*, edited by Robert C. Baron, xiii–xv. Golden, Colo.: Fulcrum/Starwood Publishing, 1993.

Introduction to *America's Treasure House: The Library of Congress* 1995 Calendar. Golden, Colo.: Fulcrum Publishing, 1994.

"Library of Congress, Washington, D.C., USA." In *Encyclopedia of Library History*, edited by Wayne A. Wiegand and Donald G. Davis, Jr., 377–81. New York: Garland Publishing, Inc., 1994.

"The World's Largest Library: The Library of Congress, a Brief History of the Giant Library." *Herald of Library Science* 33 (July–Oct. 1994): 155–63.

"Library of Congress." In *America's Treasure House: The Library of Congress 1996 Calendar*. Golden, Colo.: Fulcrum Publishing, 1995.

On These Walls: Inscriptions and Quotations in the Buildings of the Library of Congress. Washington, D.C.: Library of Congress, 1995. 106 pp. Revised edition published by Library of Congress in association with Scala Publishers, 2008. 128 pp.

"The Best of Times for American Culture? LC's New Deal Arts Collections Displayed and Discussed." *LCIB* 54 (Feb. 6, 1995): 50–52.

Afterword to *1997 Calendar Celebrating the Centennial of the Library of Congress Building*. Golden, Colo.: Fulcrum Publishing, 1996

"Lincoln and the Library: How the Collections Were Developed." *LCIB* 55 (Feb. 19, 1996): 52–53.

"Publishing at the Library of Congress: A Brief History." *Publishing Research Quarterly* 12 (Summer 1996): 38–49.

The Library of Congress: The Art and Architecture of the Thomas Jefferson Building (edited with Henry Hope Reed). New York: W. W. Norton & Co.,

1997. 320 pp. Includes "Struggle for a Structure: Ainsworth Rand Spofford and a New Building for the Library of Congress," 30–63.

"Book Palace of the American People: A Brief History of the Thomas Jefferson Building." In *The Thomas Jefferson Building: Book Palace of the American People* (exhibit brochure). Washington, D.C.: Library of Congress, 1997.

"The Library of Congress." In *Collier's Encyclopedia*, 605–6. New York: Collier's, 1997.

"The Library of Congress." In *International Encyclopedia of Information and Library Science*, edited by John Feather and Paul Sturges, 261–63. London: Routledge, 1997.

"The Thomas Jefferson Building: For Further Study and Reading." *LCIB* 56 (May 5–19, 1997): 179.

"The Library and the Declaration: LC Has a Long History with Founding Document." *LCIB* 56 (Aug. 1997): 269, 271, and 279.

"A Fitting Temple for Great Thoughts: The Jefferson Building and a New Library of Congress." *LCIB* 56 (Nov. 1997): 342–44.

"Scholars and Artisans Display Talents at Symposium and Building Crafts Demonstration." *LCIB* 56 (Dec. 1997): 365.

"Books, Reading, and the Library of Congress in a Changing America." *Libraries & Culture* 33 (Winter 1998): 34–39.

"The LC: An Incomparable American Studies Center." *American Studies Association Newsletter* 21 (Mar. 1998): 1, 3–4.

"Celebrate with the Library of Congress in the Year 2000" (with Jo Ann Jenkins). *American Libraries* 58 (Jan. 1999): 30.

"Biography and the Library of Congress: New Reference Work Introduced at Library Ceremony." *LCIB* 58 (Feb. 1999): 48–50.

"Planning the Library of Congress's Bicentennial Commemoration in 2000." *Alexandria: The Journal of National and International Library and Information Issues* 11, no. 3 (1999): 203–7.

1999–2001, Library of Congress Bicentennial Background Series

"Looking Back to Look Ahead: How the Library Celebrated Its Sesquicentennial in 1950." *LCIB* 58 (Apr. 1999): 70–73.

"The Library's Jeffersonian Legacy." *LCIB* 58 (June 1999): 120–21, 123.

"The Library, the States, and 'Local Heritage.'" *LCIB* 58 (July 1999): 156–58.

"The Library of Congress and the Library Community." *LCIB* 58 (Aug. 1999): 186–87.

"'Creativity' and the Library of Congress." *LCIB* 58 (Sept. 1999): 210–11.

"Gifts to the Nation." *LCIB* 58 (Oct. 1999): 238–39.

"The Highlands of the Mind." *LCIB* 58 (Nov. 1999): 264–65.

"A Republic Which Rests Upon the Public Intelligence." *LCIB* 58 (Dec. 1999): 286–87.

"Interpreting the Library's History." *LCIB* 59 (Jan. 2000): 6–7.

"Symbols of a National Institution." *LCIB* 59 (Feb. 2000): 28–29, 37.

"Turning Points in the Library's History." *LCIB* 59 (Mar. 2000): 52–53, 69.

"'Suitable Apartments': The Library's Buildings and Spaces, 1800–2000." *LCIB* 59 (Apr. 2000): 83–85.

"The Library's Magazines." *LCIB* 59 (May 2000): 114–16.

"Exhibition Catalogs and Brochures."*LCIB* 59 (June 2000): 134–35.

"Library of Congress Guidebooks." *LCIB* 59 (July 2000): 172–73.

"The Library's *Information Bulletin and Gazette.*" *LCIB* 59 (Aug.–Sept. 2000): 202–3.

"The Library's *Annual Report.*" *LCIB* 59 (Oct. 2000): 238–39.

"Describing the Library's Collections." *LCIB* 59 (Nov. 2000): 268–69.

"Of Time Capsules, Cornerstones, and Closet Safes." *LCIB* 59 (Dec. 2000): 306–7.

"How the Library Celebrated in 2000." *LCIB* 60 (Jan. 2001): 8–11.

2000–2010

"Debating National Culture in Nineteenth-Century Washington: The Library of Congress and the Smithsonian Institution" (with Nancy E. Gwinn). In *Getting Ready for the Nineteenth Century: Strategies and Solutions for Rare Book and Special Collections Librarians*, edited by William E. Brown, Jr., and Laura Stalker, 1–33. Chicago: American Library Association, 2000.

"The Library of Congress at 200 Looks to the Future." *Caxtonian: Journal of the Caxton Club of Chicago* 8 (June 2000): 1, 4–5.

"The Library of Congress and the Democratic Spirit." In *Libraries and Democracy: The Cornerstones of Liberty*, edited by Nancy Kranich, 169–82. Chicago: American Library Association, 2001.

"Library of Congress of the United States." In *International Dictionary of Library Histories I*, edited by David H. Stam, 407–12. Chicago: Fitzroy Dearborn Publishers, 2001.

"New Publications Highlight Library of Congress in American History." *LCIB* 63 (Apr. 2004): 74–75.

"The Library of Congress Becomes a World Library, 1815–2005," *Libraries & Culture* 40, no.3 (2005): 387.

"The Library of Congress Becomes a World Library, 1815–2005." In *Libraries & Culture: Historical Essays Honoring the Legacy of Donald G. Davis, Jr.*, edited by Cheryl Knott Malone, Hermina G. B. Anghelescu, and John Mark Tucker, 163–76. Washington, D.C.: Library of Congress, 2006.

"Mrs. Bush Inspires a National Book Festival." In *Our White House: Looking In, Looking Out*, by the National Children's Book and Literacy Alliance, 221–23. Cambridge, Mass.: Candlewick Press, 2008.

"Library of Congress." *Microsoft Encarta Online Encyclopedia*, 2008.

"Sally Hart McCallum: Why We Need Standards" (interview). In *Library Services Journal* 1 (Summer 2008): 31–35.

"Treasures on Display: More Than a Century of Library of Congress Exhibitions" (with Audrey Fischer). *LCIB* 67 (Oct. 2008): 167–73, 177.

"The Story of On These Walls." *LCIB* 67 (Oct. 2008): 186.

"Fillmore's Foundation: First White House Library Discovered, Reconstructed." *LCIB* 69 (July-August 2010): 160-61.

"An Idea Whose Time Finally Came: the Young Readers Center." In Library of Congress, *Library Services Journal* 2 (October 2010): 6.

"The Book Palace of the American People: An Introduction and Reflection." *Library Quarterly* 80 (Oct. 2010): 301-310.

"Congress, Library of (LC)." In The *Oxford Companion to the Book*, vol. 1, edited by Michael F. Suarez and H.R. Woudhuysen, 634-35. New York: Oxford University Press, 2010.

Section II: *Encyclopedia of the Library of Congress*, 2004

The *Encyclopedia of the Library of Congress*, a ten-year project, is the most comprehensive book ever published about the Library of Congress. In addition to essays and many articles by each of its two editors, it includes contributions by more than fifty Library of Congress subject specialists, nineteen color photographs of the Library's spectacular Thomas Jefferson Building, and more than three hundred black-and-white photographs.

Encyclopedia of the Library of Congress: For Congress, the Nation and the World (editor with Jane Aikin). Lanham, Md.: Library of Congress, in association with Bernan Press, 2004. 569 pp. Includes the essays "America's Library: A Brief History of the Library of Congress" (with Jane Aikin), 1–15; "The Congressional Research Service," 17–22;

"The Copyright Office" (with Jane Aikin), 33–38; "The International Role of the Library of Congress," 45–51; and "The Library of Congress and the National Archives," 103–8. Also includes the articles "Adams Building," 131–32; "Americana," 151–52; "Automation" (with Jane Aikin), 169–73; "Beckley, John James (1757–1807)," 175–76; "Billington, James H. (1929–)," 179–81; "Boorstin, Daniel J. (1914–2004)," 183–85; "Center for the Book," 203–7; "Employees and Employment," 225–31; "Evans, Luther H. (1902–1981)," 239–41; "Exhibitions," 247–50; "Jefferson, Thomas," 279–80; "Jefferson Building," 281–84; "Joint Committee on the Library," 285–88; "Librarian, Office of," 291; "Library of Congress Bicentennial," 293–95; "Library of Congress in the Capitol Building," 297–98; "Library of Congress, Administrative Reviews and Reorganizations," 299–302; "Library of Congress Strategic Plan," 303–8; "Library Services," 311; "Lincolniana," 313–14; "MacLeish, Archibald (1892–1982)," 323–25; "Madison Council," 327–28; "Madison, James," 329; "Madison Memorial Building," 331–32; "Magruder, Patrick (1778–1819)," 333–34; "Meehan, John Silva (1790–1863)," 355–56; "Mumford, L. Quincy (1903–1982)," 369–71; "National Book Festival," 383–84; "Poetry Program and Poets Laureate" (with Prosser Gifford), 397–403; "Publishing and Publications," 437–41; "Putnam, Herbert (1861–1955)," 443–45; "Rare Book and Special Collections Division and Collections" (with Jane Aikin and Daniel DeSimone), 447–55; "Reference and Research Services," 457–62; "Serial and Government Publications Division and Collections" (with Jane Aikin and Robert B. Harriman, Jr.), 471–81; "Spofford, Ainsworth Rand (1825–1908)," 487–89; "Stephenson, John G. (1828–1883)," 491–92; "Strategic Initiatives, Office of," 493; "Watterston, George (1783–1854)," 495–97; and "Young, John Russell (1840–1899)," 499–500.

Section III: Librarians of Congress and Other Library Staff

In addition to the articles listed below, biographies of the thirteen Librarians of Congress also were written for the *Encyclopedia of the Library of Congress* (above).

1970–1979

"Ainsworth Rand Spofford and the Copyright Law of 1870." *In A Century of Copyright at the Library of Congress*, 1–4. New York: Copyright

Society of the U.S.A., 1970. Reprinted in *Journal of Library History* 6 (Jan. 1971): 34–40.

"A National Monument for a National Library: Ainsworth Rand Spofford and the New Library of Congress, 1871–1897." In *Records of the Columbia Historical Society of Washington, D.C.*, vol. 48, edited by Francis Coleman Rosenberger, 468–507. Washington, D.C.: Columbia Historical Society, 1973.

"A Congenial Intellectual Occupation." Manuscripts 26 (Fall 1974): 247–53.

Ainsworth Rand Spofford: Bookman and Librarian (editor). Littleton, Colo.: Libraries Unlimited, 1975. 203 pp.

"Morsch, Lucile M." In *Encyclopedia of Library and Information Science*, vol. 18, 277–83. New York: Marcel Dekker, Inc., 1976.

"Ainsworth Rand Spofford: The Valiant and Persistent Librarian of Congress." *QJLC* 33 (Apr. 1976): 93–115. Reprinted in *Librarians of Congress* 1802–1974, 119–41. Washington, D.C.: Library of Congress, 1977.

"Herbert Putnam and the National Library." In *Milestones to the Present: Papers from Library History Seminar V*, edited by Harold Goldstein, 109–22. Syracuse, N.Y.: Gaylord Professional Publications, 1978.

"Martel, Charles (1860–1945)" (with James Bennett Childs). In *Dictionary of American Library Biography*, edited by Bohdan S. Wynar, 342–45. Littleton, Colo.: Libraries Unlimited, 1978. Also includes "Meyer, Herman H. B. (1864–1937)," 342–45; "Murray, Daniel A. P. (1852–1925)," 381–82; "Putnam, George Herbert (1861–1955)," 418–22; "Spofford, Ainsworth Rand (1825–1908)," 499–500; and "Stephenson, John Gould (1828–1883)," 506–8.

1980–1989

"MacLeish, Archibald (1892–)." In *ALA World Encyclopedia of Library and Information Services*, edited by Robert Wedgeworth, 337–38. Chicago: American Library Association, 1980. Also includes "Putnam, (George) Herbert (1861–1955)," 464–66; and "Spofford, Ainsworth Rand (1825–1908)," 542–43.

"Spofford, Ainsworth Rand." In *Encyclopedia of Library and Information Science*, vol. 28, 443–52. New York: Marcel Dekker, Inc., 1980.

"MacLeish, Archibald (1892–1982)." In *ALA World Encyclopedia of Library and Information Services*, 2nd edition, edited by Robert Wedgeworth, 507–8. Chicago: American Library Association, 1986. Also includes

"Putnam, (George) Herbert (1861–1955)," 687–88; and "Spofford, Ainsworth Rand (1825–1908)," 782–84.

"The President Appoints the Librarian, 1802–1975." *LCIB* 46 (Mar. 9, 1987): 95–98.

"James H. Billington Sworn in as Librarian of Congress." *AB Bookman's Weekly* 80 (Sept. 7, 1987): 901–5.

The Republic of Letters: Librarian of Congress Daniel J. Boorstin on Books, Reading, and Libraries (editor). Washington, D.C.: Library of Congress, 1989. 115 pp.

1990–1999

"Evans, Luther Harris (1902–1981)." In *Supplement to the Dictionary of American Library Biography*, edited by Wayne A. Wiegand, 22–26. Englewood, Colo.: Libraries Unlimited, 1990. Also includes "Mumford, L. Quincy (1903–1982)," 87–91.

"MacLeish, Archibald (1892–1982)." In *ALA World Encyclopedia of Library and Information Services*, 3rd edition, edited by Robert Wedgeworth, 529–30. Chicago: American Library Association, 1993. Also includes "Putnam, (George) Herbert (1861–1955)," 694–95; and "Spofford, Ainsworth Rand (1825–1908)," 796–97.

"Evans, Luther H. (1902–1981)." In *American National Biography*, edited by John A. Garraty and Mark C. Barnes, 7:612–14. New York: Oxford University Press, 1999. Also includes "Martel, Charles (1860–1945)," 14:582–84; "Mumford, L. Quincy (1903–1982)," 16:84–86; "Putnam, Herbert (1861–1955)," 18:9–11; and "Spofford, Ainsworth Rand (1825–1908)," 20:487–88.

2000–2010

"Daniel J. Boorstin, 1914–2004: Librarian Emeritus Dies at 89." *LCIB* 63 (Feb.–Mar. 2004): 38, 40.

"Ainsworth Rand Spofford and the New Building of the Library of Congress." *Capitol Dome* 41 (Spring 2004): 11–15.

"In Memoriam: Daniel J. Boorstin." *Perspectives: Newsmagazine of the American Historical Association* 42 (Sept. 2004): 68–69.

Daniel J. Boorstin (1914-2004). *Proceedings of the American Antiquarian Society*, Vol. 114, Part 1, 2004, 26–30. Worcester, Mass.: American Antiquarian Society, 2005.

"Ainsworth's Ashes: Final Resting Place of a Seminal Librarian of Congress." *LCIB* 64 (Mar. 2005): 75.
"Spofford, Ainsworth Rand (1825-1908). " In *The Oxford Companion to the Book*, vol. 2, edited by Michael F. Suarez and H.R. Woudhuysen, 1171. New York: Oxford University Press, 2010.

Section IV: The Center for the Book: History and Development

Included are articles about the origin of the Center for the Book, its reading promotion networks and educational outreach programs, its international activities, and its role in the National Book Festival. Each of the twelve articles in the Center for the Book 25th Anniversary Series (2001–2002) summarizes the history of a different function or activity of the Center.

1978–1979

The Center for the Book in the Library of Congress: The Planning Year. Washington, D.C.: Library of Congress, 1978. 33 pp.
Television, the Book, and the Classroom. A Seminar Cosponsored by the Center for the Book in the Library of Congress and the U.S. Department of Education and Held at the Library of Congress on April 26–27, 1978 (editor). Washington, D.C.: Library of Congress, 1978. 128 pp.
"The Center for the Book in the Library of Congress." In *The Bowker Annual*, 23rd edition, 67–68. New York: R. R. Bowker Co., 1978. Entries for the Center for the Book also appeared in the 30th (1985), 33rd (1988), and 39th through 56th editions (1995–2011).
"New Center for the Book at LC." *AB Bookman's Weekly* 61 (Mar. 13, 1978): 1763–66.
Reading in America 1978 (editor with Carol S. Gold). Washington, D.C.: Library of Congress, 1979. 98 pp.
"The Center for the Book in the Library of Congress." *QJLC* 36 (Spring 1979): 178–88, reprinted in T*he Center for the Book in the Library of Congress.* Washington, D.C.: Library of Congress, 1979.
"The Center for the Book in the Library of Congress: A Report on the First Meeting of the National Advisory Board." *LCIB* 38 (Mar. 30, 1979): 113–15.
"The Textbook in American Society." *LCIB* 38 (May 25, 1979): 189–92.
"Japanese Literature in Translation." *LCIB* 38 (June 15, 1979): 221–22.

"The Audience for Children's Books." *LCIB* 38 (June 29, 1979): 246–48.

"The International Flow of Information: A Trans-Pacific Perspective." *LCIB* 38 (Aug. 31, 1979): 355–58.

1980–1989

"A Report on a Meeting Sponsored by the Center for the Book in San Francisco." *LCIB* 39 (Jan. 18, 1980): 23–24.

"The Center for the Book in the Library of Congress: A Report on the Second Meeting of the National Advisory Board." *LCIB* 39 (May 2, 1980): 150–51.

"The Co-Responsibilities of American Publishers and Booksellers." *LCIB* 39 (May 23, 1980): 150–51.

"Broadcasting Books to Young Audiences." *LCIB* 39 (June 13, 1980): 213–16.

"Linking Books and Television." *Television and Children* 3 (Summer 1980): 67–69.

"The Rosenwald Symposium on the Illustrated Book: A Report on a Symposium Honoring Lessing J. Rosenwald, Library of Congress, May 30–31, 1980" (with William Matheson). *LCIB* 39 (Aug. 1, 1980): 271–76.

"Literacy in Historical Perspective: A Conference Sponsored by the Center for the Book and the U.S. National Institute of Education, Library of Congress, July 14–15, 1980." *LCIB* 39 (Oct. 10, 1980): 406–12.

In Celebration: The National Union Catalog, Pre-1956 Imprints (editor). Washington, D.C.: Library of Congress, 1981. 49 pp.

Responsibilities of the American Book Community (editor). Washington, D.C.: Library of Congress, 1981. 88 pp.

The Textbook in American Society. A Volume Based on a Conference at the Library of Congress on May 2–3, 1979 (editor with Thomas G. Sticht). Washington, D.C.: Library of Congress, 1981. 55 pp.

"The National Union Catalog: Pre-1956 Imprints: A Celebration of Its Completion." *LCIB* 40 (Feb. 20, 1981): 65–68.

"Good Ideas for Friends' Groups." *LCIB* 40 (Mar. 6, 1981): 79–80.

"Australia–New Zealand Library Conference." *LCIB* 40 (Mar. 13, 1981): 87–88.

"Paper for Book Longevity." *LCIB* 40 (Mar. 27, 1981): 101–4.

"The Center for the Book in the Library of Congress: A Report on the Third Meeting of the National Advisory Board." *LCIB* 40 (May 1, 1981): 149–52.

"Books Make a Difference: A Good Idea for Promoting Books and Reading in Local Communities" (with Ann Heidbreder Eastman). *LCIB* 40 (May 29, 1981): 177–78.

"Oral History and the Printed Word." *LCIB* 40 (June 12, 1981): 217–18.

"'Read More About It' Launches Third Season: A Good Idea for Linking Television and Books in Local Communities." *LCIB* 40 (Sept. 4, 1981): 305-08.

"The Center for the Book in the Library of Congress." *CSIL: Current Studies in Librarianship* 6 (Spring–Fall 1982): 1–7.

"'Read More About It' Launches Fourth Season: A Good Idea for Linking Television and Books in Local Communities." *LCIB* 41 (Oct. 8, 1982): 325-27.

"The Center for the Book in the Library of Congress: A Report Prepared for the Fourth Meeting of the National Advisory Board, October 15, 1982." In *Books That Made the Difference: What People Told Us*, by Gordon and Patricia Sabine, 196–200. Hamden, Conn.: Library Professional Publications, 1983.

Preface to *Literacy in Historical Perspective*, edited by Daniel P. Resnick. Washington, D.C.: Library of Congress, 1983.

"Scandinavian Children's Books Today: Astrid Lindgren Speaks at the Library." *LCIB* 42 (Jan. 24, 1983): 26–28.

"After Five Years: A Look at the Center for the Book." *AB Bookman's Weekly* 66 (Mar. 21, 1983): 2095–2104.

"Reading and Book Promotion: Recent Center for the Book Activities." *LCIB* 42 (May 16, 1983): 157–60.

"The Diminished Role of U.S. Books Abroad: A Report on Discussions at the Library of Congress." *LCIB* 42 (June 6, 1983): 193–96.

"Radio and Reading: A Report on a Symposium at the Library of Congress." *LCIB* 42 (July 4, 1983): 220–24.

"The History of Books: A Report on Center for the Book Activities." *LCIB* 42 (Aug. 15, 1983): 268–72.

"'Read More About It' Launches Fifth Season: A Good Idea for Linking Television and Reading." *LCIB* 42 (Oct. 3, 1983): 341–44.

"'Read More About It' Expands to CBS Radio: Books About Baseball and Football Featured." *LCIB* 42 (Oct. 10, 1983): 351-52.

"From the Exhibit Wall to the Bookshelf: 'And Now... Read About It!' Debuts." *LCIB* 42 (Nov. 14, 1983): 388–90.

"Public Lending Right: A Symposium at the Library of Congress." *LCIB* 42 (Dec. 12, 1983): 427–32.

"Books in an Electronic Age." In *Aliteracy: People Who Can Read but Won't,* edited by Nick Thimmesch, 32–35. Washington, D.C.: American Enterprise Institute, 1984.

"A New Voice: The Center for the Book's First Five Years." In *Dictionary of American Literary Biography Yearbook,* edited by Mary Broccoli and Jean W. Ross, 28–34. Detroit: Gale Research, 1984.

Preface to *ABC & XYZ: Dare to Be Creative!,* by Madeleine L'Engle. Washington, D.C.: Library of Congress, 1984.

Preface to *U.S. Books Abroad: Neglected Ambassadors,* by Curtis G. Benjamin. Washington, D.C.: Library of Congress, 1984.

"Californians James D. Hart and William Barlow, Jr. Give Engelhard Lectures on the Book." *LCIB* 43 (Jan. 9, 1984): 7.

"1983-84 'Read More About It' Reading Lists: Biography is Special Focus of the Season." *LCIB* 43 (Mar. 5, 1984): 61-64.

"Winning Ideas for Friends Groups: A Report on a Forum Sponsored by the Center for the Book and Friends of Libraries, U.S.A." *LCIB* 43 (Jan. 30, 1984): 27–28.

"Center for the Book Advisors Meet: Plans Made for Next Year's Program." *LCIB* 43 (June 11, 1984): 205–8.

"'Read More About It' Launches Sixth Season: Sports, Drama, Award Shows Featured." *LCIB* 43 (Aug. 27, 1984): 281-83.

"Calligraphy and the Japanese Word: A Symposium and Calligraphy Demonstration at the Library of Congress" (with J. Thomas Rimer). *LCIB* 43 (Sept. 3, 1984): 289–92.

"1984-85 'Read More About It' Lists: Mini-Series, Holiday Specials Featured." *LCIB* 43 (Nov. 12, 1984): 381-84.

"Images of the World: The Atlas through History: A Symposium at the Library of Congress." *LCIB* 43 (Dec. 17, 1984): 411–16.

Introduction to *Books and Other Machines: An Exhibition in the Jefferson Building of the Library of Congress, Dec. 7, 1984–June 2, 1985,* by Alice D. Schreyer. Washington, D.C.: Center for the Book, 1985.

"'Read More About It' Television Series Continues: First Lady Nancy Reagan Presents Announcement." *LCIB* 44 (Feb. 4, 1985): 19-21.

"Promoting the Study of the History of Books: Recent and Forthcoming Center for the Book Activities." *LCIB* 44 (Mar. 4, 1985): 41–44.

"1987—The Year of the Young Reader: A Do-It-Yourself Concept." *Special Libraries* 78 (Spring 1987): 144-45.

Afterword (with Jean Trebbi) to *Reading for Survival,* by John D. MacDonald, 25–26. Washington, D.C.: Library of Congress, 1987.

Books in Our Future: Perspectives and Proposals. A Supplement to Books in Our Future, a Report Transmitted in 1984 to the U.S. Congress (editor). Washington, D.C.: Library of Congress, 1987. 399 pp.

"The Center for the Book in the Library of Congress: A Decade of Promoting Books and Reading." In *The ALA Yearbook of Library and Information Services*, 198–99. Chicago: American Library Association, 1988.

"In Celebration." In *ZYX: 26 Poetic Portraits*, by Rhodes Patterson. Developed and designed by Mark Oldach and Rhonda Taira. Chicago: Society of Typographic Arts, 1989.

1990–1999

"'Explore New Worlds—READ!' Library Begins 1992 Reading Campaigns." *LCIB* 51 (Jan. 13, 1992): 11–13.

"The US's Center for the Book: An Alliance between Public and Private Interests." In *Logos: The Professional Journal of the Book World* 3, no. 1 (1992): 34–40.

"The Center for the Book in the Library of Congress and the Promotion of Books, Reading, and Book Culture." In *Encyclopedia of Library and Information Science*, vol. 49, supp. 12, edited by Allen Kent, 59–71. New York: Marcel Dekker, Inc., 1992.

"The Center for the Book in the Library of Congress." In *Dictionary of Literary Biography Yearbook: 1993*, edited by James W. Hipp, 234–39. Detroit: Gale Research, 1993.

Developing Lifetime Readers. A Report on the 1991 "Year of the Lifetime Reader" Promotion of the Library of Congress (editor). Compiled by Michael Thompson. Washington, D.C.: Library of Congress, 1993. 44 pp.

Foreword to *Publishing and Readership in Revolutionary France and America: A Symposium at the Library of Congress Sponsored by the Center for the Book and the European Division*, edited by Carol Armbruster. Westport, Conn.: Greenwood Press, 1993.

Preface to *Donated Book Programs: A Dialogue of Partners Handbook*. Washington, D.C.: Library of Congress, 1993.

"Crisis in Russian Book Culture Discussed at LC Conference" (with Barbara Bryant). *LCIB* 52 (Apr. 19, 1993): 170–73.

"About the Center for the Book." In *Dear Author: Students Write About Books That Changed Their Lives*, collected by Weekly Reader's Read Magazine. Berkeley, Calif.: Conan Press, 1995.

Books Change Lives: 1993–1994 Reading Promotion Campaign (editor). Compiled by Michael Thompson. Washington, D.C.: Library of Congress, 1996. 76 pp.

"Books Give Us Wings: The Center for the Book in the Library of Congress." *Virginia Libraries* 42 (July–Sept. 1996): 15–17.

"Great Books in the Great Hall: Television Series Celebrated." *LCIB* 45 (Sept. 30, 1996): 335–36, 348.

Foreword to *Images of the World: The Atlas through History*, edited by John A. Wolter and Ronald E. Grim. Washington, D.C.: Library of Congress, 1997.

Preface to From *Thibodaux to Tucumcari: Family Literacy in Rural Libraries*, by Molly Turner and Nancy Nober. A Report of the Viburnum Family Literacy Project. Washington, D.C.: Center for the Book, 1997.

"Libraries, Literacy, and the Library of Congress." *American Libraries* 28 (May 1997): 50–51.

IFLA Section on Reading Newsletter, no. 5 (Nov. 1997) (editor). Editorship of the Section on Reading Newsletter of the International Federation of Library Associations and Institutions (IFLA) continued for the following issues: no. 6 (July 1998), no. 7 (Nov. 1998), no. 8 (Aug. 1999), no. 9 (Dec. 1999), no. 10 (July 2000), no. 11 (Dec. 2000), no. 12 (July 2001), no. 13 (Dec. 2001), no. 14 (Aug. 2002), no. 15 (Dec. 2002), no. 16 (July 2003), no. 17 (Dec. 2003), no. 18 (Aug. 2004), no. 19 (Dec. 2004), no. 20 (Aug. 2005), no. 21 (Dec. 2005), no. 22 (Aug. 2006), no. 23 (Jan. 2007), no. 24 (Aug. 2007), and no. 25 (July 2008).

Foreword to *For the Love of Libraries: A Book of Postcards*. San Francisco, Calif.: Pomegranate, 1998.

"Partnerships for Reading: 'Building a Nation of Readers' Extends through 2000." *LCIB* 57 (Mar. 1998): 50–52.

"CFB on TV: Center for the Book Begins Third Decade of Promoting Reading on Television." *LCIB* 57 (Dec. 1998): 290–92.

Foreword to *I Hear America Reading: Why Read, What We Read*, by Jim Burke. Portsmouth, N.H.: Heinemann, 1999.

Foreword to *A Library Head Start to Literacy: The Resource Notebook for the Library–Museum–Head Start Partnership*, edited by Virginia Mathews and Susan Roman. Washington, D.C.: Center for the Book, 1999.

Preface to *The Historical Novel: A Celebration of the Achievements of Herman Wouk*, edited by Barbara A. Paulson. Washington, D.C.: Library of Congress, 1999.

"Books & Beyond: Books by Wolanin, Fadiman, and O'Toole Featured in Late 1998 Programs." *LCIB* 58 (Jan. 1999): 312–13, 315.

"Favorite Poem Project Gains Momentum: Tapes to Be Presented to the Library of Congress in April 2000." *LCIB* 58 (Feb. 1999): 19–20.

"The Gold Rush: California Historian J. S. Holliday Captivates Library Audience." *LCIB* 45 (July 1999): 159.

2000–2010

"Libraries, Literacy, and LC's Center for the Book." In *The Whole Library Catalog 3*, compiled by George M. Eberhart, 225–27. Chicago: American Library Association, 2000.

"The Indispensable Man: Washington's Legacy Discussed at Symposium." *LCIB* 59 (Feb. 2000): 30.

"'River of Words': Winners and Finalists Honored at the Library in April." *LCIB* 59 (June 2000): 132–33.

"Letters About Literature: Popular Student Essay Contest Begins 16th Year." *LCIB* 59 (July 2000): 168.

Center for the Book 25th Anniversary Series

"Publications Update." *LCIB* 60 (Apr. 2001): 98–99.

"International Update." *LCIB* 60 (July–Aug. 2001): 182–83.

"Book and Library History Update." *LCIB* 60 (Nov. 2001): 266–67.

"Reading Promotion Themes and Projects." *LCIB* 61 (Feb. 2002): 46–47.

"Symposia and Conferences." *LCIB* 61 (Mar.–Apr. 2002): 74–75.

"Lectures and Author Talks." *LCIB* 61 (May 2002): 102–3.

"Reading Promotion Partners." *LCIB* 61 (June 2002): 122–23.

"State Centers for the Book, 1984–2000." *LCIB* 61 (July–Aug. 2002): 146–47.

"Promoting Literacy, 1980–2002." *LCIB* 61 (Sept. 2002): 194–95.

"Exhibits and Displays, 1979–2002." *LCIB* 61 (Oct. 2002): 230–31.

"Promoting Libraries, 1980–2002." *LCIB* 61 (Nov. 2002): 258–59.

"25 Years of Promoting Books and Reading." *LCIB* 61 (Dec. 2002): 290–91.

"Authors and Reading Promoters at the National Book Festival." *LCIB* 60 (Oct. 2001): 242–43. Summaries of Center for the Book author and reading promotion activities at each annual National Book Festival also appeared in these *LCIB* issues: 62 (Nov. 2003): 190–91; 63 (Oct. 2004): 258–59; 64 (Nov.–Dec. 2005): 258–59; 65 (Dec. 2006): 290–91; 66 (Nov. 2007): 234–35; 67 (Nov. 2008): 234–35; and 69 (Nov. 2010): 258-59.

"Russian Librarians Visit U.S.: Book Centers to Be Established Throughout Russia." *LCIB* 60 (Dec. 2001): 274–75.

"Communities Reading Together: 'If All Seattle Read the Same Book.'" *LCIB* 61 (June 2002): 120–21.

"Center for the Book Leads Visit to Russia: 22 Reading Centers Being Established Throughout Russia." *LCIB* 61 (Nov. 2002): 256–57.

Afterword to *River of Words: Images and Poetry in Praise of Water*, edited by Pamela Michael. Berkeley, Calif.: Heyday Books, 2003.

"Promoting Books and Reading: Nationally, Internationally, and in the States." *LCIB* 62 (Jan. 2003): 9–13. Reprinted in *Best Pracice u 22 price, cultural organizacije, odnosi, biblioteka s javnoscu*, edited by Godana Stokie Simoncic, 61-69. Maticna biblioteka Istonco Sarajevo, 2009.

"Promoting Books and Reading in the Electronic Age: The Center for the Book at 25." *Publishing Research Quarterly* 19 (Spring 2003): 3–10.

"International Update: IFLA, South Africa." *LCIB* 62 (Dec. 2003): 322–23.

"Center for the Book's African Journey." In *African Research & Documentation* 96 (2004): 79–80.

"Letters About Literature Winners at National Book Festival." *LCIB* 63 (Sept. 2004): 190–91.

"'Reading Powers the Mind' Workshop Inaugurates New Family Literacy Project." *LCIB* 63 (Oct. 2004): 214–15.

"Center Leads Trip to South Africa." *LCIB* 63 (Nov. 2004): 234–35.

"State Centers Convene at Library." *LCIB* 64 (May 2005): 126–27.

"Another Successful National Book Festival." *Wyoming Library Roundup* 47, no. 4 (Fall 2005): 3.

"Reading Powers the Mind Workshop Highlights Family Literacy Partnerships." *LCIB* 64 (Oct. 2005): 230–31.

Introduction to *2006 Student Literary Awards: Letters About Literature & River of Words*. Denver: Colorado Humanities and the Colorado Center for the Book, 2006.

"One-Book Projects Grow in Popularity." *LCIB* 65 (Jan. 2006): 30–31.

"10th Anniversary of 'Books & Beyond.'" *LCIB* 65 (Mar. 2006): 74–75.

"Center Hosts Local Poets, Young Readers." *LCIB* 65 (Apr. 2006): 103.

"The Library of Congress Returns to Nebraska—Again." In *NCB News: A Publication of the Nebraska Center for the Book* 16 (Summer 2006): 2.

"State Centers Meet for Idea Exchange." *LCIB* 65 (July–Aug. 2006): 191.

"Library Hosts 'The Big Read.'" *LCIB* 65 (Sept. 2006): 219.

"A Decade of 'River of Words.'" *LCIB* 65 (Oct. 2006): 242.

"The Little Engine Still Can: 'Read for the Record' Celebrates a Children's Classic." *LCIB* 65 (Nov. 2006): 271.

"Message from the Center for the Book." In *This is Our Land: Discovering America and the World through Original Illustrations from Children's Books.* Washington, D.C.: Meridian International Center, 2006.

Building Nations of Readers: Experience, Ideas, Examples. Handbook on Reading Promotion (edited with Valeria D. Stelmakh). Moscow: NF "Pushkin Library" Bely Gorod, 2007. 225 pp. Includes "Reading Promotion in the United States: An Overview," 197–214.

Introduction to *2007 Student Literary Awards.* Denver: Colorado Humanities and the Colorado Center for the Book, 2007.

"Mr. Baldacci Goes to the Library: Author-Lawyer Writes Best Seller at Library." *LCIB* 66 (Apr. 2007): 90–91.

"River of Words Promotes Literacy, Environment." *LCIB* 66 (June 2007): 141–42.

Afterword to *River of Words: Young Poets and Artists on the Nature of Things,* edited by Pamela Michael, 279–80. Minneapolis: Milkweed Editions, 2008.

"Building Bridges with Books: Library Participates in Third Russia Book Festival" (with Seth de Matties, Harry Leich, and Vera De Buchananne). *LCIB* 67 (Jan.–Feb. 2008): 26–27.

"National Ambassador for Young People's Literature Takes Center Stage." *LCIB* 67 (Mar. 2008): 46–47.

"L'Amour Named Champion of the Book." *LCIB* 67 (Apr. 2008): 67.

"We Three Kings: Stephen King and His Family Meet Young Readers." *LCIB* 67 (May 2008): 89.

"River of Words Combines Art, Environment." *LCIB* 67 (June 2008): 118–19.

"State Centers Celebrate Ideas, Excellence." *LCIB* 67 (July–Aug. 2008): 138.

"Library of Congress Opens Its First Center for Young Readers." In International Federation of Library Associations and Institutions, Section on Literacy and Reading, *Newsletter* 28 (Jan.2010): 13-14.

"America's Reading Ambassador for Young People. " In *Library of Congress, Library Services Journal* 2 (October 2010): 7.

"Library of Congress Center for the Book. " In *The Oxford Companion to the Book*, vol. 2, edited by Michael F. Suarez and H.R. Woudhuysen, 880. New York: Oxford University Press, 2010.

Section V: The Center for the Book Viewpoint Series

Prefaces or forewords were written by Cole for the following booklets in the Center for the Book Viewpoint Series; each publication was based on a presentation at the Library of Congress during the Center's first two decades. The first, Barbara W. Tuchman's "The Book," was on Oct. 17, 1979; the last, "Readers & Libraries: Toward a History of Libraries and Culture in America" by Kenneth E. Carpenter, took place on Sept. 25, 1995.

Barbara W. Tuchman. *The Book.* No. 1, 1980.

The Audience for Children's Books. Remarks by Elaine Moss and Barbara Rollock. No. 2, 1980.

Daniel J. Boorstin. *Gresham's Law: Knowledge or Information?* No. 3, 1980.

I. R. Willison. *On the History of Libraries and Scholarship.* No. 4, 1980.

Alfred Kazin, Dan Lacy, and Ernest L. Boyer. *The State of the Book World in 1980.* No. 5, 1981.

Daniel J. Boorstin. *The World Encompassed.* No. 6, 1981.

The International Flow of Information: A Trans-Pacific Perspective (editor). No. 7, 1981.

Daniel J. Boorstin. *A Nation of Readers.* No. 8, 1982.

Dan H. Lawrence. *A Portrait of the Author as a Bibliography.* No. 9, 1983.

Harrison E. Salisbury. *The Book Enchained.* No. 10, 1984.

William P. Barlow, Jr. *Book Collecting: Personal Rewards and Public Benefits.* No. 11, 1984.

Anthony Rota. *Points at Issue: A Bookseller Looks at Bibliography.* No. 12, 1984.

Justin Kaplan. *Born to Trouble: One Hundred Years of Huckleberry Finn.* No. 13, 1985.

Robert B. Downs. *Books in My Life.* No. 14, 1985.

Daniel J. Boorstin. *The Indivisible World: Libraries and the Myth of Cultural Exchange.* No. 15, 1985.

John P. Feather and David McKitterick. *The History of Books and Libraries: Two Views.* No. 16, 1986. Includes John P. Feather, "The Book in History and the History of the Book" and David McKitterick, "The Limits of Library History."

Lawrence Clark Powell. *Next to Mother's Milk.* No. 17, 1987.

Lester Asheim. *The Reader-Viewer-Listener: An Essay in Communication.* No. 18, 1987.

David L. Vander Meulen. *Where Angels Fear to Tread: Descriptive Bibliography and Alexander Pope.* No. 19, 1988.

Donald W. Krummel. *The Memory of Sound: Observations on the History of Music on Paper.* No. 20, 1988.

R. Kathleen Molz. *The Knowledge Institutions in the Information Age: The Special Case of the Public Library.* No. 21, 1988.

James H. Billington. *Books and the World.* No. 22, 1988.

George H. Nash. *Books and the Founding Fathers.* No. 23, 1989.

Robert Vosper. *International Library Horizons: Some Personal Observations.* No. 24, 1989.

Nahum M. Sarna. *Ancient Libraries and the Ordering of the Biblical Books.* No. 25, 1989.

Bernhard Fabian. *The Future of Humanistic Scholarship* (with comments by Michael T. Ryan and Thomas F. Staley). No. 26, 1990.

Research Collections in the Information Age: The Library of Congress Looks to the Future: Views by Stephen E. Ostrow and Robert Zich (editor). No. 27, 1990.

E. L. Konigsburg. *The Mask Beneath the Face: Reading about and with, Writing about and for: Children.* No. 28, 1990.

John Malcolm Brinnan. *Travel and the Sense of Wonder* (with Jean Trebbi). No. 29, 1992.

G. Thomas Tanselle. *A Description of Descriptive Bibliography.* No. 30, 1992.

Kenneth E. Carpenter. *Readers & Libraries: Toward a History of Libraries and Culture in America.* No. 31, 1996.

Section VI: Other Publications and Contributions

Many books and articles in this section concern book, library, and cultural history. Other themes include national libraries, "great libraries," collection development, book collecting, and the pleasures of reading.

1970–1979

Foreign Newspaper Report, nos. 1–3 (editor). Washington, D.C.: Library of Congress, 1973.

Review of *The New York Public Library: A History of Its Founding and Early Years, by Phyllis Dain,* and *Open Shelves and Open Minds: A History of the Cleveland Public Library,* by C. H. Cramer. American Historical Review 78 (Oct. 1973): 1135–36.

Foreign Newspaper and Gazette Report, nos. 1–3 (editor). Washington, D.C.: Library of Congress, 1974.

"Developing a National Foreign Newspaper Microfilming Program." *Library Resources and Technical Services* 18 (Winter 1974): 5–17. Reprinted in M*icroforms in Libraries: A Reader*, edited by Albert J. Diaz, 298–310. Westport, Conn.: Microform Review, 1975.

Foreign Newspaper and Gazette Report, nos. 1–3 (editor). Washington, D.C.: Library of Congress, 1975.

Review of *The National Library of Canada*, by F. Dolores Donnelly. *Journal of Library History* 10 (Jan. 1975): 87–91.

"Foreign Official Gazette Microfilming: A Renewed Effort." *Microform Review* 4 (Apr. 1975): 101–3.

"The National Libraries of the United States and Canada." In *A Century of Service: Librarianship in the United States and Canada*, edited by Sidney L. Jackson, Elinor B. Herling, and E. J. Josey, 243–59. Chicago: American Library Association, 1976.

Review of *A History of the Oxford University Press*, by Harry Carter. *American Archivist* 39 (Apr. 1976): 212–13.

"Storehouses and Workshops: American Libraries and the Uses of Knowledge." In *The Organization of Knowledge in Modern America, 1860–1920*, edited by Alexandra Oleson and John Voss, 364–85. Baltimore, Md.: Johns Hopkins University Press, 1979.

1980–1989

"Books, Libraries, and Scholarly Traditions." *Scholarly Publishing* 13 (Oct. 1981): 3143.

U.S. International Book Programs, 1981 (editor). Washington, D.C.: Library of Congress, 1982. 61 pp.

"Frederick E. Brasch: Collector and Historian of Science." *Imprint of the Stanford University Libraries Associates* (hereafter *ISULA*) 8 (Apr. 1982): 9–12.

"For the Youth of the West: The Felton Memorial Library of American and British Literature." *ISULA* 8 (Oct. 1982): 23–27.

Preface to *Literacy in Historical Perspective*. ed. Daniel P. Resnick. Washington, D.C.: Library of Congress, 1983.

"Tattered Copies in Action: The Armed Services Editions." *LCIB* 42 (Mar. 21, 1983): 105–8.

Books in Action: The Armed Services Editions (editor). Washington, D.C.: Library of Congress, 1984. 78 pp.

"Biography: A Symposium at the Library of Congress." *LCIB* 43 (Apr. 9, 1984): 116–20.

"Buildings and Books: Leland and Jane Stanford and the University Library." *ISULA* 10 (Apr. 1984): 30–40.

Preface to *Fine Printing: The San Francisco Tradition,* by James D. Hart. Washington, D.C.: Library of Congress, 1985.

Biography & Books. A Symposium at the Library of Congress, Nov. 9–10, 1983 (editor). Washington, D.C.: Library of Congress, 1986. 75 pp.

The Community of the Book: A Directory of Selected Organizations and Programs (editor). Compiled by Carren O. Kasten. Washington, D.C.: Library of Congress, 1986. 123 pp. Includes "Is There a Community of the Book? An Introduction," 5–13. Reprinted by Transaction Books, New Brunswick, N.J., 1987. Reprinted in 2nd edition (compiled by Maurvene D. Williams, 1989, 140 pp.) and 3rd edition (compiled by Maurvene D. Williams, 1993, 150 pp.).

Preface to *The Printer & the Pardoner. An Unrecorded Indulgence Printed by William Caxton for the Hospital of St. Mary Rounceval, Charing Cross,* by Paul Needham. Washington, D.C.: Library of Congress, 1986.

"'The First Stanford Man': Timothy Hopkins." *ISULA* 12 (Oct. 1986): 12–18.

Afterword to *The Delights of Reading: Quotes, Notes & Anecdotes,* by Otto L. Bettmann, 127–28. Boston: David R. Godine, 1987.

Foreword to *Federal Copyright Records, 1790–1800,* edited by James Gilreath, compiled by Elizabeth Carter Wills. Washington, D.C.: Library of Congress, 1987.

Foreword to *Getting the Books Out: Papers of the Chicago Conference on the Book in 19th Century America,* edited by Michael Hackenberg. Washington, D.C.: Library of Congress, 1987.

Foreword to *Well Acquainted with Books: The Founding Framers of 1787,* edited by Robert A. Rutland. Washington, D.C.: Library of Congress, 1987.

Preface to *Fine Printing: The Los Angeles Tradition,* by Ward Ritchie. Washington, D.C.: Library of Congress, 1987.

Preface to *The History of Books: A Guide to Selected Resources in the Library of Congress,* by Alice D. Schreyer. Washington, D.C.: Library of Congress, 1987.

"David Starr Jordan: Stanford's Tower of Strength." *ISULA* 13 (Spring 1987): 5–9.

"Thomas Welton Stanford: A Friend in Australia." *ISULA* 13 (Fall 1987): 10–15.

The Bookseller's Art: Carl Kroch and Kroch & Brentano's (editor). Washington, D.C.: Library of Congress, 1988. 89 pp.

Foreword to *The Oxford English Dictionary and the State of the Language*, by Robert W. Burchfield and Hans Aarleff. Washington, D.C.: Library of Congress, 1988.

Foreword to *Researcher's Guide to Archives and Regional History Sources*, edited by John C. Larsen. Hamden, Conn.: Library Professional Publications, 1988.

Foreword to *Stepping Away from Tradition: Children's Books of the Twenties and Thirties*, edited by Sybille A. Jagusch. Washington, D.C.: Library of Congress, 1988.

Afterword to *The Open Door: When Writers First Learned to Read*, compiled by Steven Gilbar, 119–21. Boston: David R. Godine, 1989.

1990–1999

Introduction to *A Literary Book of Days*. New York: Library of Congress/ Phaidon Universe, 1990.

Preface to *Writing in an Era of Conflict. The National Book Week Lectures*, by Richard Rhodes and Thomas L. Friedman. Washington, D.C.: Library of Congress, 1990. Prefaces also were written for three additional books in this Center for the Book series that presented talks by recent winners of National Book Awards. The volumes were Charles Johnson and Ron Chernow, *In Search of a Voice*, 1991; Philip Levine, Orlando Patterson, and Norman Rush, *Earth, Stars and Writers*, 1992; and Paul Monette, *The Politics of Silence*, 1993.

Book Collectors of Stanford: An Eclectic Eight Who Shaped the Stanford University Libraries. Sacramento: California State Library Foundation, 1991. 79 pp. Includes the six essays cited above in the *ISULA* (beginning with "Frederick E. Brasch," 1982) and additional essays, "John Casper Branner: Bookman and University President" and "Herbert Hoover: Bibliophile and Ideal Stanford Man."

Preface to *Fanfare for Words: Bookfairs and Book Festivals in North America*, by Bernadine Clark. Washington, D.C.: Library of Congress, 1991.

"The Nation's Reading Rooms." In *Washington, D.C., A Smithsonian Book of the Nation's Capital*, 180–89. Washington, D.C.: Smithsonian Books, 1992.

Preface to *American Culture and the Marketplace: R. R. Donnelley's Four American Books Campaign 1926–1930*, by Claire Badaracco. Washington, D.C.: Library of Congress, 1992.

Capital Libraries and Librarians: A Brief History of the District of Columbia Library Association, 1894–1994. Washington, D.C.: Library of Congress, 1994. 76 pp.

"In the Company of Books: An Introduction." In *The Sign of Four,* by A. Conan Doyle. Library of Congress Centennial Bestseller Series. Bedford, Mass.: Applewood Books, 1994.

Preface to *Treasures of Florida Libraries: A Celebration of Rare and Unique Materials,* by Nora J. Quinlan and William E. Brown, Jr. Fort Lauderdale: Florida Center for the Book, 1994.

Foreword to *Justifying Jefferson: The Political Writings of John James Beckley,* edited by Gerard W. Gawalt. Washington, D.C.: Library of Congress, 1995.

Preface to *The Book in the Islamic World: The Written Word and Communication in the Middle East,* edited by George N. Atiyeh. Albany: State University of New York Press, 1995.

Afterword to *The Book in America: With Images from the Library of Congress,* by Richard W. Clement, 145–46. Golden, Colo.: Fulcrum Publishing, 1996.

Introduction to *Library: The Drama Within,* by Diane Asséo Griliches. Essay by Daniel J. Boorstin. Albuquerque: University of New Mexico Press, 1996.

Preface to *Even Anchors Need Lifelines: Public Libraries in Adult Literacy,* by Gail Spangenberg. Washington, D.C.: Center for the Book, 1996.

"Documenting Montana's Best: Heritage Project Launches Second Year." *LCIB* 55 (Sept. 2, 1996): 299–302.

Afterword to *The Most Wonderful Books: Writers on Discovering the Pleasures of Reading,* edited by Michael Dorris and Emile Buchwald, 277. Minneapolis: Milkweed Editions, 1997.

"National Archives of the United States." In I*nternational Encyclopedia of Information and Library Science,* edited by John Feather and Paul Sturges, 310–11. London: Routledge, 1997.

Afterword to *Language of the Land: The Library of Congress Book of Literary Maps,* edited by Martha Hopkins and Michael Busher, 287. Washington, D.C.: Library of Congress, 1998.

"1998 International History of the Book Projects Roundup" (with Ian R. Willison). *SHARP* News 8 (Winter 1998–99): 6–7.

"Art & Commerce: Future of Literary Publishing Discussed at NEA–Library of Congress Event." *LCIB* 58 (Oct. 1999): 246, 249.

Preface to *Thomas Jefferson and the Education of a Citizen,* edited by James Gilreath. Washington, D.C.: Library of Congress, 1999.

2000–2010

Great Libraries Series, Cosmos Club, Washington, D.C.

"Great Libraries Dinner: Librarian of Congress James H. Billington to Speak Dec. 2." *Cosmos Club Bulletin* 52 (Nov. 1999): 9

"Vatican's Librarian to Be Honored." *Cosmos Club Bulletin* 53 (Nov. 2000): 11.

"Paul LeClerc, Head of New York Library to Speak." *Cosmos Club Bulletin* 54 (Nov. 2001): 11.

"Morgan Library Director Charles E. Pierce to Speak." *Cosmos Club Bulletin* 56 (Oct. 2003): 10.

"Deutsche Bibliothek Director Elisabeth Niggemann to Speak." *Cosmos Club Bulletin* 57 (Oct. 2004): 11.

"National Archivist Allen Weinstein to Discuss Presidential Libraries." *Cosmos Club Bulletin* 58 (Oct. 2005): 16.

"Ismail Serageldin on the 'New' Bibliotheca Alexandria." *Cosmos Club Bulletin* 59 (May 2006): 10–11.

"Sidney Yerba on the Harvard University Library." *Cosmos Club Bulletin* 60 (Oct. 2007): 12.

"Ian E. Wilson on the Canadian National Library and Archives." *Cosmos Club Bulletin* 61 (Nov. 2008): 7.

"Shakespeare in Washington: Gail Kern Paster on the Folger Shakespeare Library." *Cosmos Club Bulletin* 62 (Oct. 2009): 12.

"The Crimson Collection: Robert Darnton on the Harvard University Library." *Cosmos Club Bulletin* 63 (Oct. 2010): 10.

Poets Laureate Series. Cosmos Club, Washington, D.C.

"Poet Laureate Robert Pinksy To Read, Discuss Works." *Cosmos Club Bulletin* 52 (May 1999):8

"An Evening with U.S. Poet Laureate Billy Collins." *Cosmos Club Bulletin* 55 (Oct. 2002): 11.

"U.S. Poet Laureate Ted Kooser to Read at Club." *Cosmos Club Bulletin* 58 (May 2005): 16.

"Donald Hall: Plainspoken Poet Laureate." *Cosmos Club Bulletin* 60 (May 2007): 8.

"Words from Kay Ryan, the Poet Laureate." *Cosmos Club Bulletin* 63 (May 2010): 19-20.

Foreword to *Library History Research in America: Essays Commemorating the Fiftieth Anniversary of the Library History Round Table*, edited by Andrew B. Wertheimer and Donald G. Davis, Jr. Washington, D.C.: Library of Congress, 2000.

Preface to *A Handbook for the Study of Book History in the United States*, edited by Ronald J. Zboray and Mary Saracino Zboray. Washington, D.C.: Library of Congress, 2000.

Review of *History of the British Museum Library*, by P. R. Harris. *Journal of Librarianship and Information Science* 32 (June 2000): 93–94.

Foreword to *Books, Libraries, Reading and Publishing in the Cold War*, edited by Hermina G. B. Anghelescu and Martine Poulain. Washington, D.C.: Library of Congress, 2001.

"Literacy, Libraries and IFLA: Recent Developments and a Look at the Future." *IFLA Journal* 27 (2001): 87–90.

Preface to *The Rivers of America: A Descriptive Bibliography*, by Carol Fitzgerald. 2 volumes. New Castle, Del.: Oak Knoll Press, in association with the Center for the Book, 2001.

Preface to *Collectors & Special Collections: Three Talks*. Washington, D.C.: Library of Congress, 2002.

"Book Culture during the Cold War: New Publication." *LCIB* 61 (May 2002): 92.

"Center for the Book Publications: New Items on Book History, Collecting, Collections." *LCIB* 61 (Dec. 2002): 288–89.

Foreword to *Books on the Frontier: Print Culture in the American West, 1763–1875*, by Richard W. Clement. Washington, D.C.: Library of Congress, 2003.

Introduction to *Libraries, Citizens & Advocacy: The Lasting Effects of Two White House Conferences on Library and Information Services*, by Virginia H. Mathews. Washington, D.C.: Center for the Book, 2004.

"An Evening with John Hope Franklin." *Cosmos Club Bulletin* 59 (Apr. 2006): 12.

"Shakespeare-Related Tour of the Thomas Jefferson Building." In *Shakespeare in America* (exhibit brochure). Washington, D.C.: Library of Congress, 2007.

"Introduction: For the Love of Libraries." In *Library: The Drama Within*, photographs by Diane Asséo Griliches, 5–16. Piermont, N.H.: Bunker Hill Publishing, 2008.

Preface to *Series Americana: Post Depression-Era Regional Literature, 1938-1980, A Descriptive Bibliography*, by Carol Fitzgerald. 2 volumes. New Castle, Del.: Oak Knoll Press in association with the Center for the Book, 2009.

"Donnelley & Sons, R.R." In *The Oxford Companion to the Book*, vol. 2, edited by Michael F. Suarez and H.R. Woudhuysen, 677. New York: Oxford University Press, 2010.

"Federal Writer's Project" In *The Oxford Companion to the Book*, vol. 2, edited by Michael F. Suarez and H.R. Woudhuysen, 718. New York: Oxford University Press, 2010.

"Government Printing Office (GPO)." In *The Oxford Companion to the Book*, vol. 2, edited by Michael F. Suarez and H.R. Woudhuysen, 759-760. New York: Oxford University Press, 2010.

"National Endowment for the Arts (NEA)." In T*he Oxford Companion to the Book*, vol.2, edited by Michael F. Suarez and H.R. Woudhuysen, 958. New York: Oxford University Press, 2010.

"National Endowment for the Humanities (NEH)." In *The Oxford Companion to the Book*, vol.2, edited by Michael F. Suarez and H.R. Woudhuysen, 958. New York: Oxford University Press, 2010

"Wilson, Halsey William (1868-1964)." In *The Oxford Companion to the Book*, vol. 2, edited by Michael F. Suarez and H.R. Woudhuysen, 1261. New York: Oxford University Press, 2010.

"IFLA's Section on Literacy and Reading: A History of its First Fifteen Years." In International Federation of Library Associations and Institutions. *Newsletter* No. 31 (June 2011): 6-9.

Compiled by John Y. Cole, with assistance from Staceya Sistare-Anderson of the Center for the Book, Library of Congress. Preface by Mary Niles Maack

Index